WITH A BENDED BOW

WITH A BENDED BOW

ARCHERY IN MEDIÆVAL
AND RENAISSANCE EUROPE

ERIK ROTH

SPELLMOUNT

If Robin Hood never existed, then his outlaw band
must have been led by someone else of the same name.
To that person, this book is dedicated.

First published 2012 by Spellmount,
an imprint of The History Press
The Mill, Brimscombe Port
Stroud, Gloucestershire, GL5 2QG
www.thehistorypress.co.uk

Paperback edition first published in 2017

British Library Cataloguing in Publication Data.
A catalogue record for this book is available from the British Library.

ISBN 978 0 7509 8374 7

Typesetting and origination by The History Press
Printed and bound in India by Replika Press Pvt. Ltd.

CONTENTS

PART I

THE GUILDS

On the head of the ship in the front which mariners call the prow there was a brazen child bearing an arrow with a bended bow. His face was turned toward England and thither he looked as though he was about to shoot.

Roman De Rou, Maistre Wace[1]

WOB is my name reversed;
I am a strange creature, shaped amid combat.
When I bend, and the venemous dart
goes from my bosom, I am quite ready
to sweep that danger to life far from me.
When my master who thus tormented me
released my limbs, I am longer than before,
until, fraught with destruction, I spit out
the very deadly venom I had previously swallowed.
What I am speaking about does not
easily pass away from any man,
if what flies from my belly reaches him
so that he pays for the evil drink with his strength
and quickly makes full compensation with his life.
When I am unstrung I will not obey anyone
 until I am skilfully tied. Say what I am.

THE EXETER RIDDLES

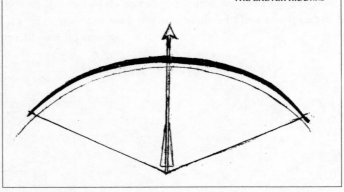

Some bows from the *Mary Rose* were in good enough condition to be tested like this one (from a photograph). Ascham really meant the arc of a circle when he wrote that a bow should come round *compasse*.

INTRODUCTION

… a bow of yew ready bent, with a tough tight string,
and a straight round shaft with a well rounded nock,
having long slender feathers of a green silk fastening,
and a sharp-edged steel head, heavy and thick and an
inch wide, of a green blue temper, that would
draw blood out of a weathercock …

Iolo Goch (bard to Owen Glendower)[2]

It has been said that archery is about two sticks and a string. That is quite true of mediaeval European archery, but we shall see that there is much more to it than that.

The origin of the longbow is unknown, although some British historians give it a Welsh pedigree. However, early examples have been found throughout Europe, such as those in Danish bog finds, dated to the Roman period. Similarly, Ötzi the Iceman (a mummy discovered in the Ötzal Alps on the border of Austria, and dated to 5300 years ago) had with him a 71¾-inch D section yew longbow and 32¼-inch taper arrows with three-vane glued and bound fletching. The arrows were – in length, materials and workmanship – nearly identical to those issued to archers on Henry VIII's carrack, the *Mary Rose*, except that Ötzi's arrowheads were of chipped stone rather than forged steel and his bow lacked the optional horn nocks. To further confuse matters, in France during the Hundred Years War, the longbow was called the 'English bow'.

The history of the bow and the longbow in particular is also the history of the wars of mediaeval England. Under King Edward I 'Longshanks', archery butts were ordered to be constructed and units of archers and crossbowmen were used during the wars in Wales and Scotland, in which Welsh mercenary archers were employed. A patent roll listed arrows an ell long with steel heads and four strings to each bow, a length indicating that they were to be used with longbows.

Military archery reached its furthest development when employed by English armies during the Hundred Years War with France. With a much smaller population than France, England could not put enough knights in the field to prevail, and had to arm its peasantry. The practical possibilities were pikes, staff weapons, crossbows and handbows. Having experienced the effectiveness of longbows in their local wars, the English chose these rather than the slower shooting and more expensive crossbows that had previously been the missile weapon of choice. But already by 1363, King Edward III complained that that the art of archery had become almost totally neglected, and demanded that everyone practise with bow and arrow or crossbows or bolts and avoid other games.

The military importance of archery, especially in mediaeval England, was such that a complex culture grew around the procurement of materials, and the manufacture and use of archery gear when archers usually outnumbered men-at-arms in English armies by three or four to one and sometimes by as much as ten to one. In hunting also, archery was more favoured in England than elsewhere, and more statutes concerning archery were proclaimed than in other kingdoms. With the end of English military archery during the reign of Elizabeth I, only vestiges of that culture remained. A late use of English military archery was during a moonlight raid by Sir Francis Drake's men on Nombre de Dios, a Spanish town in New Spain (the West Indies).

In the Market place the Spaniards saluted them with a volley shot; Drake returned their greeting with a flight of arrows, the best and ancient English compliment, which drave their enemies away.

This first part of *With a Bended Bow* will deal with the manufacture of bows, arrows, and sundry gear as produced in the Middle Ages and the Renaissance.

I

THE ARTILLERS

If you come into a shoppe and find a bowe that is small, long, heavy and strong, lyeing streyght, not windyng, not marred with knot, gaule, wyndeshake, wem, freate or pynche, bye that bowe of my warrant.

Roger Ascham, *Toxophilus*[3]

To grow in the hall
did Jarl begin.
Shields he brandished
and bow strings wound.
With bows he shot
and shafts be fashioned.
Arrows he loosed
and lances wielded.

Rigsthula[4]

In the early Middle Ages, archers probably made most of their own gear, and even a Viking jarl (earl) is described as doing so in the *Rigsthula*. In fact, Vikings of rank prided themselves on doing their own blacksmith work. By 1252 the Assize of Arms of Henry III required English freemen to own and use bow and arrows, and those of a certain income were also to have a sword, dagger and buckler. In the following year villeins and serfs were included, military age being specified as 16 to 60. The Winchester Statute of 1275 required all males under a certain rank to shoot from the age of seven. The outcome of these acts was a great deal of business for artillers, the collective name for those who manufactured bows and arrows.

Such was their importance to the country's security, the artillers of thirteenth-century Paris were exempt from watch duty on the city walls along with other guilds of craftsmen who directly supplied knights. At that time the same guild made both bows and arrows. In England The Worshipful Company of Bowyers of London were granted the right to wear liveries in 1319. The fletchers, or arrow makers, properly titled

'The Worshipful Company of Fletchers of London', formed a separate guild in 1371 and were granted liveries by King Henry VII. After the separation, a bowyer who sold arrows was subject to legal penalties, as was a fletcher who sold bows. Fletchers were however permitted to have three or four bows for personal use, as was expected of every man. In 1416 The Ancient Company of Bowstringmakers was established, although the longbow stringmakers soon formed a separate guild. They and the arrowsmiths seem to have been the poor relations among the guilds that manufactured artillery, and were not granted arms until much later. The names of the guild members often hinted at their profession; 'Flo' was once a common term for an arrow and thus men called John le Floer or Nicholas le Flouer would likely have been involved with arrow making.

The artillers supplied English citizens legally required to possess bows and arrows, as well as filling military contracts of livery (military) equipment for the crown. In this time of extreme division of labour, the well equipped archer required the services of five or more different guilds.

The guildsmen both made their product and sold it to the public in their own open fronted shops, usually located in specific areas with others of their company; Ludgate in London became known as 'Bowyerrowe'. In the morning a pair of horizontal wooden shutters would be opened. The upper one supported by two poles formed an awning while the lower one, supported on two legs, served as a counter. The craftsman and an apprentice worked in full view of prospective customers. At nightfall he retired to his residence above the shop and the shutters were locked and bolted; the guilds discouraged working at night.

The craft guilds acted much like modern trade unions. They restricted membership to guarantee full employment at decent wages to provide a fair return to all. They provided for members who were unable to work, held a local monopoly on their product and prohibited underselling below a fixed price. As no one had an advantage over another guildsman, innovation in tools or techniques was discouraged as well as claims of product superiority.

Employing extra apprentices, one's wife or young children was discouraged and thus product standards were theoretically maintained, although Ascham (author of England's first book on archery, *Toxophilus*) had some complaints on this score, criticising 'hastiness in those who work ye kinges Artillerie for war thinkynge yf they get a bowe or a sheafe of arrowes to some fashion, they be good ynough for bearynge gere.' There were other complaints as artillers had increasing difficulty in getting suitable wood and other materials. In 1385 a seller of false bowstrings was put into a London pillory and the bowstrings burned under his nose. In 1313 bowyers were accused of using poor wood, and in 1432 there were complaints about fletchers using green wood and working at night, which had been forbidden in 1371.

Each year a 'Warden of the Misterie' was chosen to oversee the guild and ensure that the *ordinances* (rules) were observed. The *misterie* was learned during an apprenticeship that would last from seven to ten years, after which the apprentice would be declared free or sworn of the city, when he would have the right to open his own shop and take on apprentices. While nearly all guild members were men, at least one female bowyer is recorded.

Some guilds and guild leaders amassed considerable wealth. The Worshipful Company of Fletchers of London still exists, although unsurprisingly it no longer has anything to do with the manufacture of arrows. Today it manages property and investments left over from the functional days of the guild.

Once a year the guildsmen held a great feast; a description of one from the time of Henry IV gives an impression of the sumptuousness and bizarre theatricality of mediaeval catering. The hall was hung with hallings of stained worsted and birch branches and the floor was covered with mats or rushes. When all had washed and wiped themselves the feast began with good bread and brown ale.

> Then came the bruets, joints, worts, gruel ailliers and other pottage, the big meat, the lamb tarts and capon pasties, the cockentrice or double roast, (griskin and pullet stitched together with thread) or great and small birds sewed together and served in a silver posnet or pottinger, the charlets, chewets, callops, mawmenies [spiced chicken], mortrews [meat in almond milk] and other such entremets of meat served in gobbets and sod in ale, wine, milk, eggs, sugar, honey, marrow, spices and verjuice made from grapes or crabs [crabapples]. Then came the subtleties, daintily worked like pigeons, curlews, or popinyays [parrots] in sugar and paste, painted in gold and silver, with mottoes coming out of their bills; and after them the spiced cake-bread, the French bread, the pastelades, doucets, dariols, flauns, painpuffs, rastons, and blancmanges, with cherries, drages, blandrells and cheese and a standing cup of good wine.

Guildsmen had various civic duties. During the fourteenth-century war with France, they were required to take turns on watch at the London waterfront, the bowyers taking theirs on Monday nights. Similarly, the guilds of the bowyers and fletchers were amongst those that supplied the torches to be borne by warders during the funeral procession of Henry V to Westminster.

Especially in the later Middle Ages, one aspect of the guilds' civic duties was the production of elaborate morality and mystery play cycles. These often lasted for days at a time and the plays had to be well performed on pain of a fine. In 1467 at Beverley the Fletchers were responsible for the pageant of Envy, while during a pageant in 1449 at Norwich the bowyers and fletchers were amongst those who bore the lights around the body of Christ.

The pressures of production on the artiller guilds during times of war were enormous, as the following orders made by the Crown attest. Hundreds of thousands of arrows and crossbow bolts were required during the Welsh campaign of 1282–83, and in 1304 the city of London supplied 130 bows and 200 quivers of arrows. In 1325 the Black Prince, running short of artillery, ordered 1000 bows and 2000 sheaves of arrows from king's ordnance, but demand exceeded supply. In 1333, the year of the Battle of Halidon Hill, the sheriffs of London were to send 4680 arrows, as it was their duty to fill the crown's quotas. In 1336 Edward III ordered the mayor and sheriffs to provide 300 bows and four chests of arrows; but the next year he claimed the throne of France and his requirements increased still further and in 1341 he ordered 7700 bows and 130,000 sheaves of arrows. In 1345 the Keeper of the King's privy wardrobe was to receive 1200 bows, 1000 sheaves of arrows and 4000 bowstrings from the City of London, and in 1359 the Keeper of the Wardrobe was ordered to buy 10,000 sheaves of 'good' arrows and 1000 sheaves of 'best' arrows.

With the renewal of the war with France by Henry V, production was again increased. In 1415 the King took an astonishing one and a half million arrows to France, some of which saved his campaign at Agincourt. In 1472 Parliament authorised a grant for a 23,000-man force of archers as a home guard. In the first year of his reign, Henry VIII imported 40,000 yew staves from Venice, without horn nocks but marked with his Rose and Crown badge, which were distributed to five bowyers. In 1523, approaching the final years of English military archery, a Tower of London inventory listed 11,000 made bows ready for use, 6000 staves, 16,000 sheaves of livery arrows, 4000 sheaves of arrows with 9-inch fletchings and 600 gross of bowstrings. With these numbers, it is not hard to see that problems with supply or quality control could arise.

As archers became an ever larger part of English armies in France during the fourteenth century, the Crown took a more active role in the production of artillery. The Royal Fletchers were established in the Tower, followed by the Maker of the King's Bows and the Keeper of the King's Bows, and both bows and arrows were made in the Tower by impressed labour at the king's wages.

However, as the cost of imported materials rose, the crown instituted price controls which, coupled with scarcity of materials, made their situation less desirable. While the companies had the advantages of monopoly, there were restrictions. In 1357 and 1369, proclamations forbade the export of bows and arrows, from 1399 there was an embargo on any weapons being sold to the Welsh rebels and in 1413 there was an embargo on selling bows and arrows to the Scots. In 1426 the Duke of Burgundy had to send a man to England to get bows for him secretly. There were also limits on the materials a craftsman could buy; in 1394 no bowyer was to buy more than 300 bowstaves for himself. At times the law strove to control even the day-to-day existence of the artisans. In 1368 sumptuary laws restricted the value of clothing and the diet of yeomen and craftsmen. They were permitted only one meal a day of meat or fish, being limited to bread, milk, butter and cheese for the rest of the day. However, these laws could not have been rigidly enforced.

Archery gear was a military necessity, and in time of need guild members were sometimes forcibly relocated to where their services were required for local supply. The Black Prince even had the fletchers of Chester arrested just to be sure of their availability. Some were attached to army units to repair equipment, such as the six bowyers and six fletchers present at the Battle of Agincourt. In 1436 a fletcher was commissioned to repair and trim used war arrows with new feathers and arrowheads.

Even before the loss of the *Mary Rose*, bowyers and fletchers lamented the decay of archery and consequent lack of work that forced them to move to Scotland and abroad to find employment. During the reign of Elizabeth I, the regulation of apprenticeships, previously managed by each guild, became controlled by the Crown, under the Statute of Artificers. For many bowyers and fletchers, Elizabeth's decision to eliminate archery for the trained bands meant an end to their craft anyway. In 1599 there were 14,204 bows and staves in the armouries of the Tower of London. By 1636 only 35 remained.

2

ARTILLERY TYPES

He purveyed him an hondred bowes,
The strenges were welle dight,
An hondred shefe of arrowes good,
The hedes burnished full bright,
And every arrowe an elle long,
With pecocke well y dight,
I nocked all with whyte silver,
It was a semly sight.

A Lytel Geste of Robyn Hode[5]

There is hardly any without a helmet, and none without bows and arrows; their bows and arrows are thicker and longer than those used by other nations, just as their bodies are stronger than other people's for they seem to have hands and arms of iron. The range of their bows is no less than our arbalests; there hangs by the side of each a sword no less long than ours, but heavy and thick as well. The sword is always accompanied by an iron shield.

Dominic Mancini[6]

As stated in the previous chapter, the combination of bows and arrows was called 'artillery'. This was the original meaning of the word, later expanded to include ordnance. Bows were of two major categories, handbows and crossbows. Most European handbows were what have come to be known as self bows, made of a single stave of wood, either straight or curved by heat bending. There is the possibility that some European bows were of composite construction but there is no real evidence of this.

Some handbows were longbows. While the British Longbow Society restricts the term 'longbow' to a Victorian ideal, we may define longbows as wooden handbows other than flatbows, long enough to take at least a draw to the ear. They would be of about the archer's own height or longer, up to six and a half feet in the case of the great longbows to shoot yard-long arrows. Most handbows were slightly wider than thick and evenly tapered to the tips. Exceptions were the Alemanni bows with some similarity to Bronze Age flat bows.

Short Saracen or 'Turkish' handbows of composite construction (a wood core strip, a sinew back and horn belly) were in limited use in Europe from the crusades onward, and the type had been in general use in Asia from time immemorial.

While handbows have been used in Europe for at least 8000 years, crossbows are a much more recent innovation. Also known as '*arbalests*' from the French, they seem to have originated in China, being first brought to Europe by Roman armies returning from the Middle East, but they did not become popular until the crusades. The Saracens were crossbow specialists but they used at least one type of European origin. The crossbow consisted of a wooden stock (tiller) and a bow (lath) of wood, composite or steel construction. The illustration below shows the one foot crossbow.

Not all bows were meant to shoot arrows, nor were all arrows meant to be shot from bows. Both handbows and crossbows had from ancient times been made for shooting stones or pellets only, and were then called stonebows. A type of crossbow for this purpose was called a *rodd*.

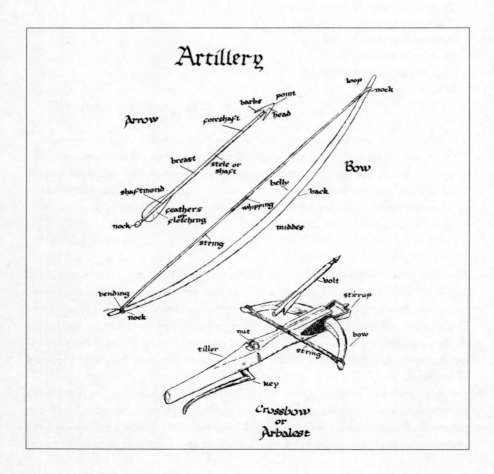

Arrows were of wood, from one foot in length for crossbows, up to five feet. The latter and others of varying lengths were intended to be thrown by hand and were called darts or javelins, favoured by 'the nimble Irish, that with darts doe warre'. Arrow throwing has remained a pastime in Yorkshire into the modern day and a length of string wrapped around the shaft enables a cast to an astonishing 280 yards. Some arrows were made to be fired from early ordnance such as muskets and bombards, the only situation in which arrows can properly be described as being 'fired', unless one wishes to include the igniting of incendiary arrows.

Bearing arrows, six feet in length, were carried ceremonially. In 1514 runners accompanying the Earl of Northumberland were provided with long arrows like 'standarts with socetts of Stell for my Lord's foutemen to bere in their hands when they ryn with my Lorde.'

Arrows were armed with heads of various types, usually of iron or steel, although stone was used in prehistoric times, and some of the Roman period Danish arrows had heads made of bone. For practice and hunting small game, large blunt heads of wood or horn were used. For a stable flight, arrows were provided with feather vanes. Crossbow shafts for war carried vanes of thin wood, parchment, leather or even copper. Some arrows, for use at short range, had no fletching at all.

Types of arrows were named according to shaft style, arrowhead style or use, for example: breasted arrow, bolt, bearing arrow, sheaf arrow, broad arrow and butt arrow. *Merke or* mark arrows, made specifically for target practice, were paired to match in weight. While the term 'bolt' is used for blunt crossbow missiles, it seems also to have been used as a designation for blunt handbow arrows and perhaps other types as well. The term 'quarrel' is derived from the French *quarré*, meaning square, and is applied to short crossbow arrows with armor piercing heads of square section.

3

STANDARDS OF LENGTH

An archar off Northumberlande
Say slean was lord Perse,
He bar a bende bowe in his hand,
Was made of trusti tre;

An arow that a cloth-yarde was lang,
Toth harde stele hayld he;
A dynt that was both sad and soar,
He sat on sir Hewe the Mongonbyrry.

The Hontyng of the Cheviat[7]

With Spanish yew so strong,
Arrows a cloth yard long,
That like to serpents stung
Piercing the weather.

Michael Drayton, Agincourt[8]

When constructing bows and arrows, craftsmen used the dimensions of their own bodies for measurement prior to standardisation. The shaftment, the fist with extended thumb was called the 'fistmele' (formerly the fist width). A 'span' was the space between thumbtip and fingertip of the spread fingers, a 'cubit' the space from point of elbow to extended fingertip, a 'thumb' from end of thumb to first joint, alternatively to the second joint. A yard of cloth was, and sometimes still is, measured between the end of the cloth between thumb and forefinger of the extended left arm and the hem held at the middle of the collarbone. Finger widths were also a useful measure.

Arrows were of various lengths according to whether they were intended to be drawn to the breast, to the ear, or to the point of the shoulder, and they also varied according to the size of the shooter. The length of the bow corresponded to the length of the arrow. In most cases, arrows were drawn to the head, and arrow length was measured from the base of the nock to the points of the arrowhead barbs or shouldering of the head. The word 'nock' means notch and it refers to the notches at the ends of the bow to hold the string, as well as the notch in the end of an arrow shaft to fit the string.

A bow casts an arrow by its speed of recovery from full draw. All other things being equal, the shorter the bow the faster it will be, for as the twentieth-century American bowyer/archer Howard Hill's axiom states: 'The more a bow limb is bent, the faster it returns.' The optimum length of a bow is determined by how far the material of which it is made will bend without breaking. Mediaeval bows were made long enough to provide a safety factor, but those used for flight shooting to maximum distance were very close to breaking at full draw.

With regard to standard lengths, for longbows the earliest reference to mediaeval proportions is the French *Book of Roi Modus* written after the Battle of Crecy, around 1370. The term 'long bow' was not much used, even in the later Tudor period; *Lartdarcherie* (see below) uses the term '*arc a main*'. *Roi Modus*, which is mainly concerned with hunting, was probably written in Normandy. It states that the 'English bow' of yew is to be 22 *poignees*, measured between nocks, and the arrow is to be 10 poignees from base of nock to points of barbs, 'poignee' meaning a grasp or the width of a fist, a distance that varies from person to person. The stave and shaft could be measured by grasping with alternate hands, taking care to press one well down on the other, a method of measurement used by English country people well into the nineteenth century. It should be noted that a person who gains weight will find his poignee measurement increased, but in any case the crucial relationship will remain proportional.

As an example, I am 5′ 8″ tall and 22 poignees measured using my fists gave me a bow of 5′ 11″ and arrows of 31½″. *Roi Modus* says to draw to the ear and draw up the arrow to its head. The arrow worked out exactly right for this kind of draw at maximum stretch with a weaker bow, but if the arrow is too long to fully draw in practice, as mine were, Ascham (see below) says to cut it shorter. *Roi Modus* adds that the bowstring should be of silk, braced at a height of a palm and two fingers from the bow.

In 1515, *Lartdarcherie*, written in the Picard dialect, was printed in Paris. The Hundred Years War was long over and Paris was again a French city. *Lartdarcherie*, citing *Roi Modus,* tells us that according to custom the arrow should be ten poignees and the bow should be two poignees more than double the arrow length, exactly as previously specified. Flight bows should be a poignee shorter but only two or three arrows a day should be shot from them. It states that many archers draw longer arrows but many of these shoot a weaker arrow by doing so. There are also many who use a shorter shaft, still making long shots and shooting as strongly as others, but the book's author suggests that they would be finer archers by using the 10 poignee draw length and adds; 'I venture to say that it is impossible to shoot a long arrow in an ungraceful way, if the bow is pushed forward, that is, pressed toward the target when the arrow is loosed.'

Roger Ascham's *Toxophilus,* printed during the reign of Henry VIII, was England's first book on archery. Writing about longbows when practice with them was still compulsory, Ascham refrains from giving measurements of bows or arrows on the grounds that individual variations make that impossible. However, as the English also drew to the ear and drew the arrow to the head, the length of arrows shot in this way could hardly have been much different from the 10 poignee French arrows.

We now come to the famous 'clothyard' arrows, that supposedly had shafts three feet in length. Were they really used, or did the term refer to smaller arrows of perhaps 30 inches as author T. Roberts suggested in 1801 in his book *The English Bowman*? The Iron Ulna, an iron rod three feet long (an *ell*), was made in the thirteenth century to fix the measurement for cloth, and was also used for land measurements. The term 'clothyard', referring to this iron stick and applied to arrows, dates from 1465, and clearly describes an exceptionally impressive arrow. In 1336, the ninth year of the reign of Edward III, the mayor and sheriffs were to provide

> … three hundred good and sufficient bows, with strings proportionable to them, and also fair chests of arrows of the length of one ell, made of good well seasoned wood; the heads of the said arrows to be duly sharpened, and the flukes or barbs of a large size.

In mediaeval and Renaissance writings, the terms 'clothyard', 'clothier's yard' and 'tailor's yard' are sometimes used interchangeably with the word 'ell'. But there was some confusion caused by local variations of measurements that had the same name. The 'Statute of the Staple' fixed the yard at 36 inches and the English ell was newly designated as five-fourths of the standard, or 45 inches. The Scottish ell was 37 inches, as was the yard of three Rhineland feet used by Flemish clothmakers brought to England under the Plantagenets, this yard being abolished in 1533. However the clothyard remained three feet of 12 inches, 36 inches in length. Such an arrow would require a longer bow and preferably a tall and strong archer. Archers with these characteristics were sought after and skeletons of archers on the *Mary Rose* were indeed taller than the average crewman. A contemporary wrote of the English archers at Agincourt that 'the most part of them drew a yarde.'

In 1825 a Mr A.J. Kempe saw some arrows in Cornwall, which he believed to be old English, that were 3 feet two inches long. This measurement probably included the head. Cornish archers of the rebel party who defended the high road at Deptford Bridge in 1446 were reported to have shot arrows 'in length a full yarde'. Francis Bacon (1561–1626) also reported the Cornish rebels as using arrows of a 'tailor's yard'. Richard Carew, in *The Survey of Cornwall* of 1602, tells us that the Cornishmen used shafts of a 'cloth yard in length' for long shooting. The English Board of Trade presently considers the 37-inch Flemish yard to have been the clothyard. These sources suggest that Cornishmen used arrows of a good 36 inches in length.

In 1590 Sir John Smythe wrote in his *Certaine Discourses Military* 'Our English bows, arrows and archers do exceed all other bows used by foreign nations, not only in thickness and strength, but also in the length and size of the arrows.' He doesn't say just how large and thick they were, but Paulus Jovius does. A sixteenth-century traveller, he reported that the English shot arrows somewhat thicker than a man's little finger and two cubits long, headed with barbed steel points from bows of extraordinary size and strength. These were war arrows. As mentioned above, a cubit is the measure of a man's forearm from elbow to the extended middle fingertip, and my two cubits make 36 inches, our clothyard. This is a very thick and heavy arrow by modern standards, even taking into consideration that it was probably tapered and made of light aspen. *Mary Rose* arrows were of ½-inch maximum thickness.

Many modern archers might consider such an arrow impossible to shoot effectively. However Dr Pope, an archery enthusiast and researcher in the early twentieth century, tested a Chinese or Mongolian bow that his brother had purchased in China from a Chinese man who had demonstrated shooting with it. The accompanying arrow was 38 inches long by ½ inch in diameter with a forged iron head. Though it was tapered in the foreshaft it still weighed four ounces. By comparison, a modern hunting arrow weighs an ounce and a half or less. This Chinese arrow was scarcely to be differentiated from the late mediaeval clothyard.

The reflexed composite bow that accompanied this arrow drew 98lbs at 28 inches, a long way from full draw. Neither Pope nor his companions could draw it more than a foot and proper testing was impossible. Finally Dr Pope, a seasoned bowhunter, shot the arrow from his 85lb hunting bow, the strongest he could command. It flew only 115 yards.

Pope then made up an arrow based on a sixteenth-century Italian painting showing a bow and arrow realistically portrayed. The arrow, considering the bow length as six feet, worked out to a ½ inch shaft 35 inches in length with feathers nine inches long and 1½ inches high. The broadhead was 3½ inches long and weighed more than an ounce, the entire arrow weighing three ounces. It was doubtless with growing feelings of inadequacy that Pope, who had killed bears and lions with his arrows, managed to shoot this arrow 117 yards from a longbow of 72lbs at 36 inches.

The Winchester Statute of 1275 allowed bowstaves of six and a half feet long to be imported free of duty. A great longbow for shooting a yard-long arrow must have been at least six and a half feet between nocks, and staves of this length were ordered. Some statutes specified seven foot staves, squared, and 3 fingers thick, and a 6′ 11″ bow was found on the *Mary Rose*. In his book *Longbow: A Social and Military History*, Robert Hardy mentions a record of Edward II giving a longbow of two ells in length to shoot a 'clotharrow'. A bow twice as long as the arrow would not be long enough to fully draw safely.

It seems that clothyard arrows were too long to be fully drawn in a draw to the ear and may have been drawn to the right breast or the shoulder of the drawing arm. They were probably shot only at roving or flight distances with the bow hand elevated. For my part, I find that in drawing to the right breast, 36 inches is a bit more than the maximum length that I can draw. Drawing beyond the shoulder, as the Japanese did, is very difficult with a powerful bow. We may consider the yard-long arrows to have been the maximum length in use with handbows in mediaeval Europe. Longer then this, they would be used as javelins.

In the second half of the fifteenth century, Edward IV issued a curious statute, his fifth act. Referring to Ireland, it specified that every Englishman, or Irishman living with Englishmen, provide himself with an English bow of his own height plus a fistmele and with twelve shafts of the length of three-quarters of 'the Standard'. (The word 'fistmele' at this time referred to the width of a fist, the 'poignee', and now included the extended thumb to determine a bow's brace height.) This length of bow works out the same as the *Roi Modus* method, and also corresponds to an old rule that the bowstring should be the length of the shooter; bows used by Scottish mounted archers in the service of Louis XI and his opponent Charles of Burgundy in the wars of 1475–1477 were equal to a man's height.

The arrow lengths required by the statute are another matter. 'The Standard' is the 36-inch yard fixed in the 'Statute of the Staple', and three-quarters of the Standard was 27 inches. No explanation was given for a variable bow measurement coupled with a fixed, and proportionally short, arrow measurement for anyone over 4′ 5″ tall. This arrow measurement would appear to have been a standardisation for military purposes in a land in which small bows (Irish bows) and arrows had come into use. Perhaps Edward wanted the Irish who had not learned longbow shooting in child-hood to at least become accustomed to longbows. Longbows and arrows were sent to Ireland to be sold to the King's subjects but a statute of 1515 suggested that in default of longbows in Ireland, the people should apply themselves to the Irish bows.

A reference to a short arrow like those required in the statute can be found in a thirteenth-century Leicestershire coroner's report. The de Banco Roll gives particu-lars of the killing of one Simon de Skeffington in 1298, the year of William Wallace's defeat at Falkirk. The yew bow was one and one half elles (4′ 6″) long with a hemp string, while the arrow was a peacock-fletched ash stele three-quarters of an ell long, again 27 inches, and one inch in circumference. That would be $^5/_{16}$ or at most $^3/_8$ inches thick. It bore a head of iron and steel 3 inches long and 2 inches wide. This large head for a slight arrow would have to have been a swallowtail hunting broadhead.

Curiously, according to T. Roberts, writing in 1801, when men still drew to the ear and 5′ 6″ was considered average height, 27-inch arrows were used with six-foot bows as standard practice although many archers sensibly cut the bows down to 5′ 8″ or less. Of course by this time, bows were made with a stiff handgrip area rather than the even bend of mediaeval times, and thus had to be long. These 27-inch arrows may be considered the shortest that could be used with longbows and are better suited to use with the short handbows that were used throughout Europe during the Middle Ages.

Le Livre de Chasse gives specifications for the short handbow, called a 'Turkish' bow, referring to its length rather than its construction, also known as a 'smallbow', and its arrows. It was written in the fourteen century by Count Gaston de Foix, Foix being a county on the northern side of the Pyrenees. During the Hundred Years War he refused to aid either English or French forces and was passionately fond of hunting, in which pursuit a short bow has certain advantages. It is less cumbersome in brush country and can be readily shot from a kneeling position. It is also quick of cast although its light arrow has less impact than that of the longbow, making it suitable for killing deer but less so for warfare. Bows of this type changed little through the centuries and are pictured in manuscripts more frequently than longbows.

De Foix suggests a shaft of 8 poignees from nock to barbs. This gives me a 26½-inch shaft, the same length as a method of recent tradition of placing an end of the shaft against the base of the neck, the other end between the extended fingertips of both outstretched arms. The bow is to be 20 *poulcees* between nocks. Under the assumption that this measurement is the length of the thumb from tip to second joint, I get a bow that measures 4′ 8″ between nocks. The completed bow matches those in the illustrations for the fifteenth-century edition of the book, which are shown being drawn variously to the breast or face. De Foix adds that the bow, designed for short-range shooting, should be 'weak', that the silk bowstring should be braced to the height of a *'paume de large'*, a palm's breadth, and that the well filed and sharpened broadhead should be four fingers broad and five fingers in length, of course a swallowtail broadhead. The resulting bow is shorter than one made using the *Roi Modus* specifications, but as it is necessarily thinner than a longbow, it tolerates a greater bend. The 'six small bows with a sheaf of long arrows' that Sir Peter Courtney sent to France for the king's gamekeeper in the time of Richard II would have been of this type. The one complete twelfth-century Waterford bow measures 4′ 12″, still a smallbow.

In all the foregoing examples we find equipment made to fit the size of the bowman, with the exceptions of the clothyard and the three-fourths of the Standard arrows. The 'traditional' English longbow of recent times most nearly matches the one described in the atypical Fifth Act of Edward IV, the only precisely specified old English measurements. This so-called 'traditional' six-foot longbow and 28-inch arrow left the archer with a bow that was, by other mediaeval standards, ten inches too long for optimum casting power. Because of the post-medieval fashion of the stiff handgrip and tips of the 'traditional' longbow, some of this additional length was necessary to avoid breakage, but some practical archers such as Dr Pope cut their bows to 5′ 8″ in length, thereby increasing their efficiency.

The *Mary Rose* find illustrates the specifications given above. Sir John Smythe had noted that military bows were made long enough that they 'did but seldom break'. Most of the arrows were 30 inches, the longest nearly 32 inches. A bow measured as specified above would be 5′ 11″. The *Mary Rose* military bows, except for the very long one cited above, exceeded this by from two to six inches. A minority of the arrows, about a third, were about 28 inches, the shortest 24 inches. Both the long and the short arrows were bound together in the same sheaves to be shot from longbows of a minimum of six feet in length. A biography of Charlemagne describes the Emperor's fondness for his hunting weapons, 'a good silver-hilted Frankish sword, a spear, and a bow with long and short arrows'. It seems clear that both long and short arrows were shot from longbows.

4

BOWS

'Behind their wall,' he was told, 'There was a woman, covered with a green mantle, who kept shooting arrows with a wooden bow. She wounded several of us. She was finally overcome by several men. We killed her and brought her bow to the sultan. He was amazed at this happening.'

Baha ed Din[9]

A good bowe in his hand,
A brod arwe ther ine,
And foure and twenty goode arwys,
Trusyd in a thrumme

Robyn and Gandelyn[10]

Both longbows and shorter handbows were in use in Europe from prehistoric times. The longbow casts a heavier arrow that a short bow doesn't have the mass to cast effectively, and weight means penetration. The long draw keeps the bowstring on the arrow longer, maximising the thrust. Also, the necessarily heavier arrow flies more steadily than a short one and stands better in a wind. These characteristics meant that the English found the longbow in the hands of a practiced archer a more effective war weapon than the crossbow, which was favoured by their French enemies during the Hundred Years War. At the Battle of Crecy, the Genoese crossbowmen shot first but their bolts fell far short, while the English longbowmen's arrows did not. However, without a culture of longbow use from early childhood, most nations retained the crossbow. English livery (military) bows were often hurriedly mass produced and not always with the best materials. Yew bows were classified as yew 'of the best sort', others of 'the second sort', still others of 'the coarser sort'.

We know most about the longbow, but shorter handbows were more usual in mediaeval times, especially for hunting. They were drawn to the breast, sometimes to the face. In both England and France, the longbow was used in practice shooting at

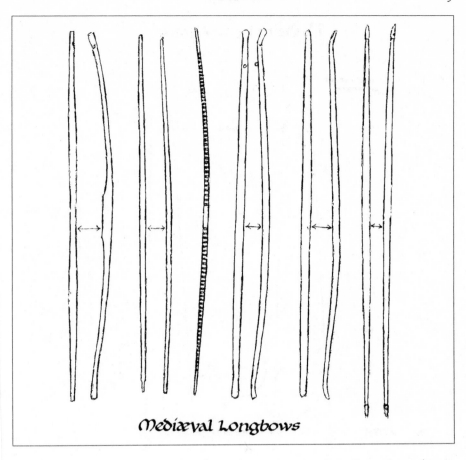

Mediæval Longbows

marks. Serious archers brought several bows to practice. Of differing strengths, lengths and cross sections, they were for specific purposes like butt or clout/prick shooting (see p. 165), or for flight shooting, the latter being a favorite French game for wagers.

Cross Sections

Some sharp their swords, some right their murrians set;
Their greaves and pouldrons rivet fast. The archers now their bearded arrows whet,
Whilst every where the clam'rous drums are bras'd.

Drayton, *Polyolbion*[11]

The Parisian *Lartdarcherie* describes the advantages of variations in cross section.

Bows are made of two patterns that is to say, square and round, which are used for three kinds of shooting. The square are best for butt shooting for three reasons

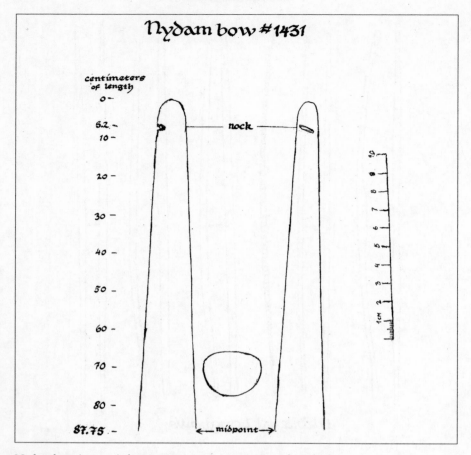

Nydam bow #1431

Nydam bow (see p. 57) showing measurements at points of one limb.

– first, because they have more back and therefore last longer; secondly, because the arrow lies better against their side, and thirdly because they shoot straighter and keep their cast longer. A bow should be of the same shape for the butt and chapperon shooting.

While most mediaeval archery terms are directly translatable from one language to the other, it seems clear from the context that the word 'back' here means what in England is called the belly. French nomenclature of the present day continues to refer to a bow's belly as the 'back' while the back is called the 'face'. Through the FITA, the international archery federation based in France, these terms have become standard.

Round bows are recommended for chapperon and flight shooting.

Those made for chapperon shooting have a broader back than the others, as more arrows are shot with it, for if they had too narrow a back, they would not last. Those made for flight shooting have narrower backs and are the better for it, as the back only makes them slower and more sluggish.

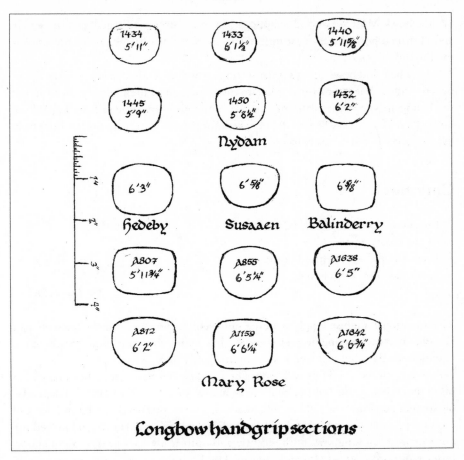

1434 5'11"

1433 6'1½"

1440 5'11⅝"

1445 5'9"

1450 5'8½"

1432 6'2"

Nydam

6'3"

6'5⅞"

6'⅞"

Hedeby

Susaaen

Balinderry

A807 5'11¾"

A855 6'5¼"

A1638 6'5"

A812 6'2"

A1159 6'6¼"

A1842 6'6¾"

Mary Rose

Longbow handgrip sections

The cross-sections are of the grip area of mediaeval longbows that were evenly tapered to the tips to bend in an arc. This measurement together with the length enables us to make a replica bow or to estimate draw weight of the originals. These are beyond the strength of most of today's archers. We can see the increase in draw weight through the centuries.

The explanation for this is that the shearing line of a rectangular bow, the point between tension and compression, is midway between back and belly, so that tension of the back and compression of the belly are equal. In a narrow bow with a narrow belly section approaching a triangular shape, the shearing line, which can be found by balancing a paper cutout of the cross-section of the bow on a pinpoint, is closer to the back. The belly is then subjected to disproportionate compression. While this gives the bow a fast recovery and consequently excellent cast, it also causes an early crushing of the fibres on the belly and the bow soon loses efficiency. For this reason flight bows were used sparingly. Ascham felt that bows that were flat should be gathered round to have a faster cast for distance shooting as well as being more accurate at close range.

On the *Mary Rose* D section longbows were found, the only shape recognised as longbows by the British Longbow Society, as well as some rectangular and some trapezoidal bows. Most are of oval (elliptical) section, a compromise between the square and D shaped bows. Livery gear for military use was often hastily produced, explaining the lack of standardisation.

Viking bog find bows are of similar sections as well as lenticular. The ratio of thickness to width varies from 1-1 in the rare round section to the slightly wider 1-1.1 at the handgrip, sometimes flattening to 1-2 in the limbs of some self-nocked Viking bows. ('Thickness' here means depth, width means the section across the bow from left to right when held ready to use.)

Curvatures

My curving bows adorn my bench,
My mailcoats are of gold.
Brightest of all my helm and shield,
Heirlooms from kings of old.

The Lay of Atli[12]

The 'traditional' English longbow of the nineteenth century was made of a stave as it had grown. Heat bending began to be experimented with in the United States in the twentieth century but was well known in mediaeval Europe.

A bow with recurved tips will shoot faster and farther than a straight-end bow, all other things being equal, although it can be argued that the more stable and dependable straight end longbow is the best kind. The latter was preferred by Saxton Pope and Howard Hill (1899–1975), who had tried reflexed and recurved bows, and indeed the great majority of longbows both recently and historically have been straight ended. Horace A. Ford (1822–1880) and Howard Hill both found the reflex or recurve to be a bad form, detracting from the steadiness of the bow, although Asian archers shot with considerable accuracy with their sharply reflexed hornbows.

Mediaeval manuscripts show many types of curvature that indicate considerable use of heat bending, especially with short handbows. These curvatures have been used throughout history by peoples ranging from the Assyrians to Native Americans, from Andaman Islanders to ancient Egyptians.

'Round Compasse'

This term of Ascham's in his *Toxophilus* refers to the bending of a bow in the arc of a circle at full draw. Because a longbow is not of nearly uniform thickness like flat bows, the middle of the bow is subject to greater tension and compression at back and belly than the thinner parts.

This type of bow does not kick excessively and its cast is fully as good as that of the type with stiff handgrip, if not better. Ascham mentions bows that fret at the handgrip and assumes this to be because of the heat of the hand. I however believe that this is due to the crushing of belly fibres, which is most likely at the handgrip with this type of bend, as often portrayed in old illustrations.

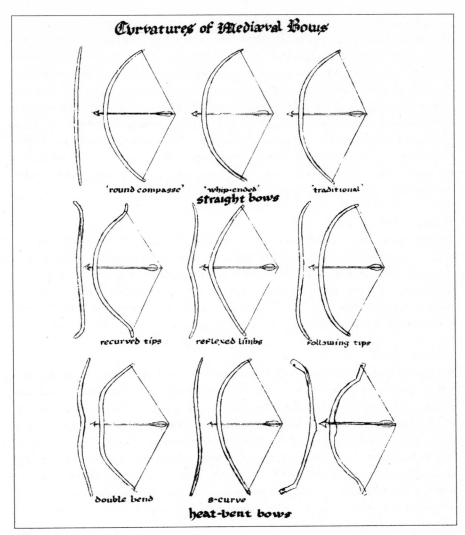

Various curvatures of bows. Heat bending was regularly used, mostly for smallbows.

Whip ended

Recommended by Ascham for the adjusted and finished bow., the tips are thinned to increase the bend at that part of the limb. The wood here will, being thinner, take a greater bend without breakage or crushing. Whip ends increase cast and lessen any hand shock at the loose, but have not been much in favour recently because the modern practice of completing a bow before it is shot in means that the whip ends come under considerable strain when the bow is braced, causing bad string follow near the tips. If the ends are whipped after string follow has developed in the bow, the strain on the ends is lessened. Ascham cautions 'not too muche lest they whip in sunder,' meaning that the ends should be thinned as much as possible short of danger of breakage.

Traditional

An old illustration shows this apparent type of bend on a drawn longbow but it may be the result of the curvature of the bow at rest. The bow is reduced at the midlimb, leaving stiff a handgrip area and tips: This is the main style of modern 'traditional' longbows. The stiff handgrip area is believed to reduce kick and the stiff, almost round tips are intended to reduce strain on the ends of the bow. The midlimb is overstressed, other parts under-stressed and for this reason modern longbows must be longer for the draw length than mediaeval bows. The type of bend that would give even stress on a longbow would be one steadily increasing toward the tips, a double involute curve. Other curvatures would have been the result of heat bending, either with steam or dry heat.

Recurved tips

These were by far the commonest curvature. In mediaeval bows the recurve was not as great as in modern ones, the curvature being only enough to bring the extended tips of the bent-up bow into line with the bowstring, which did not touch the bow anywhere but at the nocks. Recurved tips are also seen on some longbows on the continent, particularly those of the fifteenth century or later, some shown in Flemish paintings. All of the following types of bows might also have had recurved tips.

Reflexed limbs

A type of curvature seen on the Norman bows in the Bayeux Tapestry is also seen more clearly on a French fifteenth-century unicorn tapestry. The bow at midpoint is sharply bent toward the string, the limbs being reflexed. When the bow is bent up, the limbs bend straight. Some of the bows of this type were definitely short. Representations of longbows in the margins of the Bayeux Tapestry may be due to artistic licence or incompetence, but one chronicler stated that the Normans did use longbows. Some late mediaeval manuscript illustrations portray longbows with a reflexed lower limb, while others, representing Normans versus Saxons, show Saxon longbows as straight ended while the Norman longbows have slight recurves.

Double bend

This type, restricted to smallbows, also has a bend at midpoint but in this case toward the back. At midlimb, bends are toward the belly, sometimes closer to the midpoint, sometimes closer to the tips. In some of these bows, these bends are extreme. This type of bow usually also has recurved tips. The appearance of this bow when bent up is similar to that of Asiatic composites, with which it is sometimes confused. This form appears in illustrations from the twelfth century to the sixteenth. A fifteenth-century Spanish painting shows a bow of this type with horn nocks similar to nineteenth-century English ones.

Bows of this curvature were sometimes formed differently from the usual even-tapered stave, being made thickest and widest at the midlimb apexes of both outward bends. This may be clearly seen in fifteenth-century paintings and manuscript illustrations from England, Flanders, Spain and Germany, showing that the style was widely disseminated. At full draw the bow assumes a fairly even curve. If it did not have the double bend curvature, such a bow would soon break at its midpoint.

S-curve

The S form of curvature has been found in a wide spectrum of cultures. The pygmies of the Andaman Islands made such bows into the present century, intentionally curving them in this way, and an s-curve bow is clearly pictured along with a recurved longbow and a double bend bow in an early Stone Age painting from Alpera Cave in south-west Spain. The bend toward the string is in the upper limb of the bow. In both the Viking bows found at Susaaen (see p.58) and Ballinderry (see p.59), one limb is quite straight, while the other follows the string. That a bow that has been evenly tapered to both ends should have come so much in one limb and not at all in the other, is noteworthy. Were it only in one bow, one would suspect the curvature to be the result of 1000 years of burial in the earth, but when found in two bows, both Viking, coincidence begins to be stretched a little. Both bows appear to have been bent to a light S curve before use. Most of the bows illustrated in a fifteenth-century edition of *Froissart's Chronicles* show a noticeably greater curve in the upper limb.

Following tips

Another type of curvature seen occasionally illustrated has both limbs of the bow bent toward the string above midlimb. I can offer no reason that such a bow would be desirable. This curvature was used by the ancient Egyptians and three of the aboriginal bows pictured in Pope's *Bows and Arrows* have just such an intentional curvature. The only one in condition to be tested was a Mojave bow, used by the most warlike of the Californian Native American tribes. Its performance was not particularly impressive, although it was no longer in its original condition and had been displayed bent up.

Static recurve

Bows portrayed in several illustrations found in the thirteenth-century Maciejowski Bible are something of a mystery, in that they show the expected period dress and weaponry of Western Europe except for the use of camels as mounts and the bows which, unlike any other illustrations or archaeological finds from western sources, are shown with the enlarged handgrip and static recurve tips of Asian composite bows. These bows are shown as being about the height of the archer's chin but some are shown being drawn to the ear, a long draw for a wooden bow of this length. However, the bow limbs are shown thicker than those of a composite. Asiatic tribes of northern Russia, such as the Ostjak, made wooden bows of this type, as have some modern craftsmen. It is possible that the artist had seen an Asiatic bow and pictured it in his illustrations of Biblical events. An imperfectly preserved painting in the thirteenth-century Sainte Chapelle in Paris also seems to show such a bow.

Stone and Pellet Bows

An arowe of an elle longe,
In hys bowe he it throng
And to thr head he gave it hale;
There is no deere in this forest,
An it would on him feste,
But it should spill his shale.

The Kynge and the Hermit (fourteenth-century poem)[13]

The stonebow was a bow adapted to cast stones or pellets. Sometimes the adaptation would be confined to a different type of string, a double string equipped with a pair of wooden or ivory rods as spacers and a pouch or other holder between them, sometimes the bow itself was of a specialised form. Bows of this type have been used all over the world, the oldest known specimen, a pelletbow, being found in Japan. Two means of ensuring that the pellet clears the stave (and the shooter's hand), are either a built-up handgrip that will permit holding the bow with the necessary torque or twist to throw the pellet to the side of the bow, or more rarely to have an opening within the bow through which the pellet passes.

The earliest European illustration is in *The Book of Hours of Catherine of Cleves*, written in the Netherlands around 1440 and now in the Pierpont Morgan Library. In the framing margin of the page for the feast day of St Fabian and St Sebastian, bows, crossbows, bolts and other accessories are illustrated. Amongst the bows a pelletbow with double string and square pellet cradle is carefully portrayed; a special feature is the depiction of a central brace of steel with a round eye for the passage of the pellet. The two arms of the bow are separately fitted into sockets on either side of the eye. Since with this type of bow the pellet did not have to be shot with a twist, there was no need for a special built up handgrip. Double-pouches of white and blue are shown above and below this bow, used for carrying pellets. The different colours of the pouches imply that two types of pellets were carried, such as steel, lead or clay. A mosque lamp made for the Mamluk emir Ad-Din the Bowman (1216–1285) shows pellet bows of similar type.

Stone and pellet bows appear in the historical record, as in 1327, when rowdys were recorded as annoying Londoners with stonebows and crossbows ('*balistas et arcus pro lapidibus*') with which they shot stones and clay pellets up lanes and alleyways. Later, in 1479, Louis XI of France purchased stone-throwing steel crossbows and stonebows together with moulds for making the pellets. A pelletbow is listed in a will of 1567, and when Henry VIII died in 1574 the inventory of his armoury in the stores at Greenwich listed two longbows with a leather bag containing moulds to make pellets of lead or clay; at Westminster were 'Twoo Longe Bowes of Ewghe to shote stones in withe cases of Lether to them.'

Pellets used in India in 1830 were made of blue or yellow clay, mixed with a little oil and dried in the shade so as not to dry out too much. They were described as larger than a musket ball, but not heavier than a lead ball at about 24 to the pound, that is, about an ounce and a half, or the weight of a respectable arrow. No aim was taken with these bows, although the naturalist Henry Forbes claimed to have killed a squirrel at 80 yards and said these bows could be deadly.

Another type of bow used to shoot a ball was the slurbow. This was equipped with an arrow permanently attached to the string. A weak spring on each side of the head lightly held the ball, which was thrown when the arrow was loosed. The arrow could also be headed with a 3–4 foot tube containing shot which was similarly discharged. The slurbow was probably not used prior to the invention of hand held firearms.

Bowtips

Horn bowtips are shown in a tenth-century Saxon drawing in the Cotton manuscripts. An Italian fourteenth-century manuscript, and others, in which the bowtips are black, may also indicate horn tips, such as those found on the *Mary Rose* bows. They do not seem to have come into general use until the fifteenth century. In 1561, 6′ 6″ bowstaves 'ready made except the horns' are recorded as having been procured from Naples. The *Mary Rose* bows seem to have all had horn nocks to fit bowtips that measured about 12mm in circumference, evidently standardised. Only one horn nock from the *Mary Rose* has been preserved. It is less than three inches long, with rather thin walls, the notch cut in only one side, as was usual with earlier wooden bows. It is suitable for an upper nock, to be used with a string loop. A lower nock could be the same. Antler and iron spikes on the tips of two Nydam bows (see p.57) have been mistaken for nocks, but seems unlikely. Horn nocks seem to have been used in the fourteenth century and came into general, although not universal, use in the fifteenth century.

Horn nocks have continued in use until the present day in England, where a longbow is not considered complete without them. When they were glued in place with animal glue, wet weather could cause the horns as well as fletching to come loose, as reported by Elizabethan archers in Ireland. *Lartdarcherie* describes them as being

> ... usually made of cows horn, the reason being that it is softer and less elastic than that of other horns, and it is well suited for the square and round bows used for chapperon shooting as it is not too springy. But for flight shooting they are best when made from the tips of stag horns, for the harder the horn, the greater the spring it will give to the bow. And you should know that all horns should be fairly large when they fit on the bow, so as to keep the string away from the wood, and the shorter they are the better, as long as the bow can be strung. Some people have silver horns put on their bows, but I have found this neither useful or profitable, and I have tried both.

The purpose of the horn tips would seem to have been, in addition to keeping the string from touching the limb, as Mongols accomplished with the little transverse bone blocks at their bowtips, to enable the wooden bowtips to be given the

maximum thinning, or 'whipping'. *Lartdarcherie* specifies the greatest reduction
within a palm's breadth of the tips to maximise cast. 'Every well made bow should be
reduced as much as can be safely done near the horns.' A personal bow might have the
tips reduced even more than the 12mm warbows, and one *Mary Rose* bow had been
treated thus after the horn nocks had been affixed.

5

ARROWS

… his armourer came to present him with six new arrows, Rufus took the arrows, tested them for their suppleness and complimented the armourer on his fine workmanship. Rufus, keeping four of the arrows himself, gave the other two to his best friend and companion Walter Tyrell, saying that the sharpest arrows should go to him who was best able to kill with them.

Odericus Vitalis[14]

The arrows from the ramparts fall like hail
Upon the pagan enemy below,
And piercing shrieks the sky with fear assail,
Arising from the Christians and their foe.

Ludovico Ariosto, *Orlando Furioso*[15]

Arrows were made in three forms for butt, prick (clout), or flight shooting respectively. Feathers were attached to the 'shaftment', the nock end of the stele. A shaftment was 6½ inches until the twelfth century, then 6 inches. *Lartdarcherie* divides arrows into two kinds according to the means of fastening the feathers: glued and waxed. In the first case, the feathers were glued to a shaftment; in the second, the feathers were bound to a waxed shaftment.

The glue used would have likely been animal glue, which, not being waterproof, was not stable in wet conditions. Elizabethan archers stationed in Ireland complained that their fletching, apparently glued, was coming loose in the damp climate and that their bowstrings, treated with hoof glue, were damaged. Isinglass (fish glue) might have been preferable, but being produced from the bladders of sturgeon, was not available in quantity. Arrows pictured with red binding at both ends of the fletching would probably have been glued. *Lartdarcherie* claims that the English preferred glued fletching, but those found on the *Mary Rose* were waxed.

The waxed arrows from the *Mary Rose* were probably coated under the fletching with sealing wax, a mixture of green verdigris, beeswax and pitch, the fletching then

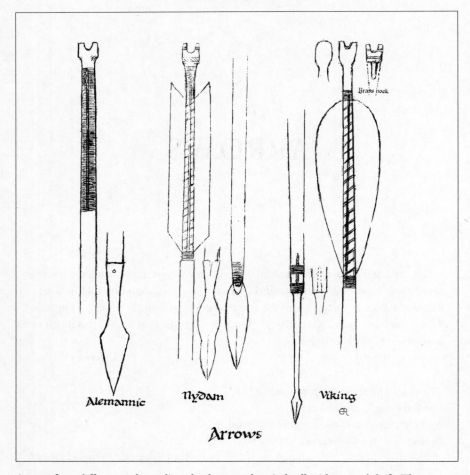

Arrows from different early mediaeval cultures and periods, all with tapered shafts. The Alemannic arrow is short, to be used with a stiff handled bow, fletching style unknown. Short arrows for smallbows might simply be cylindrical.

being bound in place with red silk thread and heated to fuse the shaft, fletching and binding. Unlike glued fletching, this was waterproof. This method evolved from the fletching with birch tar and binding of earlier times including the Nydam find (see p.57) and the Alemmanic (see p.58) arrows.

According to *Lartdarcherie*, there were two sorts of glued arrows: sheaf and flight. The sheaf arrows were usually thick with high swan feathers, cut large, in the same shape as those of flight arrows, and with round iron heads. They were the regular arrows that the English used for butt and chapperon shooting because they were truer than any waxed arrow. The English called every glued and iron headed shaft, whether big or little, a sheaf arrow.

Glued flight arrows were headed with horn or iron heads and were fletched with the first pinion feathers of the wings of pigeons or ducks, variously with three, six or nine feathers. Three feathers were considered best, to be three small finger widths long. The six-feather fletching added three lower feathers between them and the horn nocking. Nine-feather arrows were considered good only for show. Some were made hollow, bored from the head to within three fingers breadth of the feathers which themselves were the breadth of three small fingers in length. The nock was of horn. Some shooters filled the hollow arrows with lead, others with quicksilver, the latter being more effective. However, the use of hollow arrows, which looked like solid ones, was considered dishonourable through giving an unfair advantage. It is hard to imagine how a lead core would cause arrows to fly farther, but *Lartdarcherie* claimed they did. Some Turkish flight arrows had lead inserted in a hole drilled in the base of the nock to bring the balance point toward the rear for a farther flight.

Waxed arrows were used for butt, chapperon and flight shooting, with appropriate feathering for each use, bound with silk on wax. These were preferably swan feathers, the front wing feather for butt shooting, the hinder wing feathers for chapperon shooting. *Lartdarcherie* considered goose feathers, though commonly used, to be suitable only for war arrows and although many shafts were made of ash, aspen was thought best. Ascham, however, found ash preferable to lightweight aspen.

For flight shooting with waxed arrows tipped with very light iron heads, gerfaulcon feathers were recommended. Shafts were to be of a light, stiff wood like birch or cherry. These might also be 'made hollow with a long head and varnished above and below.' *Lartdarcherie* states that English flight arrows were considered the best because the wood available in England was lighter and stiffer than that found in France. To judge by the amount of space given to flight shooting equipment in *Lartdarcherie*, it was a popular activity. Some flight arrows were made to shoot better with the wind, some to shoot better against it, the two appearing identical.

Stele Types

> A shaft hath three principal parts, the stele, the feather, and the head; each of which must be severally spoken of.'
>
> Roger Ascham, *Toxophilus*

The stele is the wooden part of the arrow, usually with a nock at one end to receive the bowstring. Steles were of a variety of shapes of which Ascham names two: the 'breasted' and the 'taper', the latter also called 'reshe-(rush) grown' or 'bob-tail', and there were others as well. All these forms at least up to the mid-fifteenth century seem to have had nocks as thick as, or thicker than, the maximum thickness of the shaft. The *Mary Rose* arrows, perhaps for faster production, have no expansion of nocks but have horn slips to reinforce the nocks.

Steles were made of a single piece of wood or they were pieced in the foreshaft like arrows in the Stone Age or more modern 'footed' arrows, but also sometimes in the shaftment with a heavier wood 'to counterwey with the heade'. Sometimes an arrow had more than one piecing. Archers also liked the decorative effect.

Arrow nocks were secured against splitting by being enlarged, as in many of the Nydam and Hedeby arrows, by brass nocks with a tang inserted in a hole drilled in the stele end as in a few Vendel period Norse arrows, by tanged horn nocks as mentioned in *Lartdarcherie* and pictured in John Gower's book, or by a horn slip inserted in a saw cut at a right angle to the nock, as the *Mary Rose* arrows.

Ascham defined the requirements simply: an arrow should be 'strong enough to stand in a bow, and light enough to fly farre'. This will be further considered in Chapter 11.

Breasted

The breast is the area forward of the shaftmond, the part of the arrow at the nock end measured by the fist and outstretched thumb. The stele is tapered from the breast forward to the head and backward to the nock. This shaft has the flattest trajectory due to the balance point being farther back than the midpoint. It also is lighter than a parallel shaft for a bow of a given strength. Ascham wrote that 'the bigge breasted shaft is fit for him which shooteth right afore him but is not good for him that shooteth under hand for it will hobble.' This shaft is good for long shots from powerful bows and was considered best except for very short lengths or in a rough wind. Saracens began the forward taper from the midpoint of the stele.

Taper

This shaft is thickest at the head, tapering to the nock. The taper may be increased in the shaftmond. Ascham says that these steles 'stress not a shaft much in the breast where the weight of the bow lieth as you may see by the wearing of every shaft', but that 'a little breasted shaft is not good for him that shooteth above the hand (right afore him) because it will start.' Saracens felt that the taper arrow with low fletching was swiftest. This shaft is good at short distances, especially for weaker bows. It tends to shoot to the left. The longer *Mary Rose* arrows were of this type, ½ inch thick at the head, tapering evenly to a ⅜-inch nock. Taper arrows are also seen in the *Luttrell Psalter* depiction of archers at the butts (see picture 15 in the colour section). Howard Hill and other modern archers found lightly tapered arrows most accurate and forgiving for general shooting. A dissenting *Lartdarcherie* however, considers taper arrows, of ash, fit only for proving armour. Certainly the thick foreshaft reduces the breaking off of arrowheads. In England the taper was considered the most accurate for short range shooting until the time of Horace Ford's unqualified endorsement (based on incorrect assumptions) of parallel shafts.

Parallel

This stele is of the same diameter throughout except perhaps for a taper in the shaftmond. Although it is by far the most popular form at the present time, Ascham considered it too weak in the breast. Saracens found it not as good as other types for long arrows but better for short arrows that might otherwise be too light for anything but flight shooting. However, many arrows in manuscript illustrations appear to be of the parallel type. The shorter *Mary Rose* arrows were around ½ inch in diameter for

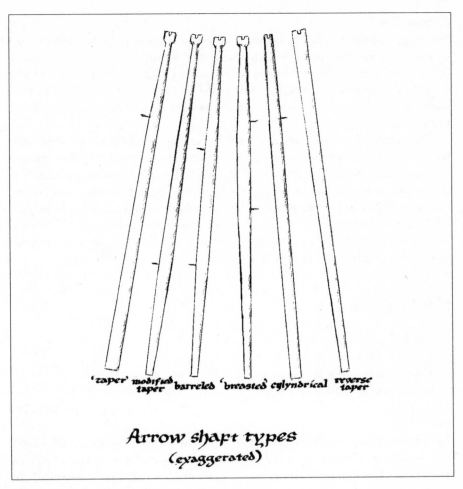

Arrow shaft types
(exaggerated)

Forms of arrow steles of mediaeval and Renaissance arrows.

about two-thirds of their length then tapered to a ⅜-inch nock. Thinner shafts tend to be parallel when it is not practical to reduce the nock width.

Barreled
Similar to the breasted type but tapering evenly to both ends from the middle third of its length. Saracens considered this style most accurate and generally best and classified it as a variant of breasted arrow, as Europeans may also have done.

Modified Taper
This stele has its thickest portion toward the head and is otherwise tapered toward head and nock like the breasted and barreled arrows. A Viking arrow from Norway with a long spread nock for fast nocking in war is of this type, as is the Chapter House arrow in England.

Reverse Taper

This type of stele has the expanded end of the taper at the nock and appears clearly in several illustrations and one statue of the early Renaissance, shown as a short arrow with a long or heavy head. This style could only be practical to give weight and a narrow foreshaft to a short arrow for penetration purposes. The head would have to be heavy enough to keep the balance point of the arrow from being too far back.

Arrows tapered to both ends will shoot farther than a parallel arrow of the same weight and can be shot from a stronger bow because less of the thrust of the string is dissipated through bending, When a parallel arrow is shot, it bends almost entirely in the middle, so there is a lot of wood in the shaftment and foreshaft that does nothing to enable the arrow to stand in a bow. The taper in the shaftment is meant to cause the loosed arrow to stabilise more quickly. Some *Mary Rose* arrows were found to be thinner at their midpoint. It is extremely doubtful that they were made that way, and may be due to shrinkage from water damage.

Fletching Styles

> The dynt yt was both sad and sar,
> That he of Mongonberry sete,
> The swan-fethars, that his arrowe bar,
> With his hart-blood the wear wete.

The Hontyng of the Cheviat[16]

To affix fletching, birch tar made from the thin bark of the European white birch was used as an adhesive from the Stone Age. The bark must be heated to over 350 degrees Celsius, in the absence of oxygen, otherwise it will simply char. The resultant brittle black mass is liquid when heated and can be painted on, hardening as it cools. It can be softened again by careful heating to make adjustments in position. Thought to be no longer used in Britain by Roman times, its usage continued in northern Europe. Ancient methods of production remain a mystery. Glue from bluebell bulbs boiled with a little water has reportedly been found on Bronze Age arrows for fletching and was suggested for that purpose in a sixteenth-century herbal. It works well on porous surfaces such as paper and was used to starch lace in Tudor times.

Later, fish glue such as isinglass or animal glue was used. *Mary Rose* arrows that may have been fletched with isinglass show green colouring of viridian on the shaftment. Animal glue was in use by fletchers until recently. It is water soluble, and Tudor English archers in Ireland regularly lost their fletching in the rain.

Feathers on mediaeval arrows were cut in a variety of styles, some of which had specific names. Ascham mentions several styles.

Square shorn

This is the simplest type. The rib is cut to length and the feather is trimmed parallel to the rib. This style, pictured in early continental manuscripts, is suitable for short range hunting arrows. The Japanese and Chinese used it on all types of arrows meant for excellent archers. Because this style has the most air resistance, fletchers fixed the vanes in line with the axis of the shaft rather than helical.

Swine backed

This type is so named because of the similarity of its curve to the ridge of the back of a wild boar. It was a popular style and often pictured in early manuscripts. It is still popular today.

Saddle backed

The name apparently is derived from the appearance of an early type of mediaeval saddle with a high cantle and no pommel. Ascham writes: 'The swyne backed fashion maketh the shaft deader, for it gathereth more ayre than the saddle backed, and therefore the saddle backed is surer for daunger of weather, and fitter for smooth flying.' Arabs called this style with an untrimmed tail the 'martin trim' because of its resemblance to the wing of a martin.

Round

Ascham writes of the round cut feather as good and much used before his own time. It is necessarily the shortest feather and Ascham mentions that it may therefore be mounted lower on the shaft. This style had been used by ancient Greeks. It cannot be cut to a perfect semicircle because of the slant of the barbs of the feather.

Tryangel

This is cut with straight edges as the name suggests and probably means right triangles. Ascham writes of it as being the most popular style in his own time. It is very common in manuscript illustrations of the fifteenth century.

There were usually three vanes to an arrow though *Lartdarcherie* describes flight arrows with six or even nine. With three-vane fletching, one vane, a different colour than the others, was called the cock feather because it stood upright when the arrow was nocked on a horizontal bow. The two shaft feathers would ride equally on the bow when the arrow was loosed. Less common was the use of four vanes, used on the Danish arrows from Nydam, and also those of the Saracens, which permitted faster nocking and the use of the cross nocks mentioned by Ascham. Some modern archers also feel that four-vane fletching helps accuracy. The usual fletching was made of goose wing feathers plucked while the bird was alive. While some writers emphasise grey goose feathers, manuscript illustrations usually show white ones, and Ascham's advice to have a cock feather of black or grey implies that the remaining feathers were of another colour, probably white. Peacock feathers, the brown wing feathers, were more highly prized although Ascham found them too rough and heavy.

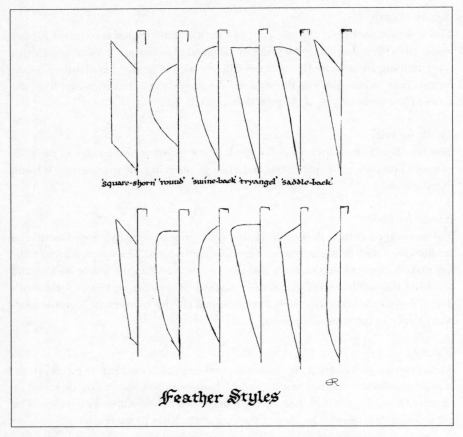

'square-shorn' 'round' 'swine-back' 'tryangel' 'saddle-back'

ℰℛ

Feather Styles

No mediaeval or Renaissance feather fletching has been preserved but the styles are well known from manuscript illustrations, verbal descriptions and impressions in the birch tar or wax used in fletching.

If the head of the arrow is light, the feathers should be cut low and short. For heavy heads the feathers should be higher and longer. An English inventory of 1475 lists arrows with the new long style 9-, 8-, and 7-inch feathers, the latter being more than half the total, and the 1397 Arundell inventory lists 10-inch peacock and 9-inch peahen fletchings. A Tower of London inventory of 1523 lists 4000 sheaves with 9-inch fletching. A round fletch would be only a few inches long. For comparison, the Chinese war arrow tested by Pope (see p.21) had feathers a foot long.

Two-vane feather fletching was rarely used on arrows for handbows but was used on crossbow arrows and bolts, as well as wood, horn, leather, parchment, or even copper vanes. For very short range, some arrows had no fletching at all. Fletching will be further considered in Chapter 11.

Arrowheads

Ane othir court thare saw I consequent,
Cupide the king wyth bow in handy bent,
And dredefull arowis grundyn scharp and square.

William Dunbar, *The Golden Targe* (fifteenth century)[17]

In mediaeval times, blunt and whistling arrowheads were made of wood or horn, and normal arrowheads, while occasionally still made of bone or antler, were mostly made of steel in a number of different forms. To fix arrowheads to the shaft, some early ones were made with a tang inserted in a hole drilled in a stele, and some flat blades such as forked or chisel type blades were fixed in a saw cut in the end of the stele, these types having the stele reinforced with wire binding. Arrowheads made with a socket to receive the stele became nearly universal after the time of the Vikings. Early sockets were about ⅞-inch outside diameter, Tudor ones ½ inch for the bobtailed shafts. For some hunting arrows, a pin through socket and stele prevented arrowheads from becoming detached. War arrows were designed so that the arrowhead would detach, meaning that the arrowhead would remain in a wound, making injuries more severe and preventing the enemy shooting the arrow back. Ascham notes three types of arrowheads 'used in old tyme'. They are the 'brode arrow hede' or 'swallow tayle', the 'forke hede', and the 'Englyshe heades' which were the best for war, these being the barbed heads now classified as type 16. The Arundel Archive of 1422 lists 'sperehedes, bykere, dokebyll, hoked, broadhoked, horsehead' and 'forker' arrowheads.

Broadheads

These have flat pointed blades with sharp edges, sometimes with a central rib, or are of lozenge section. Often they are 'bearded' (barbed). Broadheads an inch wide from barb to barb were ordered by Edward III at the beginning of the Hundred Years War until improvements in armour reduced their effectiveness. Broadheads continued to be used for hunting, and are still used for that purpose. The terms 'hooked' and 'broadhooked' may refer to the long barbs of swallowtail broadheads. Their barbs are not intended to hang in an animal's flesh, but to reduce the weight and wind planing for the length of the edge. The *sperehedes* would be lanceolate, leaf shaped, without barbs. These were suitable for either war or hunting. Dr Saxton Pope's experiments showed that broadheads penetrated better than bodkins in yielding animal tissue, the central blade cutting a path for the two lower blades to pass through with lessened friction, but they could also pierce a mail hauberk.

The type 16 war arrowheads, called 'English heads' and perhaps 'bykere' heads, a compromise between broadhead and bodkin, were barbed, designed to make them difficult to remove from a wound. Ascham however, felt that they interfered with the rotation of the arrow that he thought necessary for maximum penetration. They may be the horseheads mentioned in the Arundel Archive, the small barbs forming the horse's ears. These were effective against man or horse, and a horse hit with a few long barbed arrows would run mad.

Mediaeval hunters were warned about the danger of being on the opposite side of a game trail from another hunter because of the risk of injury from an arrow passing completely through a deer. However a huge 'swallowtail' broadhead such as the one four fingers wide and five fingers long recommended in *Le Livre de Chasse* is clearly intended to cause extreme blood loss rather than deep penetration, as is an *angell* (angle) head with edges forming a right angle. Similarly a Viking broadhead with an additional transverse blade made a cross-shaped wound which was nearly impossible to close. This may have been the *flein* that took the life of Haakon the Good, the third king of Norway, at the Battle of Fitjar in 961.

Small barbed broadheads with very long tangs were used for fire arrows, the exposed tang wrapped with flammable material and the barbs bent into an S section to hang in a thatched roof until it was well ignited.

Bodkins

The word bodkin was applied to any object used for piercing, including awls as well as arrowheads. Designed to pierce armour, narrow bodkin arrows were used only in warfare, and could have square, triangular or lozenge cross sections. Those from the early Middle Ages were slender in order to be effective against a mail hauberk. If an arrow had enough force to snap one link, it went on through. Some Viking arrowheads were slender enough to pass through the link. Shorter, stouter bodkins 2–5 inches long came into use as plate armour developed. Short triangular bodkins had a can opener effect, the three sharp edges cutting, and the sides pressing the corners of the cut inwards. Dr Pope's experiments showed that while the broadhead penetrated best in yielding animal tissue where the bodkin would bind, his square bodkin penetrated best in boards, metal plate, and chain mail. 'Quarrels', from the French 'quarré' and specific to crossbows, had four-sided points.

Some Tudor bodkins recently tested were not hardened. These may have been used in practice shooting at round boards used as targets.

Forked and chisel heads

Also with flat blades, forked heads, 'forkers' differed from broadheads in having two points with a cutting edge between them. They were used in hunting both large game and waterfowl from the Scottish highlands to Siberia. Those with crescent heads could cut off a wing or head of a waterfowl and a body hit would kill, even without cutting through the feathers; the Roman emperor Commodus is recorded as having used forked arrows to decapitate running ostriches.

A forked arrow may have been the 'slotted arrow' that killed King Harald Hardrada, and in the later Middle Ages, forkers may have been used for cutting sails, shrouds and lines on ships during sea battles. Their suitability for cutting such lines was shown in a very different setting in the early twentieth century, when a number of bowmen were being auditioned for work on the movie *Robin Hood* starring Errol Flynn. They were asked to attempt to cut a gallows rope, which Howard Hill cut with a forked arrowhead that he had devised. When asked if he could do it again, he asked 'How many times?' He got the job.

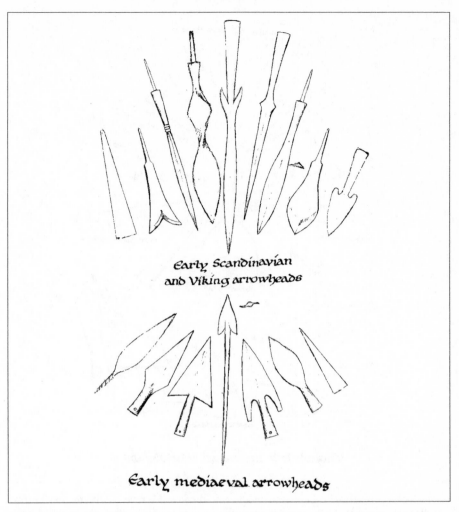

Early Scandinavian
and Viking arrowheads

Early mediaeval arrowheads

The arrowheads depicted above are all preserved steel heads now in museums. The central early mediaeval arrowhead is for a fire arrow. The Viking arrowheads show attention to mail piercing. Up to this period, arrowheads continued to be a mix of tanged and socketed arrowheads, like those from Nydam. The one with a second blade at a right angle, perhaps a *flein*, would make a cross-shaped wound, difficult to close.

Uncommon chisel-shaped arrowheads, perhaps the duckbills ('dokebyll') mentioned in the Arundel Archive, may have been similarly used. Experiments have shown their penetration to be as effective as broadheads.

Piles
Round in cross section, they were made with pointed or rounded ends like bullets. They were usually used in target practice but may have occasionally have been used in war. Ascham mentions a late mediaeval type of pile called a silver spoon head from

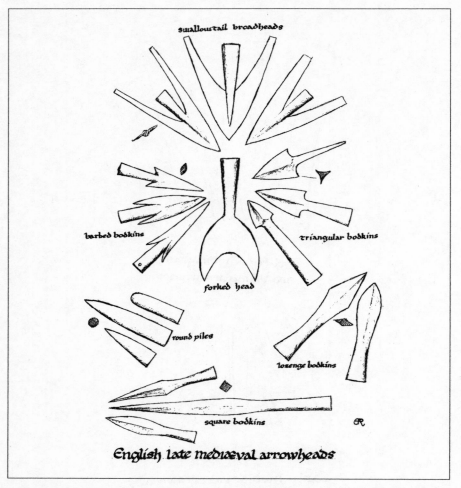

swallowtail broadheads

barbed bodkins

triangular bodkins

forked head

round piles

lozenge bodkins

square bodkins

English late mediæval arrowheads

Of the barbed English arrowheads, the middle type, the so called type 16 with the small barbs, was the most common. English bodkins were from two to five inches long and weighed from ½ to 1¾ ounces. The English swallowtail broadheads were used in both war and hunting at this time.

its resemblance to the ornament on the ends of some silver spoon handles. This pile had a ridged shoulder at the opening of the socket so that the archer could tell by feel when he had come to full draw. Drayton's poems refer to any kind of arrowhead as a pile, and an old Saxon meaning of the word is 'arrow'. '*Pil*' is also the Old Norse word for arrow.

Blunts

Large bulky arrowheads made of horn, antler or wood and made with a round or sometimes pentagonal cross section were used for popinjay shooting and for hunting small game such as birds and squirrels, in order to stun the animal without damaging the skin or flesh. In 1247 the Earl of Winton, with exclusive hunting rights in Bradgate Park, agreed to allow a neighbouring baron to hunt there with nine bows and six hounds. However, the archers were to use no barbed arrowheads but only '*sagittas pilettas*,' arrows with rounded knobs on the shafts to prevent complete penetration. Blunts were also used for target practice, usually at short range, and sometimes had a projection at the tip so that they would stick in a butt. Archaeological finds at the Viking town of Hedeby include wooden blunts that are of one piece with the stele.

Whistling arrows

Heads similar to blunts, but hollow and with holes cut in such a way as to produce a whistling or howling sound while flying, were used from ancient times in China and were used by Mongols for signalling and for psychological effect. The earliest mention of them in European records is from the reign of Henry VIII.

Fire arrows

The fire arrowhead had a very long shank, most of which was left exposed to wrap with impregnated tow. The barbs were bent into an S cross section to hang in a thatched roof while the fire took hold. The use of fire arrows by the English was noted by Matthew Paris. Arrows carrying an ounce of combustible material, called 'fireworks,' could apparently be shot 'twelve score'. According to Vegetius this material was composed of pitch, resin, oil or naphtha on cotton or tow, wrapped on the end in the form of a ball. Its use was especially effective in naval operations.

Incendiary crossbow bolts at the Swiss National Museum have been analysed and it was fould that their cloth wrappings were saturated with the following ingredients:

	outer layer	inner layer
sulphur	88%	13.7%
salpeter	10.4%	83.5%
charcoal	2.8%	2.8%

A type of fire arrow used by the Saracens was headed with a little glass bottle of naphtha. The arrow shaft was fixed in the opening of the bottle which would shatter on impact and was sprinkled with powdered black sulphur to ignite while flying through the air. A combination of phosphorus and magnesium, carried separately and applied just before shooting, ignited from the friction of flight. Saracens also used larger flaming bottles of naphtha as a kind of Molotov cocktail against armoured crusaders. The little bottles were also used in yet another variant of chemical warfare. In sea fights bottles of quicklime were used to blind the eyes and disorder the foe, according to Matthew Paris.

Some think that the famous Greek fire was produced from crude oil with added sulphur, pitch and quicklime. The seventh-century addition of salpeter could produce spontaneous combustion.

Poisoned arrows

For large game, Spanish hunters poisoned the heads of their crossbow bolts with the pressed juice of the white hellebore (veratum album) plant. Poisoned arrows are not known to have been otherwise used in Europe, despite French suspicions about English arrows and English medical treatments for poisoned arrows.

6

OUT OF ASIA

And there came with him thirty and six Kings, and one Moorish Queen, who was a negress, a queen called in Arabic 'Nugueymat Turya', Star of the Archers, and she brought with her two hundred horsewomen, all negresses like herself, all having their hair shorn save a tuft on the top, and this was in token that they came as if upon a pilgrimage, and to obtain the remission of their sins; and they were all armed in coats of mail and with Turkish bows.

The Chronicle of the Cid[18]

The angels attend no human sport save archery.

The Prophet Mohammed

Reflexed Asiatic composite bows were used by horse archer nomads who ranged the steppes and deserts of Asia. They were made of layers of horn, wood and sinew and were capable of an extraordinary flexion which enabled them to shoot an arrow of nearly their own length. The resultant speed of recovery sent arrows farther than a longbow, and eyewitness accounts reported their phenomenal accuracy. Marco Polo had plenty of opportunity to observe the archery of Kublai Khan's Mongols. Some of these bows found their way to Europe, such as those of the Huns, Alans, Avars, Magyars, Mongols, Saracens and Turks, in slightly varying forms. The Viking name *Hornbogi* implies possession of such bows. Remains of several bows of this type have been found in the Viking town of Birka, which was an end station of the Silk Road and the site of a Khazar trading post, the Khazar traders bringing their bows with them from their steppe homeland. These kinds of bows came to be used by Byzantine fighters and were used in Saracen settlements in Sicily.

The wooden strip used as a basis for the composite bow was preferably of bamboo. Other kinds of wood could be used but bamboo, being extremely flexible, was ideal. Sinew was next glued to the inner curve of the reflexed bamboo strip. The kind of sinew specified was that from the backs of cattle, thick pieces lying along both sides of the ridge bone of the spine. These pieces were dried, then soaked and softened, then separated. The 'northern barbarians' (the Mongols and others) lacking silk or the hemp from which the Chinese made their bowstrings, used sinew for this purpose also and made glue from fish bladders.

The wooden core, the sinew and the horn, were about equally thick. Shredded sinew bundles soaked in glue were overlapped, and each layer was allowed to dry before the next was put on. For the horn belly plates the Chinese used two pieces of oxhorn while the northern 'barbarians' used four pieces of sheep horn. The Chinese made their bows wider toward the tips than the handgrip, and at the tips were rigid pieces of wood angled forward from the back. Near the ends of these, the nocks were cut. The completed bow was dried over a low fire for ten days to two months, and the nock was covered with thick leather or soft wood.

This was the basic type of bow construction of all the Mongolian and Saracen bows that came to be used in Europe, primarily in Italy. Saracen settlements in Sicily were a source of competent archers and crossbowmen that were employed by Christian kings and emperors in the early Middle Ages. While Muslims were skilled with crossbows, handbows were very popular, partly because of their resemblance to the Muslim crescent as opposed to the Christian cross suggested by crossbows. While the Christian church declared archery hateful to God, the Prophet Mohammed felt otherwise.

The bows of the Huns were from 4' 7″ to 5' in length. None have been completely preserved but remains found in burials give a picture of their specifications. They were made with bone plates attached at handgrip and tips to make those areas rigid. The reflexed limbs were elliptical in section. A gold foil covering for a bow in a grave shows parallel sides up to the bone tips that angle to a point. The working limbs were a flattened oval, each only about a foot in length, and the curved upper tip was longer than the lower, bringing the arrow pass to the middle of the bow.

The Alans, though not Mongolian, rode with the Huns and their bows seem to have been identical. One from Alanian kurgan # 2 was 4′ 7″ long. Bows of this type were also used by Germanic tribesmen such as the Ostrogoths who rode with the Huns.

The later Avar bows of seventh and eighth-century Hungary were as much as a foot shorter and were sharply curved at the juncture of ear and limb. The Avars were Asiatic and in fact were still called Huns by contemporary Europeans. Shortening the bow and increasing the recurve increased the distance the bow would cast. Remains of a Magyar bow show only the ear plates with no plates at the handgrip. Arrows used with these bows were usually between 75–90cm.

The *Thorsdrapa* of 990 AD (a Viking skaldic poem) mentions '*tvividar*,' double-wood bows, two-ply laminates that were in early times a product of the Finno-Ugric hunting tribes inhabiting northern Russia and Scandinavia. Those of the northern Russian tribes such as the Ostjak, usually with sharply recurved tips, were almost identical in appearance to the hornbows of the Asian horse archers. Not infrequently they also had a thin layer of sinew on the back, protected by birch bark, but horn was not used. They were made of a flexible wood for the back and a stiff coniferous wood for the belly. The ears were sometimes a part of the back strip, at other times separate pieces fitted in various ways, glued and bound.

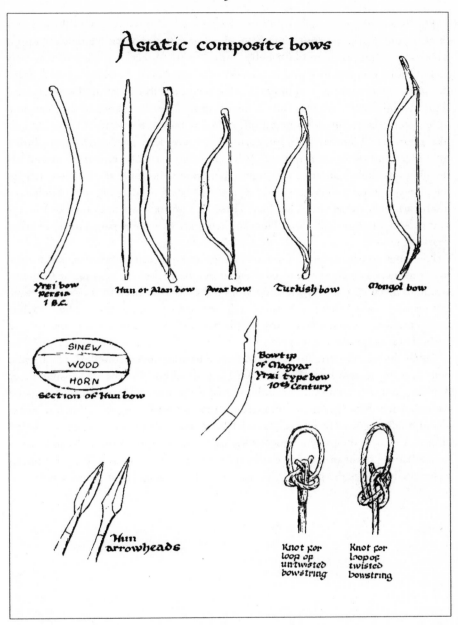

Asiatic composite bows

Yrzi bow Persia 1 B.C.

Hun or Alan bow

Awar bow

Turkish bow

Mongol bow

SINEW
WOOD
HORN

Section of Hun bow

Bow tip of Magyar Yrzi type bow 10th Century

Hun arrowheads

Knot for loop of untwisted bowstring

Knot for loop of twisted bowstring

The Roman historian Tacitus mentions the 'Fenni' of 'Ultima Thule' who lived east of the Baltic and hunted with bows and bone tipped arrows. They lived by reindeer herding and hunting in Arctic regions where there was limited choice of wood. Their descendants in northern Scandinavia, the Lapps and Finns whom the Vikings knew collectively as Finns, made and used double-wood bows ranging from short hand-bows to six-foot longbows with bone tipped arrows.

The bows were made of a thin birch back which also formed the tips, and of a thicker pine (Furu, Norway Pine) belly glued together, providing a tension-strong back and compression-resistant belly similar to the effect of a stave of yew that includes sapwood and heartwood. Travellers described how the glue was made from the skins of large freshly caught perch. One account tells us that the Lapps laid the skins in cold water until the scales came off easily. They then cooked the skins in a little water, continually skimming it off, and stirred until the contents become thick like a porridge. This was dried for storing. Whenever they needed glue, they broke off a piece and dissolved it in water. When the two parts of a bow were assembled the glue was applied and the parts tightly bound together until the bow was dry. As the glue was water soluble, it had to be protected by an overlapping spiral binding of birch bark strip, the bow tips left bare. These bows were sometimes used by Vikings as well as by Finns or half-blood Finns in their service, as the personal name *Finnbogi* bears witness.

The longbows remained in use long enough to be described by seventeenth-century travellers as well as being represented by one preserved example at Orbyhus Castle in Sweden. The Orbyhus bow does not quite date back to the Middle Ages, but we may assume that very similar ones were used in earlier times. The Orbyhus bow is fitted at one end with an iron ferrule that includes a spike and a groove to bind a wooden ring for use as a ski pole.

Other finds of Finnish bows in Scandinavia have not been complete. The broken belly sections of two bows are fairly well preserved but the tips are missing. Early drawings of bows used by Finns indicate that these were seldom recurved. Finland has no ancient bow specimens but there is a mediaeval painting in a church showing a saint holding a short handbow. The tips are recurved but the string, instead of being affixed at or near the extreme ends of the ears as in the case of the Russian bows, is nocked at the point of curvature several inches from the end as in most European examples. However, the painting may have been by a foreign artist, as many were.

7

CROSSBOWS

Artem autem illam mortiferam etDeo odibilem ballistoriorum et saggitariorum, adversus christianos et catholicos de cetero sub anathemate prohibemus. (We prohibit under anathema that murderous art of crossbowmen and archers, which is hated by God, to be employed against Christians and Catholics from now on.)

The 29th Canon, Second Lateran Council, 1139[19]

The Genoways did them great trouble with their cross-bows.

Froissart's Chronicles[20]

Although Roman armies used crossbows, there are no records of their use in northern Europe before the Norman invasion of Britain. However, they soon became a standard missile weapon. In 1139 at the Second Lateran Council, Pope Innocent II condemned the use of crossbows (and bows) against Christians. However he did permit their use against heathens, and the popularity of crossbows continued to increase. Crossbows, first used in any numbers in the eleventh century, were popularised in France and England by Richard the Lionheart who learned to appreciate them during the crusades.

Making crossbows was a craft outside the province of the bowyer and became the province of the arbalastier (see Chaper 15). A Berwick Castle inventory of 1298 lists 7 crossbows with winches, 6 two-foot crossbows, 8 one-foot crossbows and 189 goose wings for fletching bolts. However, at that time Roxborough Castle had only 20 crossbowmen but 92 archers, so the traditional bow was clearly more common. In he wider world, Venetian traders, crewing their swift eastbound galleys, are recorded as being each equipped with abacus and crossbow while their Genoese rivals specialised as mercenary crossbowmen. King Henry VII restricted crossbows to those with 200 marks annual rental but by that time crossbow makers were beginning to change over to firearms.

An early type of crossbow mechanism was one in which the string rested in a groove in the tiller and was released by an upward moving pin. Crossbows of this kind

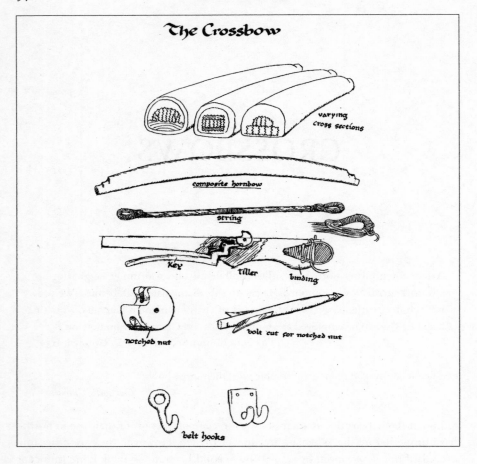

The Crossbow

varying cross sections

composite hornbow

string

Key   Tiller   binding

notched nut   bolt cut for notched nut

belt hooks

were still used in Norwegian whale hunts until the introduction of harpoon guns. One composite crossbow in the Swiss National Museum has a tiller with this type of mechanism, its only metal part being the iron stirrup.

Early crossbows were made with a wooden bow about a yard long, called a 'lath' or 'prod'. Some early European manuscripts show bows with their backs covered with bumps; a bow made from a yew branch gives this effect because of the many pins left raised. More elaborate forms were soon produced. Composite laths of wood, horn and sinew were developed in the twelfth century (hunting crossbows illustrated in *Le Livre de Chasse* seem to have both composite prods and wooden ones) and a revolving nut improved upon the hole and peg tiller (stock), which some continued to use. Forward of the nut, the tiller was grooved to take the bolt. The tiller (stock) was made of hard wood such as pear, walnut or oak; it had to be heavy enough to compensate for the shock of release and was matched to the strength of the bow for steadiness.

In *Le Livre de Chasse* the crossbow arrows are pictured as cylindrical shafts about 15 inches long with heavy broadheads and two-vane feather fletching. Bolts for the later military crossbows were of wood, up to ¾ inch thick and from 12–18 inches in length for the hand-held crossbows. Of course those for the great wall crossbows were much larger. The shafts were often tapered slightly toward the butt, which had no nock. In many bolts, the end of the shaft was vertically thinned to fit a notched nut. French bolts were generally made of beech, although some were of yew.

Bolts were fletched with a variety of materials, usually thin strips of wood, two vanes being glued into deep grooves cut into the shaft with a fence plow plane on a curved track. These were curved considerably, especially toward the butt, in order to make the bolt spin in flight. Although feathers were generally used, some bolts were fletched with pieces of leather, others with copper vanes affixed to the shaft with rivets; the author has seen one example with straight vanes of parchment glued to the shaft. Some bolts, however, had no fletching at all. Crossbow strings were always of the double loop type, sometimes of sinew, more often of hempen thread.

Steel crossbows were first made in about 1314. As crossbows became ever more powerful, the cranequin, a ratchet working on a small wheel turned by a windlass, enabled the crossbowman to cock them more easily. The Burgundians, always on the lookout for new technology, began using steel crossbows in 1426 and used them in the final war of that duchy. They had to have many spare bows because they had a tendency to break in cold weather. In spite of this difficulty, the arctic Lapps used steel crossbows until fairly recently. Steel bows did not have as good a cast as composites but had other advantages. They could be left braced and did not lose effectiveness on hot days or come apart in damp conditions. The steel bow was forged by a blacksmith, the steel strip being tapered and the nocks specially shaped to prevent them cutting the string. These bows, less bulky than the composites, could be fixed with wedges into a slot in the tiller. In the sixteenth century, Italy, Spain, and Germany made the best steel crossbows.

Even Saracens used crossbows with tillers of boxwood or orange and a bow made of two opposing staves of yew. These were used during naval engagements when composites were not employed because of the damp salt air. The use of two opposed staves may imply a construction like that of the Arab 'Filq' type of handbow in which the two pieces of wood were joined side by side in a diagonal line running nearly the length of the stave. Some wooden bows continued in use even after being made obsolete by composite or steel bows.

The composite was the most common type of crossbow in use during the Middle Ages and it persisted as a sporting weapon even after the introduction of steel bows and firearms. The Swiss were still using only composite bows in 1504 when most countries had changed over to steel, and the 'arbrust,' the stone casting crossbow, became popular for birding.

8

THE ARCHAEOLOGY OF ARCHERY

… as the Saxons came first into this realme in Kyng Vortigers dayes, when they had bene here a whyle and at last began to faull out with the Brittons, they troubled and subdewed the Brittons wyth nothynge so much as with their bowe and shafte, whiche wepon beynge straunge, and not sene here before, was wonderfull terrible unto them, and this beginninge I can thynke verie well to be true.

Roger Ascham, Toxophilus[21]

The ravens wheeled, the eagles screamed,
On earth was noise of fray!
From hand was hurled the sharp-filed
spear, the whetted arrow flew.
The bow was busy, shield met spear and
Fierce the combat grew.

The Battle of Maldon[22]

In the nineteenth century, a number of bows and arrows of the Roman period (fifth century) were found in Danish bogs, perfectly preserved by the peat. Curiously, finds from earlier periods in this area contain no archery gear of any kind. Saxo Grammaticus, a twelfth-century Danish monk who wrote down much that had been oral tradition, related a tale of the greatest (legendary) battle that had ever been fought in the Northlands: the Battle of Bravalla Heath where King Harald Wartooth met his end:

The skilled archers of the Gotlanders strung their bows so hard that the shafts pierced through even their shields … for the arrow points made their way through hauberk and helmet as if they were men's defenceless bodies.

Roman historians recorded that the northern barbarians sacrificed everything they captured to their gods. Literary licence aside, this might help to explain the presence of these weapons in bogs that have also yielded human sacrifices.

Danish Bog Finds

On the Jutish peninsula, from whence the troops of Hengist and Horsa crossed the channel into Britain in the wake of the Roman withdrawal, three galleys were unearthed at Nydam Bog. With the galleys were found dozens of bows and arrows as well as many iron and bone arrowheads. There was also a wooden quiver that could have held perhaps a dozen arrows, and bronze mounts for another quiver or possibly a drinking horn.

The bows from Nydam Bog are nearly all longbows of yew, from 5′ 7″–6′ in length and 2.8–3cm in width. One of pine was made like those of yew. They were made from saplings or boles 4.5–10cm in diameter with 7–20 yearly growth rings per centimetre. Cross sections range from a D through rounded D through oval to round. The limbs are evenly tapered and most flatten toward the tips. Sapwood was of the same thickness for the full length of some of the staves, leaving hardly any heartwood at the tips. Some knots were raised while most were worked flat. A typical bow from this find is 178cm in length, 2.8cm wide and 2.6cm thick at the middle. Another is 197.5cm x 2.75cm x 2.6cm.

Nocks vary: a notch in each end on opposite sides, upper left and lower right at 5.5–8.5cm from the tips; a groove around the bowtip; shouldered ends; or a notch in one end with two small holes in the other. Some had no nocks so the strings must have been tied on. Some had a protruding bronze nail 1½–2½ inches below a nock to keep the bowstring loop from slipping down the limb. One bow was furnished with a sharply pointed iron cone (not a nock) at one tip, enabling it to be used as a stabbing weapon. Another bow had a similar spike made from an antler, reminiscent of a Robin Hood ballad in which the hero decapitated the sheriff and stuck the head on the end of his bow.

The arrows were also of pine, 29–37 inches long, the measurement including the arrowheads of iron and some of bone. The arrows, of 9mm maximum thickness, show little or no tapering in the foreshaft but extreme tapering in the shaftment with nobbed nocks cut to 5mm to fit a thicker bowstring than the ⅛-inch ones used with the later *Mary Rose* arrows. The strings may have been made of intestine or sinew, like the strings the Liangulu archers of Kenya made for their very powerful longbows. The Nydam arrows had four-vane fletching, believed to have been eagle feathers, 4¹⁄₁₆ inches to 5¹⁄₁₆ inches (10–13cm) long, the now missing feathers set in birch tar and spirally bound in place with long nettle fibres spaced 10mm apart. Binding extends past the fletching to the nobbed nock to prevent splitting. The carefully made arrows had strange markings, as cresting or perhaps of a symbolic nature, cut into the shafts. Some arrowheads were broadheads but most of the arrowheads were of the bodkin type meant to pierce a mail hauberk. Some had sockets while others were tanged to be glued and bound in slits cut in the foreshaft.

Bows found at Vimose are similar to those from Nydam and are from 66–77½ inches long. These lengths are from tip to tip, not from nock to nock. One of the bows has three parallel grooves cut lengthwise in one face. Several bows had bindings of thread. In one example 1cm wide bands were placed 1cm apart for the length of the bow except for the tips and the handgrip indicating an arrow pass at midpoint.

Another had a spiral band the length of the bow except for the tips. Still another had criss-crossing bands spiralling in opposite directions. The workmanship is painstaking and of excellent quality. Arrow shafts from Thorsberg of ½-inch maximum diameter were from 26 to 35 inches long.

Some other bows from roughly the same period have been found in other locations. One from Heechterp near Leeuwarden in Dutch Friesland is round in section, 2.45cm in circumference. With one end broken off it is 59 inches (151cm) long. The original length has been estimated at 168cm.

Another Danish longbow from Susaaen, Sjaelland, is 185cm long. It has a D section and a light but very definite and even S curve. There are opposed side nocks near the tips, with two small holes at the tip of one end. This bow has a transverse line 70cm from one end and 115cm from the other on the convex belly side. This line has additional design that has caused the bow to be classified as of late migration period. I would personally consider the ornament to be Viking in style.

Alemannic Gear

The Alemanni, a Germanic tribe, settled in southwestern Germany and eastern Switzerland. Several of their bows have been found, dating from the sixth and seventh centuries, and all of the same type. They are of yew five to six feet in length (although one example is seven feet) with sapwood left on the back. A well preserved specimen, the Oberflacht bow, is 5′ 9½″ long, 5′ 6¾″ between nocks. The bows have a long stiffened grip area narrower and thicker than the flattened pentagonal limbs. This kind of handgrip has not been found on other mediaeval bows but some Stone Age and Bronze Age bows are similar. Nocks, seen from the belly, are on the upper left and lower right, about 50mm from the ends. At the tips of the upper limbs there appears to be a drilled hole or a double grooved nock, perhaps to attach a string keeper.

Two well preserved arrows attributed to the Alemanni have also been found, both about two feet long. They are of taper form, 1cm thick at the shouldering of the head to 57.4mm just below the nock which is left 1cm thick. The area to receive the fletching was wrapped with fine yarn, then painted with birch tar to affix the feathers. The Altdorf arrow is only 27½ inches long, including the socketed arrowhead which is 3¼ inches long, glued to the conical point of the foreshaft. The headless Oberflacht arrow is 22½ inches long including the 1-inch conical point. These are very short arrows, especially for a bow of the length presumed to have been used – but a shower of Alemanni arrows was enough to prevent a Roman crossing of the Rhine in 354 AD. The Alemanni used bows similar to Victorian longbows, bending mostly at the midlimb, so longer arrows would have caused breakage as recent reproductions have shown.

A longbow found at Kragehul Bog, dated to about 500 AD, has an end broken off. A nock is cut two thumbs from the end and there are two protruding nails with silvered heads four thumbs from the end. Near the middle of the bow are two differently ornamented carved transverse lines, believed to be sight marks. If one is a sight mark, the second may have been made be to aid in the correct placing of the bowhand.

There is little remaining of archery gear in Anglo-Saxon England. A warrior's grave at Chessel on the Isle of Wight contained a five-foot bow and 24 arrows. This is a smallbow of the length described in *Le Livre de Chasse*. However the double sheaf of arrows, more than were appropriate for hunting, implies use in warfare.

Viking Gear

Excavations at the former Viking settlement of Hedeby have yielded a complete yew longbow and parts of several others, one of which is made of elm. The remains have been dated to the period from the ninth century to 1066, when the town was destroyed. The complete longbow is 191cm, 6′ 2½″ long with slightly expanded tips bent toward the shooter at 9cm and 7cm from each end. Oddly enough, these bends are toward the belly of the bow as in the manuscript illustration depicting the execution of St Edmund (see illustration 24 in the colour section). This would counter slippage of the single loop bowstring tied in place on the lower limb, and the upper limb is bent to match. Several inches below the upper nock cut on the bowhand side, a metal boss keeps the bowstring loop from sliding down the limb. As it had been made from a 5–6cm sapling, the cross section, the same shape for the length of the bow, is necessarily more oval than D shaped to maximise sapwood. Several reproductions of this bow range from 83–100lbs draw weight (38–36 kg) because of variations in the wood. Other bows found had tips flattened to a lenticular section.

No complete arrows were recovered at Hedeby and we do not know what length of arrow was used with the complete bow. Partly preserved arrows are of modified taper form, tapering to ⅜ inch just below the nock. Most fletching was of three vanes. Four- and two-vane fletching has also been found. While no feathers have survived, drawings of the period show swine-back and squareshorn fletching. Remains of birch tar covering the entire fletching area show impressions of spiral binding and helical (slightly spiralling) fletching of 4½ inches. Some Viking fletching was also done on a base of tar coated yarn wrapping, while some had tar in bands at the ends of the feathers only. With tanged arrowheads, the shaft tip was reinforced with a binding of thin brass or copper wire.

While complete arrows were lacking, many war and hunting arrowheads were found at Hedeby. Remnants of a tapered leather and wood quiver measure 62cm long. The fletching beyond the mouth of the quiver would add another few inches of arrow, as would the large arrowheads used by the Vikings, allowing one to approximate the length of a complete arrow.

Other Viking finds include a yew bow found with a sword at Ballinderry, in Ireland. It is 185cm, 6′ ¾″ long and the cross section is a rounded rectangle approaching a trapezoid at the handgrip. The limbs progressively flatten toward the tips, which, like those of Hedeby bows, have been heat-bent toward the belly side. Several fragments of yew bows have also been found in Waterford, Ireland with one complete bow 4′ 12″ long. Their date has been fixed from the end of the thirteenth century to the beginning of the fourteenth. The bow tips appear to be bent like the earlier Viking bows, and Waterford was originally a Viking town. These bows are the first found to have nocks cut in flattened bowtips from both sides rather than sidenocks.

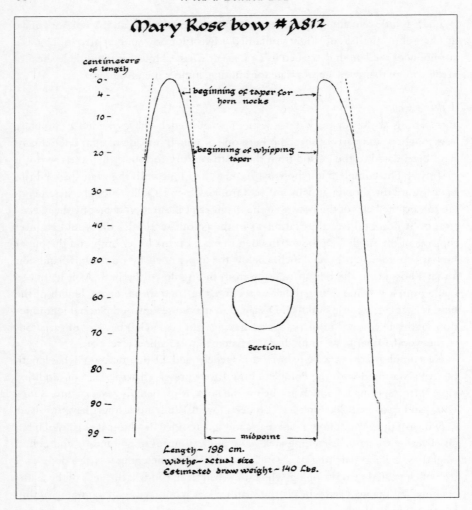

The Mary Rose

In 1545 Henry VIII's carrack, the *Mary Rose*, one of his finest warships, set sail with more than 400 soldiers and sailors to take part in an expedition against the French. Tragedy struck in the Solent, the straights north of the Isle of Wight, when before Henry's eyes, his ship sank to the bottom with nearly all hands. The anti-boarding nets had already been placed over the deck, so that those men who managed to get up from below deck were trapped, and there were fewer than 35 survivors.

The Roll of the King's Ships lists an inventory of 250 yew longbows, 6 gross of bowstrings and 400 sheaves (24 arrows per sheaf) of livery arrows on board. Salvage began in the nineteenth century when a number of bows were recovered, of which several are still kept in the Tower of London. More have been found recently: 138 yew longbows and some 3000 arrows, 12 leather bracers and one of bone or ivory. No shooting gloves were found (see Chapter 16), but there were two left handed mittens.

This gear is of the sort Ascham was writing about in *Toxophilus*, the ship having sunk in his time.

The pointed tips of all these bows show stains where horn nocks had been glued in place, as was usual by that time. Only one of these nocks has been preserved, though the wood is in good condition except for cellular deterioration. No bowstrings have been found and no flax remains, though some hemp cordage which may have been tarred, and some silk, have been preserved. Small iron objects, including arrowheads, have rusted away, though some stains have left sufficient trace of the form to recognise the types.

Bow lengths vary in length from 6´ 3¾˝ to 6´ 9⅛˝. The longer ones would permit a clothyard shaft to be drawn to the head. The typical length is 6´ 6˝ without the horn tips, which would have placed the nocks at about an inch in from the tips which were covered to 1½ inches. The wood is of a good close-grain yew, 50 rings to the inch, with sapwood. Some show string follow, some are straight, but most show a slight reflex. These may have been amonstg the bows produced by five bowyers from 40,000 staves Henry VIII purchased from the Doge of Venice in 1510.

In section, the bows vary from almost rectangular to trapezoid to nearly circular, slightly flattened on the back, the most common form being a modified D section or oval. At the point that the horn nocks are affixed, the sections are circular, and some had the bowtips further thinned after the nocks had been applied. Sides of the tapering staves are slightly curved, the taper increasing considerably at the ends to increase cast, the 'whipped' ends mentioned by Ascham. Only one of the bows found had originally been bent up and it retained its bend showing a brace height of about seven inches. One of the bows, drawn to 30 inches, nearly full arrow length, forms a nearly perfect arc of a circle. Some of the bows are a trifle heavier in one limb. According to *Lartdacherie* this would be the lower limb. Some of the bows are marked just above the arrow pass with indentations in various simple designs, probably bowyers' marks. Replicas of these bows nearly all draw more than 100lbs at 30 inches, one estimated at 180lbs.

The *Mary Rose* arrows were found in sheaves of 24, the majority being bound together with cord or leather strips, while some sheaves were mounted in punched leather discs, through 24 half-inch holes, not larger than the arrow shafts. Arrows in these discs, which would keep the feathers from being crushed, were located at battle stations on the upper deck and the main gundeck of the ship, although in one puzzling case, a young six-foot archer had the disc with arrows tied to his waist.

Most of the shafts are made of aspen (poplar), a few being ash, beech, birch, hazel and even oak. No arrow fletchings have been preserved, although the traces of feather ribs and bindings can be clearly seen; the fletching was probably of wax. Arrow nocks had been reinforced with horn slips, most of which have disappeared. Shaftments are coated with greenish colour from verdigris, mentioned among components for the arrows of a Scottish king. The feathers were also bound with thread, spirally wound at about five turns to the inch. Only a trace of the red silk binding thread has survived. The quills were from 6 inches to 6½ inches long. Their position and distance from the nocks implies that the ends were left untrimmed and the cutting style was prob-

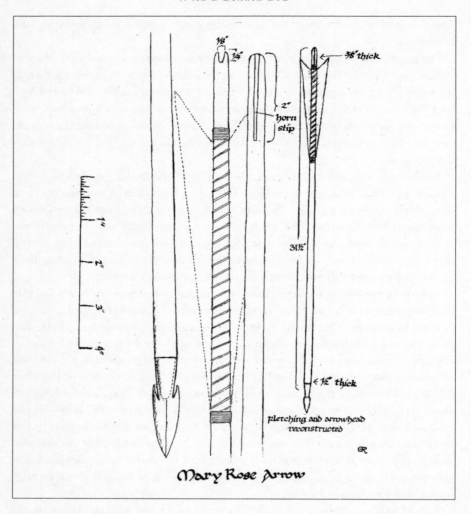

Mary Rose Arrow

ably saddle-backed. According to *Lartdacherie*, the English did not normally bind the fletching of sheaf arrows. It may be that the binding was an adaptation to counter the dampness that goes with use at sea.

Nock widths indicate the probably maximum thickness of the bowstring. One was measured as ¼ inch deep and ⅛ inch wide at the opening narrowing slightly to the base. Considering that bowstrings for livery bows were of hemp, this would indicate a surprisingly thin string for a bow drawing over 100lbs, where a thick string is to be expected.

Most of the arrows were of taper form ½ inch thick at the head to ⅜ inch at the nock, the average being 30½ inches in length. These were clearly intended for armour piercing at short range, up to 200 yards or so. A second group of arrows had parallel shafts ⁷⁄₁₆ inches in diameter. There were two groups of arrow length, the longer ones around 31½ inches and the shorter ones around 28 inches. The proportion of 18 long shafts to 6 of the shorter ones matches Sir John Smythe's advice (written in 1590) to provide flight arrows in that proportion. In tests, the shorter, lighter arrows did indeed fly farther despite being short for the longbow length.

The *Mary Rose* arrows average about 31 inches from nock to barbs, and the bows about 6′ 4″ between nocks, with few great variations. The arrows are thus about the length determined by *Roi Modus* specifications and the bows about a fistmele or more longer, as one might expect in view of Smythe's comment that military bows were made longer so that they seldom broke.

British Finds

Several other bows believed to be roughly contemporary with the *Mary Rose* bows have been found in England. The Flodden Bow, thought to have been used at the Battle of Flodden, is a D section yew bow, six feet long, which has been described as 'rather roughly made'.

The Mendelsham Bow is thought to be from the time of Henry VIII. One end is broken off leaving it 53 inches long, but it has been and estimated to have originally been nearly six feet long. The cross section is a rectangle with rounded edges and it is whip ended in the last foot of length, and shaped for a horn nock.

The Hedgeley Moor Bow is supposed to have been used at the battle of the same name during the Wars of the Roses. It is 65½ inches long, 1½ inches maximum width, and 3½ inches girth at that point. It had no horn nocks, the ends having been notched to take a string. There are two deep cuts at midpoint, of unknown origin or purpose.

The Spencer-Stanhope longbow is of yew with sapwood on the back, 6′ 7″ in length and appears to have had horn or other applied nocks. Its girth has been reported as 5¼ inches at midpoint tapering to 1¾ inches circumference at each tip; width and thickness are not given. Assuming a D section of usual proportion, the middle would be about 1½ inches by 1¼ inches, matching the heavy bows found on the *Mary Rose*.

The Chapter House arrow, or Westminster Abbey arrow, was found in one of the towers of the abbey. It is 29 inches long, plus the socketed steel arrowhead, 4 or 5 inches in length, which seems to have been barbed. The shaft is of modified taper form, made of what seems to be ash. Twelve inches from the head at its maximum thickness of .45 inches (1.15cm), nearly a half inch thick, it tapers to .41 inches (1.05cm) at the arrowhead and to .33 inches (0.85cm) at the nock, a plain nock with a transverse slit for a reinforcement, probably a horn slip. The arrow once had long fletching fixed with what might have been pitch, spirally bound with thread and with green colouring on the shaftment. Other measurements differ slightly. No one knows how the arrow, a war arrow of Tudor type, got into the tower. However, in 1376, two employees of a London farrier were charged with having shot at pigeons on houses with bolts and arrows, some 'sticking in houses'. This or a similar event may explain the arrow's presence.

We have here enough examples from both the early mediaeval and the late Renaissance periods in which archery was in serious use in hunting and warfare, to see the minor changes that took place. While the D shape was a popular cross section, some of the earlier bows tended to flatten toward the tips while the *Mary Rose* bows retained the same proportion of width to thickness right to the tips where they became round and conical for fitting the horn bowtips that were rarely used in earlier periods but became usual if not universal in later periods. In the earlier periods, yew sapwood sometimes retained the same thickness throughout while in later bows it was trimmed proportionally to the heartwood. Both earlier and later bowyers sometimes left knots and pins raised and sometimes worked them flat.

Although the sixteenth century was considered a period of decline in archery, archery practice was compulsory, and the bows from the *Mary Rose* are much more powerful than most earlier ones. A seventeenth-century Norwegian bow from Vinje in Telemark, when bows were still used in hunting, is described as of a 'hard kind of wood', and has a nearly oval cross section with a flat underside and rounded overside. One end is broken off, the length of the remaining stave being 53 inches (1.35m). The greatest width is 3.2cm, about 1¼ inches. While we have no bows remaining from intermediate periods, we do have the written information from *Roi Modus* and *Le Livre de Chasse*.

9

RANGE AND
PENETRATION

...such English archers as were there shot so wholly together that their arrows pierced man and horse and when the horses were full of arrows they fell one upon the other.

Froissart's Chronicles[23]

'And boy'quoth he, 'I've heard thy grandsire say,
That once he did an English archer see,
Who shooting at a French, twelve score away,
Quite through the body nailed him to a tree.'

Drayton, *Polyolbion*

Range

How far could the mediaeval archer shoot his arrows? The bowshot was a common measure of distance, especially among men with military experience, and references to siege camps being set up a little more than a bowshot from a castle wall imply a real distance. The Franks who captured Jerusalem in the First Crusade reckoned its dimensions in terms of bowshots: 'From the Latin monastery, built in honour of St Mary to the Temple of the Lord, built by Solomon, the distance is two bowshots,' and again, 'Within, from wall to wall it is four bowshots. On the south is Mount Zion, a little closer than a bowshot.' Maps of Jerusalem as it was at that time show this distance unit to fit in the several instances. The distance between the Latin monastery and the Temple is about 408 yards. A bowshot then was standardised at about 204 yards. At this time compulsory archery practice, which made possible the use of more powerful bows, had not yet been instituted.

A Viking specification for the bowshot, or rather the arrowshot, in Iceland's *Gragas 352* (Grey goose) law states: 'Örskotshelgr er nu 2 hunruð lögfaöma tolfroeö a slettum velli.' This defines the area of legally recognised sanctuary around a man's home as having the radius of an arrowshot, specified as 200 fathoms on level ground. Unfortunately, we don't know for sure what this distance was. The Icelandic fathom is presently believed to have been 3 or 3½ ells, the old Icelandic ell of 1200 being 19¼ inch (49.2cm). Germanic peoples used to reckon 100 as ten twelves rather than ten tens. The arrowshot would then be at least 324.72m or 355 yards. A recent official revised estimate suggests that 200 Icelandic fathoms equal 480m.

An anonymous manuscript from fifteenth-century France, *La Fachon de Tirer de L'arc a Main*, gives the normal range for a yew bow in *chapperon* (clout/prick) shooting (see p.165) as 300 paces with the more skilful archers frequently shooting at 400 paces. The sixteenth-century *Lartdarcherie* based on the above manuscript, repeated these distances, specifying the use of a round bow. One would expect these distances to be surpassed by English bowmen who shot 'wyth strength of bodye'.

In mediaeval England, distances shot were given in scores, 20 paces or yards. A fifteenth-century source tells us that 'the pace conteyneth five feet.' This, the Roman pace, was measured between successive positions of the same foot. Another source gives a particular distance as 1125 feet or 225 paces, again a five-foot pace. A military pace, measured between alternate feet, would be about two and a half feet, but may not have been used in mediaeval archery.

Sometimes the length was given in yards, which were three feet. In the early twentieth century Sir Ralph Payne-Gallway, reportedly, using a fifteenth-century steel crossbow, shot several crossbow bolts 450 yards across the Menai Straits, and two mediaeval writers have told us that a longbowman could shoot as far or farther than a crossbow. Hardy reported coming across an authentic example of an archer in 1976, using a self-yew longbow of 116lb draw weight, who consistently and in the presence of witnesses, shot arrows 350 yards. Other modern archers with reproduction longbows and flight arrows have also reported 450 yards or even longer distances shot. Additionally, in his 1346 book *Nuova Cronica*, the Florentine banker Giovanni Villani reported that English longbowmen shot three arrows for every bolt from a crossbowman.

One of Henry VIII's many statutes concerning archery stated that; 'No person above the said age of twenty four years, shall shoot at any mark of eleven score yards or under, with any prick shaft or flight, under the pain to forfeit for every shoot six shillings and eightpence.' This statute covered the compulsory universal archery practice in England, but was not always strictly enforced. Henry, a notable athlete in his youth, demonstrated his shooting ability at the request of the French King Francis I during their meeting at the Field of the Cloth of Gold from 7 June to 24 June 1520. Shooting at a length of twelve score, he repeatedly shot arrows into the white, a performance that crossbowmen of the French king's bodyguard were not able to equal.

England was one of the last countries in Europe to retain archers in its armies. In 1590, Sir Roger Williams published a book vigorously advocating that archery be discontinued in favour of firearms. He wrote disparagingly of the archers of his time that 'few or none doo anie great hurt 12 or 14 score off.' The nature of this source establishes that in this time that was universally recognised as a period of decline in archery, war arrows were shot in battle to a distance of from 240–280 yards at the very least, this information coming from one of archery's severest critics.

In the same year Sir John Smythe published his book *Certaine Discourses Military* in favour of retaining military archers. He claimed that the heavy war arrows could be shot 12 score, or 240 yards, and that 'many archers can shoot 24 or 20 scores with their flights'. That brings the possible military range up to 480 yards, albeit with flight arrows having less impact than the heavier sort of war arrows. Smythe's book was suppressed, and five years later Williams had his way. In 1595 the Privy Council abolished bows and arrows as a weapon of war.

Not everyone considered this the end of the matter. In 1602 Richard Carew wrote of the Cornishmen of an earlier day that 'they were good shooters and far shooters' and that 'for long shooting, their shaft was a clothyard in length and their pricks 24 score paces, equal to 480 yards; and for strength they would pierce any ordinary armour, and one Robert Arundell, whom I well knew, could shoot twelve score paces with his right hand, with his left, and from behind his neck.' So Smythe and Carew, writing at about the same period, agree on a respectable 480 paces.

The 1628 guide sheet for the archery range established just outside London, *Ayme for Finsbury Archers*, lists distances of up to 19 score and 14, that is 393 yards between rovers. Marks 'within every man's reach' were at 18 score and 18 or 373 yards. It should be borne in mind that these distances do not refer to individual exceptional shots, but were lengths commonly shot. In the same year a small book was published proposing a new type of fire arrow for military purposes. It consisted of an ordinary shaft at the end of which was a brass tube to hold the combustible material. The author claims that with his 'practised arm of common strength' he can shoot these arrows, hardly flight shafts, 14 score.

During Cromwell's repressive rule, archery declined in popularity, but revived as a sport upon the restoration of the monarchy in 1660. In a celebratory contest on that occasion, the flight record was 22 score, 440 yards.

It is interesting to compare these distances with self longbow records in more modern times. In 1891 a man named Maxon, using a 'new improved' longbow, set an American flight record with a shot of 290 yards. Thirty-six years later the record was bettered by three yards. But Howard Hill, the American bowyer/archer/hunter brought back something of the Middle Ages. In 1928, with a 'longbow' of his own design of 172lbs draw weight, he shot an arrow 391 yards.

Recently the recovered *Mary Rose* bows and arrows have inspired still more people to take up the sport. In England Mark Stretton, a strong archer, shoots with *Mary Rose* replica gear, his bows drawing 150lbs at 30 inches. He finds that the bow only really starts to work properly at 30 inches or more. Arrows made as copies, ½ inch thick at the head, were found to weigh between 865–1550 grains. At a 30-inch draw the bow cast a 1181 grain arrow over 250 yards and a 1547 grain arrow well over 200 yards. He has also managed a longbow of 200lbs draw weight. Simon Stanley has shot with a 180lb bow and using a 150lb bow, draws an arrow 33 inches to below his ear as we see in some mediaeval illustrations. He shot a 1500 grain arrow 370 yards.

Penetration

> Sigurd Hog-Head was in the lead, with a thin round shield in one hand and a hunt-
> ing spear in the other. Gunnar sighted him and shot an arrow at him; Sigurd raised
> his shield when he saw the arrow curving high, but the arrow went right through
> the shield, pierced his eye and came out the back of his neck.
>
> *Njal's Saga*[24]

> All made of Spanish yew, their bows were wond'rous strong.
>
> Drayton, *Polyolbion*[25]

Penetration is determined by the speed and momentum of the arrow. Momentum is
derived from the weight of the arrow, and the length of push from the loosed string.
Speed is determined by the draw weight of the bow and its speed of recovery from
the loose. For these reasons, an arrow of 30 inches or more shot from a powerful longbow has great penetration potential.

Viking shields of wood and light enough for combat did not always stop arrows
as we see in the Njal's Saga excerpt above. Another is from Magnus Erlingson's saga
describing a period of civil warfare involving the *birkebeins* (birchlegs). 'Nikolas had a
red shield in which were gilt nails, and about it was a border of stars. The Birkebeins
shot so that the arrows went in up to the arrow feathers.'

Mail armour made of linked steel rings, began to be supplanted by plate armour
in the thirteenth century. Penetration is better achieved by weight than speed and
the heavy bodkin pointed arrows of the English longbowmen spurred the development of defensive armour to a frenzied pace during the fourteenth century. By the
fifteenth century a knight was completely covered in steel plate. Jousting armour
could be made as heavy as a horse could carry, but combat armour had to be light
enough that the wearer could wield weapons other than a couched lance, and move
about on foot.

A long narrow bodkin point would readily penetrate mail but the increasing use
of plate armour led to less acutely pointed bodkins that would penetrate and not
break easily.

Giraldus Cambrensis wrote of a Welsh tribe during the reign of Henry II:

> There is a particular tribe in Wales named the Venta; a people brave and warlike,
> and who far excel the other inhabitants of that country in the practice of archery.
> During a siege, it came about that two soldiers, running in haste towards a tower
> situated some distance from them, were attacked with a number of arrows from
> the Welsh; which being shot with prodigious violence, some penetrated through
> the oak doors of a portal, although they were the breadth of four fingers in
> thickness. The heads of these arrows were afterwards driven out and preserved,
> in order to continue the rememberance of such extraordinary force in shooting
> with the bow.

Giraldus Cambrensis continues:

It happened also in a battle, in the time of William de Breuas, as he himself relates, that a Welshman, having directed his arrow at a horse soldier who was clad in armour and had his leather coat under it, the arrow, beside piercing the man through the hip, struck also in the saddle and mortally wounded the horse on which he sat: another Welsh soldier, having shot a horseman who was covered with strong armour in the same manner, the shaft penetrated through his hip and fixed it in the saddle. What is most remarkable is that as the horseman drew his bridle aside to turn around, he received another arrow in his hip on the opposite side, which, passing through it, he was firmly fastened to the saddle on both sides.

These accounts hint that such strong shooting was considered exceptional by the Norman English, who were themselves no mean archers at this time.

The arrows and bolts of Richard the Lionheart's archers and Genoese crossbowmen at Arsuf were reported to pierce Saracen armour 'like eggshells'. Carew wrote that the Cornish cloth yard arrows for strength would pierce any ordinary armour, and Potritius (1544) wrote that an English arrow with a little wax on the point of the head will pass through any ordinary corselette or cuirass.

Giovanni Michele reported that the 'English draw the bow with such force and dexterity that some are said to penetrate corselettes and body-armour ... such is their opinion of archery and their esteem for it that they prefer it to all sorts of arms and harquebusiers ... contrary to the judgement of the captains and soldiers of other nations.' It was also stated that the more experienced archers could pierce not only corselettes, but a complete suit of armour.

In the Hundred Years War Tito Livio reported that French knights were killed or wounded with arrows and the *Gesta Henrici Quinti* reports that at Agincourt the English arrows shot against the French 'by their very force penetrated the sides and visors of their helmets.' However at the Battle of Poitiers, French horsemen equipped to ride down archers had especially effective armour. Geoffrey le Baker reports that 'their chests were so well protected with mail, plate, and leather shields that arrows shot at them were broken or deflected.'

During the reign of Henry VII, the Earl of Douglas led a force of Scottish raiders into Northumberland. Confronted by the Earl of Northumberland's forces, he made a stand at Homildon Hill where they came under a hail of arrows. The Earl of Douglas and his nobles had been improving their armour for three years and they confidently couched their lances and charged the English archers, but 'the archers, although they retreated, were still shooting and with such vigour, determination and effect that they pierced the armour, perforated the helmets, pitted the swords, split the lances and penetrated all the Scot's equipment with ease.' Despite his new armour the Earl of Douglas, when taken prisoner, was found to have taken five deep wounds; his head had been pierced and he had lost an eye. But within a year he was again in combat and again wounded and captured. It should be noted that the speed of a charging horse will significantly increase the penetration of an arrow shot at it, approximately an inch if the horse is moving at the average charging speed of 20 miles per hour.

Linen jackets could also be effective against arrows. It was said of those produced during the reign of Louis XI that 'few were killed by stabs or arrow wounds in these jacks.'

Armourers did their best to keep up with the innovations in arrowheads and increased effectiveness of archers. In 1448 the Guild of Armourers offered their best proof armour, which they claimed could withstand a quarrel from one of the powerful crossbows with a windlass, and their second best, proof against a bow. *Lartdarcherie* mentions that taper arrows, the shafts least likely to break above the head, were used to test the armour.

At the Battle of Flodden in 1513, archers were still used but seem not to have been effective against the Scottish armour. 'Except it hit in some bare spot [the arrows] did them no harm.' By the late sixteenth century, arrows were no longer expected to penetrate armour and armoured enemies no longer needed heavy pavises to protect themselves from the weakened English archery. Sir John Smythe still maintained that archers shooting four or five arrows to every bullet could 'hurt, wound, gall, and sometimes kill at nine, ten and eleven score as well as the fiery weapons can do.' A caliver had a range of 400 yards, a musket 600 yards. Smythe conceded that handgunners were best in skirmishes, but thought archers better in pitched battle. He still claimed that war arrows could be shot to 12 score and some could shoot 24 score with flight arrows.

Modern tests of more or less validity have been conducted; both Dr Saxton Pope and Stephen Grancsay of the Metropolitan Museum of Art conducted penetration tests against sixteenth-century mail shirts, one from the Middle East and one from Europe. Both were penetrated by bodkin arrows shot at close range from less powerful bows than those that were contemporary with the mail shirts. A seventeenth-century helmet was penetrated by a direct hit but not by a hit on the side, which glanced off. A bolt shot from a crossbow of 740lb draw weight penetrated the helmet by hitting one of the rivets, while a second bolt glanced off.

Surprisingly, the bolt flew less than 3 per cent faster than the arrow as measured by chronograph. A musket made in about 1600 pierced both front and back of a seventeenth-century lobstertail helmet. It should be remembered that John Smythe pointed out that an arrow can kill or wound throughout its entire flight, unlike musket balls that lose so much velocity at extreme range as to be ineffective. Arrows shot in a high arc gain more velocity and therefore greater penetration in their downward flight than is maintained by a level shot at the same distance.

In modern times an Englishman, C.J.Longman, using a 65lb bow, shot an English pine target arrow weighing one ounce and tipped with a conical steel pile through an oak board one inch in thickness so that the point projected an inch on the other side. The modern Englishmen Mark Stretton and Simon Stanley mentioned in the previous section, armed with their replica *Mary Rose* bows and arrows, conducted tests that would duplicated the Tudor capability. A replica breastplate of mild steel was stuffed with a sandbag, and an arrow headed with a square pyramid-shaped head shot from a 160lb bow penetrated well, as did a ⅜-inch 865 grain arrow shot from a 120lb bow.

The revival of warbow shooting in England has given us new and better testing opportunities. Mark Stretton, who shoots warbows as strong as those used in Tudor wars, also forges beautiful replica medieval arrowheads and has tested them on marks similar to those of the period. Although he has drawn 200lb bows, the tests were done with a replica yew warbow drawing 144lbs at 32 inches with 31½-inch ash arrows, ½ inch in diameter, tapered at the nock. These arrows were headed with six arrowheads of different types and shot at fifteen yards.

A riveted mail hauberk fitted over a tailor's dummy was penetrated by all test arrows including a crescent forker, a leaf shaped broadhead and a swallowtail broadhead as well as three bodkin points. All had penetrated through the back of the shirt nearly undamaged but a heavy quarrel type bodkin had penetrated furthest.

A newly slaughtered pig, still warm, was obtained from a farmer to simulate a human. As expected, all arrows penetrated. The bladed arrows made gaping wounds, but the skin closed tightly around the bodkin arrow shaft. Later examination showed that the heavy quarrel type bodkin had passed through the shoulder, smashed through the ribs and protruded an inch beyond the opposite shoulder. Both the swallowtail broadhead and the crescent forker had broken the spine, the latter being stopped by the vertebrae. Both had rotated slightly after entry, increasing damage and bleeding. In the end the broadhead had to be cut out. The pig had also been fitted with a reenactment quality mild steel breastplate 1.6mm thick. A heavy quarrel type bodkin penetrated several inches into the flesh making what would have been a fatal wound, as claimed by mediaeval chroniclers.

A breastplate with slightly higher carbon content was tested with all the arrows. The quarrel-type bodkin penetrated as before and the short bodkin pierced the plate and jammed at the socket, probably a fatal wound. The long bodkin, the leaf shaped head and the crescent forker all curled in the points and were snapped from the shaft. Surprisingly, the swallowtail cut through the plate but was stopped by the barbs. The improved lozenge bodkin punched through, penetrating to halfway up the socket.

A dummy was then fitted with a brigandine consisting of a leather vest to which were riveted 1.2–1.4mm overlapping metal plates, which were covered with fine-quality velvet affixed by decorative rivets. All the arrow types were shot at both front and back. The bodkin points appeared to bounce off and the only penetration was the leaf shaped blade which slid through the plates but only got ½ inch past the leather lining. Close inspection showed that the heavy quarrel head had penetrated enough to pierce the leather before bouncing off. There were no fatal injuries simulated. A new arrowhead, reduced in thickness at its widest part, penetrated 3½ inches through the brigandine. It would be interesting to have similar tests done on linen jacks.

Procurement of a dead Canada goose enabled more tests of the crescent forker. It was found that, unlike the broadhead, the forker did not penetrate the feathers it bunched up but caused fatal trauma without damage to the meat. The forker would cut through the neck, but only if the rotation of the arrow permitted. In mediaeval and Renaissance times this type of arrow was sometimes used to slash sails and sever line on a ship.

MODERN REPRODUCTIONS

'Draw archers, draw your arrows to the head!'

William Shakespeare, *Richard III*[26]

On the bench he sat, a bowstring twining,
bent the elmwood and arrows shafted.

Rigsthula[27]

My *Mary Rose* bow

From an Oregon dealer, I procured a yew stave 6½ feet long, 60 rings to the inch, and
with no blemish save for a single pin in the back. From this stave I made a bow to
the measurements of the *Mary Rose* bow given in the 1894 book *Badminton Archery*,
volume 24 of the series *The Badminton Library of Sports and Pastimes*.

In addition to the measurements relayed by Dr Saxton Pope in *Bows and Arrows*,
Badminton Archery includes the information that the bow is 1½ inches by 1¼ inches
at midpoint. At one foot from the tip, the girth is 3¼ inches, at two feet, a girth of
4 inches, and at 2′ 10″, the maximum 4½ inches girth, maintained for 8¾ inches.
Additionally, bowtips from the *Mary Rose* are shaped for horn nocks in a rounded taper
5cm long and 12mm at the round base. Bows of all lengths and strengths were so uniformly of these dimensions as to seem to represent a specified standard for livery bows.

At the ends of the stave I cut pin nocks. I made a linen string and with the greatest difficulty managed to brace the bow, which snapped one string after the other at
brace height. I well recall the months of strain and struggle to master the bow and
eventually, at the very limit of my strength, managed to draw some 95lbs at around
28 inches, still several inches from full draw, at which it would have drawn about
110lbs. I was definitely overbowed and doubtless set my shooting form back several
years. Although drawing and loosing this bow gave the feeling of being caught in an
earthquake, there was no noticeable kick or shock in the bowhand despite the even

curve and bending in the hand. Unable to develop sufficient strength to test the bow properly, I had no alternative but to trim the bow down to the point I could shoot with it, about 85lbs.

This was the second bow I had made to the same specifications, the first having been of two billets united by a double fishtail splice. One day while shooting it, there was a loud report like a gunshot and I stood holding a handful of 'many shivers' in my bowhand. Spliced staves do not seem suited to the making of powerful bows. Both copies originally had about the same draw weight, well in excess of 100lbs at full draw.

While I have no wish to contradict Dr Pope, I would nonetheless gape in disbelief were anyone to show me any yew longbow of the above dimensions and tell me it drew less than 80lbs, even at a 28-inch draw. At least I can now draw a bow of 65lbs with minimal effort, even when out of practice.

Length between nocks	6′ 3″
Midpoint	1½ inches x 1¼inches
Midlimb	1⅛ inches x ⅞ inch
Nocks	½ inch x ½ inch
arrow length	31½ inches
Draw weight	110lbs

My Ballinderry/*Roi Modus* bow

As the Ballinderry yew longbow, though found in Ireland, can be assigned to a Viking origin with considerable certainty, and as Vikings frequently made bows of elm, I decided to find a suitable stave of this wood. Eventually I learned of a wood turner in a Swiss hamlet (I lived in Switzerland at that time) who had air-dried elm. I purchased two staves cut off the edges of a slab and made a bow according to drawings of the back, side, and sections of the Ballinderry bow.

I was unable to get measurements other than overall length and handgrip section. In section it is squarish, the back and belly slightly convex. The sides angle from the back to a narrower belly in the middle part of the stave. I removed the sapwood which might better have been left on. Lacking a specific Viking formula, I used the *Roi Modus* specifications for bow and arrow length, the bow, in accordance with Ascham's writings being left 4½ inches overlong for the draw length with peg nocks in this, its first stage. It was made to be within my strength and measured as follows.

Length between nocks	6′ 3″
Midpoint	1¼ inches x ¹⁵⁄₁₆ inch
Circumference	3⅞ inches
Midlimb	1³⁄₁₆ inch x ¾ inch – 3½ inches
Nocks	¾ inch x ⅜ inch – 2 inches
Brace height	a shaftmond (6¼ inches)
Draw weight	65lbs at 31 inches

The bow, tillered to round compass, bent in an arc like the new moon and was long enough by mediaeval standards to shoot a flight arrow of a full yard, but I didn't wish to risk it, as it is very difficult to get bow staves. I wanted to test its cast against my more powerful yew bow, which at this point was tillered more nearly in the modern manner. Accordingly, I went to a friendly nearby golf course with a driving range where I was assured that the marked distances were correct, except for the 250-yard marker, which was five yards short, to be clear of the fence that marked the actual distance.

In a moderate side wind both bows shot commercial 29-inch barreled arrows with field points to the 200-yard marker. A commercial 31-inch parallel target arrow flew a couple of yards further from the elm bow and 215 yards from the yew bow.

I next tried a highly breasted 31½-inch steel-tipped beech arrow with small triangular feathers. This arrow, of my own manufacture, weighs in at an ounce and a quarter. I call it a flight arrow. It flew 220 yards when shot from the elm bow while the yew bow cast it beyond a marker of 240 yards.

I was surprised by these results as both bows were still several inches overlong. They both shot a heavier arrow farther than any of the aboriginal bows tested by Pope. I was especially surprised about my elm bow. Elm has always been acknowledged to be the inferior bow wood of the two, but in spite of having a fairly thick string and bending in the hand, it nearly equalled the performance of my yew bow. Pope's best personal longbow cast 250 yards, with a very light and efficient flight arrow. I concluded that a bend of a perfect arc is at any rate not inferior to a stiff handgrip and tips, contrary to popular belief.

I then finished the bow, whipping the outer limbs, recurving the tips and cutting the final side nocks leaving 2¼ inch projecting beyond them, applied sun-thickened linseed oil and set on a new silk string. To sink the draw weight, which had of course increased with the shortening, I also trimmed down the belly slightly. The bow shoots sweetly, with no kick. The measurements are now:

Length between nocks	5′ 11″
Midpoint	1¼ inches x ⅞ inch
Midlimb	1⅛ inches x ¾ inch
Nocks	¾ inch x ⁵⁄₁₆ inch
Brace height	a palm and two fingers
Arrow length	31½ inches
Draw weight	67lbs at 31 inches

In the next test, with a wind slightly in my favour, I again shot the flight arrow and had to look for it on the other side of the fence that marked 250 yards.

My *Le Livre de Chasse* bow

This is the short, relatively weak hunting bow to be used at short range. It is made of Osage orange, an American wood that has been considered by some bowmen to be the equal of yew. It is what remains of my first attempt at making a bow. In my ignorance, I went to a local lumber yard (in California) specialising in hardwoods and upon being told that they had no yew or lemonwood, asked for Osage Orange that had not been through a kiln. In the next room was a great beautiful yellow slab sawn from a bole, sapwood and bark intact, still damp enough to be cool to the touch. I had a piece with sapwood cut from the edge. It had been felled several months before. I finished a longbow about a year later. Eventually I had to shorten it due to a bad spot near the end of one limb, and I reduced it to *Le Livre de Chasse* dimensions. While the arrows are measured in poignees, the bow is measured in poulcees or thumbs. An old Danish measurement, the thumb is the length of the end joint from thumbtip to bent knuckle. That is clearly not what is meant in this case. The measurement that fits here includes both joints of the thumb. The bow was made to match old manuscript illustrations of short hunting bows, dyed black and smoothly tapered, with recurved tips projecting ¾ inch beyond both side nocks.

Length between nocks	4′ 8″
Midpoint	1¹⁄₁₆ inch x ¹³⁄₁₆ inch
Midlimb	⅞ inch x ¹¹⁄₁₆ inch
nocks	½ inch x ⅜ inch
brace height	A palm including thumb width
arrow length	26½ inches
draw weight	50lbs at 25½ inches

Because of the short arrow length, it may be held either vertically or horizontally and shot from a standing or kneeling position. These possibilities make it very convenient in field conditions, although it is rather light in the hand. The bow between nocks is only half a poignee longer than twice the arrow length, which for a longbow, would not be considered enough leeway even for a flight bow. However, it is not too short for the draw length. In fact, I have frequently shot 28-inch arrows with it. A bow of this length must be made so slender – to bring down the draw weight – that it will take a rather greater bend than a longbow will, consequently increasing the cast.

This bow shoots a 26½-inch hunting arrow of modified taper form 170 yards. It used to be stronger but has developed string follow, and the string is no longer taut enough at brace height.

These bows do not provide a demonstration of the best of mediaeval archery. I do not have the physical strength to master the powerful bows formerly used by men who practised archery from childhood and were pressed to use ever stronger bows. They do however demonstrate that self-taught bowyery and fletchery can produce authentic gear.

II

THE BOWYER

Ewe of all things is that whereof perfite shooting would have a Bow made.

Roger Ascham, *Toxophilus*[28]

Materials

Ascham lists the types of wood considered suitable for bows: 'Ewe, Elme, Wych and Ashe'. Yew was considered by far the best, the others being classified as 'meane woodes'. The yew tree is a singly growing evergreen with 'death green' poisonous needles and non-poisonous red berries on the female trees, small cones on the male. In the British Isles it has been traditionally planted in churchyard cemeteries since at least the twelfth century. Those trees were exempt from harvesting for the English war longbows, most of which were made of yew. The English crown regulated propagation and cutting of yew trees and English agents eventually had to search Europe for new sources. Vikings also used yew as well as elm for bows, bows at both Ballinderry and Hedeby being of yew. Ullr the Boga As, god of the bow and skiing, was said to have his Asgard home in *Ydalir*, the Yew Dales. Yew has tough, ivory-coloured sapwood that will bend far without fracture and more brittle reddish to yellowish heartwood that has excellent springiness, both of which are used in a bow. These qualities made yew the favoured bow wood from the Stone Age until the present day.

There are a number of species of yew with similar qualities. English yew was not considered the best, that from dry mountain areas where slow growth resulted in close grain being preferable. Spanish or Venetian yew was especially prized, the latter 'by reason of the heat of the sun, which drieth up the humiditie and moisture of the sappe.' Spanish yew became scarce when the Spaniards, following the visit of the Black Prince, destroyed their yew trees so that they would not again suffer at the hands of Englishmen with bows of Spanish yew. Yew from Switzerland above Basel was also prized. Even Saracens used yew in crossbows designed for use in sea battles, for fear of their usual composites becoming ineffective in damp conditions.

Lartdarcherie recognises two types of yew: the white and the red. The white is the Portuguese yew, soft and of open grain, the more open the grain, the softer the wood. The redder Italian yew is of straighter grain than any other, has a sharper cast, and quickly regains its strength, but is harder to work and to string at first, and breaks more easily than the Portuguese yew. In *Le Livre de Chasse* Gaston de Foix also recommends boxwood for bows. Ascham's preferred yew, in which the sapwood and heartwood were much alike, may have been the Portuguese yew. As well as yew, *Lartdarcherie* mentions two other kinds of wood, whitethorn and sushuz used in flight bows, but good for only one shot, becoming sluggish after one or two shots.

All English livery or war bows were to be made of yew, but civilian demand meant that the Crown had to introduce controls to ensure that military supply was not jeopardised. A law was passed that no one under seventeen (until which age bows were to be supplied by a parent or guardian) was to use a yew bow unless his father or mother possessed lands of annual value of 10 pounds or he himself had goods to the value of 40 marks. An act of 1541 required the bowyer to make four bows of 'elme, wyche, basil, ashe' or other suitable wood for every one of yew, or two such bows for every one of yew if he lived in the vicinity of London. The bows of a man's height that Edward IV mandated for Ireland were to be made of 'yew, wych, hazel, ash, auborne or any other reasonable tree'.

In his 1684 book *The Art of Archery*, Gervase Markham wrote that the best bow is of yew, the worst of *witchen* (wych), or elm. Elm seems to have been a poor second in preference but the most favoured among the 'meane woodes'. It is a large leafy tree with spreading top branches and is more common than yew. In Viking war poems elm bows are mentioned more often than those of yew, and the remnants of an elm bow were found at the Hedeby Viking settlement along with yew ones. The coarse wood is hard and strong and has great tensile strength. A present-day bowyer of my acquaintance finds elm, treated with dry heat on the belly, to be as good or better than yew.

Giraldus Cambrensis wrote in 1198 that the renowned Welsh Venta archers used only bows of forest elm, '*solum ex ulmellis silvestribus,*' although there are yew trees in Welsh mountains and they did use yew later in the Middle Ages. The wych (*wyche*) elm, very similar to elm, may be the wood referred to by Cambrensis.

Ash, a tree with feathery leaves and red berries, can be found in the mountains. It is a tough flexible wood formerly preferred by wagon makers. Goethe's secretary, Eckerman, while in Brabant, had researched suitable bow woods. He learned that 'there is a lot of difference between ash and ash,' depending on area and conditions of growth. His best ash bow was of tough wood from the 'winterside' of a bole. It was soft to draw and fast, but after a few months it developed string follow and lost cast.

The fifth kind of wood listed in the statute mentioned is 'basil' or 'brazil'. This had to be imported from southeast Asia. The wood is heavy with a porous grain and is of a reddish brown colour darkening with age, and was a source of red dye in the thirteenth century. Marco Polo brought home a brasil tree seed but it failed to grow in Italy. A very similar wood was later found in South America, giving its name to the area where it was found. It is also known as Pernambuco wood.

Giraldus Cambrensis specified that the Venta of southern Wales did not use bows of 'cornus, laburnum or yew', these evidently being materials he would have expected to find used. *Cornus* is a Latin word meaning horn (Cambrensis wrote in Latin) but was also used to mean dogwood (*cornus sanguinea*) as Ascham used it in his list of arrow woods. The tree has white or pink blossoms. The wood is fine-grained, hard, heavy, brown and tough and was used when those qualities were needed.

Laburnum is a poisonous tree with bright yellow flowers. Supposedly used for bows by the ancient Gauls, it was used for by bowyers in southern France until recently. It may not yet have been grown in England in Giraldus Cambrensis's time, thus explaining its absence from the historical record.

Ascham informs us that 'everie bowe is commonlye made eyther of a boughe, or a plante, or of the boole of the tree.' Bows made from a 'boughe' or a branch, are usually full of pins and subject to string follow. They were thought good enough for children and beginners. Bows made from a 'plante', a sapling, could be quick of cast and flexible if 'of good and clene growth' but the bole or trunk of a tree, the almost exclusive source of bow staves nowadays, 'is cleanest without knot or pin, having fast and hard woode, by reason of his full groweth, strong and mightie of caste, and best for a bowe, if the staves be even cloven.' The yew bows from Hedeby were from 5–6cm saplings, the root end being used for the upper limb. The cross section of the yew bow is partly determined by the original thickness of the wood in order to use the sapwood fully. An act of 1566 required bowyers to be prepared to supply 50 bows of elm, witchhazel or ash within 20 days – more than two a day. Medieval handbows were made from a single stave. When good yew became scarce, two billets might be joined in the middle with a double fishtail splice. A will of 1569 lists one of these new 'peaced' bows.

Manufacture

What follows is the process of making a bow of yew, using both heartwood and sapwood of a stave from a bole. Finding a suitable tree for staves required some experience. It should be found in the mountains, as yew grown near sea level is inferior. The bole should be five to ten inches in diameter, free of branches, not twisted by wind, of sound wood and preferably straight. The *Mary Rose* bows had been made from boles of eight or more inches in diameter.

Wood from the north side, or winterside, of trees in northern areas has closer, finer annual rings and makes the best bows. It was considered essential to fell the tree in winter when the sap was down and not 'cut out of season in the month of April, the sap being in them'. Bowmen have found winter-cut wood stronger, more durable, and less likely to follow the string.

The cut length of bole is then split into staves like the segments of an orange with a pair of iron or oaken wedges and a large heavy mallet. As splitting follows the grain it can now be seen if there is any previously undetected twist or unsound wood. According to Ascham the staves should:

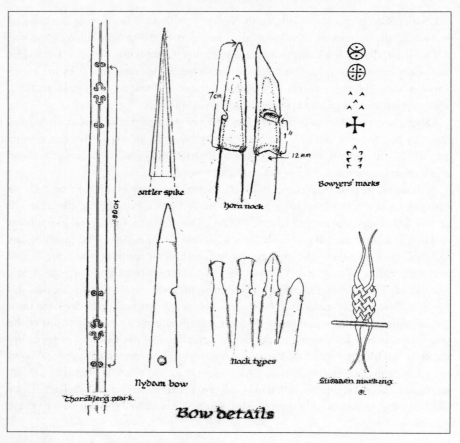

antler spike

horn nock

Bowyers' marks

7cm

1"

12 mm

Nydam bow

nock types

Susaaen marking

Thorsbjerg mark

Bow details

The Thorsbjerg mark shows the incised mid-portion of a longbow with broken tips. Estimated original length would have been near six feet. With nearly parallel straight sides, it then tapers to the usual slender tips from the outer circle markings. The antler spike is not a nock, but a stabbing weapon. A sidenock is cut an inch below it, and a brass boss keeps the string loop from slipping down. A similar spike was of iron. The cattle horn nock, also a sidenock, is from the *Mary Rose,* as are bowyer's marks that identify the craftsman. These are small and cut in just above the arrow pass on the bowhand side on some of the *Mary Rose* bows. The bow tips from Waterford are our only mediaeval examples of nocks cut in from both sides on flattened tips. The only complete bow in this find is 125cm long, a smallbow. The Susaaen bow has a transverse line of unknown purpose 70cm from one end and 115cm from the other on the convex belly.

> ... be even cloven, and afterwards wrought, not overthwarte the woode, but as the graine and streighte growinge of the woode leadeth a man, or els, by all reason it must sone breake, and that in many shivers. This must be considered in the roughe woode, and when the bowe staves be overwroughte and fashioned. For in dressinge and pykinge it up for a bowe, it is too late to loke for it.

With some kinds of wood cloven immediately after felling, the stave may warp towards the back (the bark side), forming a reflexed stave. This can be tested by removing a sample strip and it can be avoided by seasoning the log before splitting, but the reflex is not undesirable, especially if the bow is to be backed. Many of the *Mary Rose* bows have this sort of reflex, which might also be the result of heat treatment.

The cloven staves are trimmed with a hatchet or riving knife. All trimming must follow the grain as Ascham says. A law of Edward IV required imported staves to be 'three fingers thick, and squared, and seven feet long, to be well got up, polished and without knots'. Some completed *Mary Rose* bows were nearly seven feet long. In the first stages of making the bow, the stave should be left about six inches longer than the finished bow is to be.

The bow staves then have to be seasoned. In 1394 individual bowyers were prohibited from purchasing more than 300 bowstaves at a time but were required to always have finished bows in stock. Staves in large numbers may be stacked in a room out of direct sunlight in criss cross layers to allow free circulation of air. We do not know how long they were seasoned in mediaeval times but more recent traditional English bowyers have seasoned staves for five years, a little wood being trimmed off each year. Less conservative American bowyers have left staves, cut before Christmas with the bark on and the ends painted, for three or four months in an unheated room out of direct sunlight, then removed the bark and trimmed the stave to nearly the finished size. They are then left for another three or four months through the summer in a warm room without artificial heat, after which time the staves are ready to work.

A bowyers' tools are listed in a will of 1569 as gravers, files, a hatchett, a 'turning wheel' or lathe, and flotes (floats). With these he would begin the real work. The first part of the bow to be completed is the back, the sapwood side, then the sides, then the belly. If sapwood is to be included, as in the case of yew or elm, its eventual thickness must be decided on. If yew is being worked, it is important to avoid breathing the poisonous dust from rasping or sanding. The back is usually left $^3/_{16}$ inch to $^1/_4$ inch thick, about one fourth the maximum thickness of the finished bow. If it is left thick, the tips may consist entirely of sapwood as in certain of the old Danish longbows in which the back was trimmed to the surface of a single annual ring. Alternatively, the sapwood is trimmed to keep its proportion to the heartwood, necessarily crossing the grain. The back will seldom be perfectly flat in section but will be more or less convex depending on the circumference of the bole from which the stave was cloven.

Knots or pins in the surface were worked flat in the case of a bow found in the Nydam Bog and in the case of some of the *Mary Rose* bows, while in other *Mary Rose* bows they were left raised, as Ascham advised, because

> … freates begin many times in a pinne, for there the good woode is corrupted, that it must needs be weake, and because it is weake, therefore it freates. Good bowyers therefore do raise every pinne and alowe it more woode for feare of freatinge.

One old longbow, though not mediaeval, had left them raised in squarish lumps. I find a float file and a coarse half round file suitable for working the back. In working, the stave must not be pressed against any hard surface, or it may dent.

This completed, the back is marked with a line crossing the midpoint of the stave. Then a cord or thread is fastened by pins in the ends of the stave, ideally bisecting both tips and the transverse line at midpoint, and the centre of the back is marked with a straight line from end to end.

The side lines of the bow are now laid out according to a tried and true prototype. Some *Mary Rose* bows taper evenly to near the tips. With others the sides slightly curve, tapering little until within a foot or so from the tips, where the taper sharply increases to very slender whipped ends, all 12mm thick, also found in Nydam bows. This reduces hand shock and increases cast. It is advisable to leave the bow a little stronger than the finished one is expected to be because of variance in the strength of individual specimens of wood, bearing in mind Ascham's admonition that 'a bowe is not well made that hath not woode plentye in the hande.' Marks indicating the widths at mid point, midlimb, and near the tips will suffice for the usual mediaeval type bow. Maximum thickness would usually not be more than 1½ inches wide and 1¼ inches thick.

These marks are now joined in a smooth curve and the byewood removed. A hatchet may be used as far as skill and safety permit. Hatchets formerly used in this way were beveled on one side only, the flat side coming against the surface to be cut. Some bowyers use a finely set plane close to the line but I do not feel safe with it; having had unhappy experiences when the blade hit a curl in the grain from the wrong direction, I prefer a drawknife or rasp and, quite close to the grain, a float file. This kind of single cut file is a happy medium between the effects of filing and planing, producing a smooth, straight surface quickly without tearing up the grain. The mediaeval bowyer would have used his float, similar to a wooden plane block but with a float file mounted on its base so that he could file lengthwise along the stave. The float, a very rare charge in heraldry, appears on the arms of the Bowyers of London, and apparently was peculiar to the bowyers' trade. Marks of this tool may be seen in the finish on the *Mary Rose* bows, without further smoothing. Perhaps some personal bows were polished with a boar's tooth and an oilcloth, like some seventeenth-century ones. Ascham writes:

> The best colour of a bowe that I find, is when the back and bellye in workinge be much after one maner, for such oftentimes in wearinge do prove like virgin wax or golde, having a fine long graine, even from one end of the bowe to the other; the short graine, althoughe such prove well sometimes, are for the most part very brittle.

The sides having been finished relatively easily, we may start on the belly, which requires more care. For this, a spoke shave is an appropriate tool, and a shoemaker's rasp is useful when the bow is braced. As it is unwise to finish the bow with a thickness greater than a 1 to 1.1 ratio to the back, a safe beginning is to reduce the thickness of the belly to the width of the back, a square cross section. Marks made are measured from the back; the marks are connected to form a smooth gradual taper and the byewood removed.

The so-called 'traditional' English longbows of the recent past were made with a stiff handgrip area to avoid a jarring loose, and with stiffened tips, so that the bending was primarily at mid-limb. In Tudor longbows however, the bow was tillered to bend in an even arc. Ascham's term 'round compasse' meant that the bow should bend in the arc of a circle. Archers using replicas of this style have encountered no problem from the even bend.

I personally prefer to leave the bow squared off at this point. Now the bowyer sets one end of the stave against the floor, placing one hand at the middle of the bow, the other at the upper tip and flexes it, always toward the belly. This is to test its strength and accustom it to bending. Any obviously stiff spots should be further reduced, and obvious weak spots should have adjacent parts reduced on the belly only. Reduction of the belly has a much greater effect than reduction of the sides. A bow twice as wide is twice as strong, but a bow twice as thick is eight times as strong.

At this point the chosen cross section, nearly round, D shaped, trapezoid or nearly rectangular, may begin to be shaped; the rounded D cross section was usual in the *Mary Rose* bows. The tillering nocks may now be cut. The *Mary Rose* bows were fitted with horn tips and the remnants of nocks are still visible after the trimming. These were not tillering nocks, but are where the horn nocks were cut through. Seen from the belly side, these nocks were cut in the upper left and lower right tips of the limb, but these were used after the bows had been shortened to their final length, and I prefer to use temporary peg nocks while the stave is still at full length. When the bend is as even as possible, the sides are cut in about half an inch from the tips, leaving pegs projecting from the ends.

A thick single loop bowstring is put on, braced low (see Chapter 13). The upper loop of the bowstring is slipped over the end of the bow and made to reach to about three fingers below the nock by adjustment of the timber hitch at the lower nock. Then the right leg is placed between bow and string with the midpoint of the belly of the bow against the right thigh. The lower tip of the bow is placed across the instep of the left foot. The left hand pulls the upper bowtip forward and the right hand adjusts the string to the upper nock, making sure that the bowstring is centred on both bow tips.

The bow is now braced, in mediaeval parlance 'bent up'. The bow is checked for even curvature, and the back examined to see if any part of it is slanting rather than horizontal. If so, the reason is that one side of the bow is stiffer than the other, so the belly must be reduced on the lower side. When the bow bends evenly at brace height, it can start to be drawn a few inches at a time. Bows are very stiff at first, but will shortly develop some string follow, a set curve toward the string, which make them easier to bend.

This is the most crucial stage of bow making, as the wood must be gradually taught to bend. Ascham wished that all bowyers would give their staves 'tillerings plentye'; a tiller is a thick board the length of the intended arrow with a padded concave depression at one end in which the midpoint of the bow is set. Along one edge, there are notches to catch the bowstring. The bow is set on the tiller, drawn a few inches, and the curve checked. The bow must not be on the tiller a moment longer than necessary, only a few seconds at the most. In these moments, the back and sides must be checked as before, and the belly shaped and reduced. Since the aim is an arc, some bowyers find that it helps to have several arcs of suitable radii drawn on a large piece of paper, to maintain an even curve as the bow is drawn a little farther each time. These arcs may be drawn with a pencil tied to a piece of string.

When the bow has been tillered to nearly the desired draw length, its strength may be tested. The beginner bowyer is unlikely to be able to do this by feel alone, and can use a spring scale, commonly used to weigh objects up to 50lbs. The braced bow is set on its back on the padded floor, held in position with the feet at midpoint, with the spring scale hooked on the midpoint of the string. The bow is pulled up with both hands while an assistant measures the distance between the back of the bow and the string while noting the reading on the scale. It is not necessary to fully draw the bow if a force-draw curve is plotted using draw weight readings at every few inches of draw, especially in the last few dangerous inches. If the bow is at the desired ratio, usually a thickness of 1 to a width of 1.1, and is too strong for the shooter to draw, it will have to be reduced in both sides and belly.

If no further reductions are necessary, the bow is ready to shoot. The nocks are checked to make sure that they will hold the string; at this point the bow must not be allowed to get wet. This is the stage of manufacture in which the 'white' bow would be found in a mediaeval bowyer's shop. Bear in mind Ascham's caution:

> That bowe, which at the first byinge without any more proof and trimming, is fitte and easy to shoote in, shall neither be profitable to last longe, nor yet pleasant to shoot well, and therefore as a young horse full of courage, with handling and breakinge, is brought into a sure pace and goinge, so shall a new bowe, fresh and quick of caste, by sinking and cutting, be brought to a stedfast shootinge.

The mediaeval archer could buy a completed bow without further adjustment but Ascham suggested that, having chosen a bow, 'take your bowe into the fields, shoote in him, sinke him with deade heavye shaftes, look where he cometh moste, provide for that place betimes, lest it pinche, and so freate.' The shooting in the fields is to bring the bow to its hopefully final set. There is little danger to the bow as it should be several inches too long for the shooter's draw length. Some 200 arrows should be enough, and the bow can lose up to 8–10lbs of draw weight in the process. The purchaser had the duty of a bit of filing if necessary to even out overly sharp curves, 'Freetes', nowadays called 'chrysals', occur when the pressure of excessive compression causes a transverse line of crushed fibres across the belly, which can eventually work its way into the wood as far as the neutral axis.

> When you have thus shotte in him, and perceyved good shooting woode in him you must have him agayne to a good cunning and trusty workman, which shall cut him shorter, and pike him and dress him fitter, make him come round compasse everywhere, and whipping of the endes but with discretion, lest he whippe in sunder, or els freete, soner than he is ware of; he must also laye him streight, if

he be caste, or otherwise need requyre or if he be flat made, gather him rounde, [optional] and so shall he both shoote the faster, for farre shooting, and also be surer for near prickinge.

We have come to the final shaping of the bow. The new tillering nocks are cut to the owner's measurement or longer. As mentioned above, they are cut on the left side of the upper limb and the right side of the lower limb, seen from the belly. The nocks should be more than ⅛ inch deep to be sure the loops will hold, and the edges rounded; I find a thin rat-tail file the best tool for cutting the nocks. The bow tips are left to project an inch or two beyond the nocks whether for protection of the nocks and bending or for the final fitting of horn nocks. The bow is now tapered to reduce the point at which the nocks are cut to the width and thickness of the first stage nock area. The draw weight will now have increased and the entire bow may be reduced and re-tillered to the desired draw weight if necessary, but the back of the bow is not to be tampered with. A bow that is 'cast' is one warped out of line with the string. If the above methods do not help, it is necessary to resort to heat bending, which is also required to recurve tips or produce other curvatures.

At this point the ends of the bow are whipped. In this context 'whipping' means thinning the ends to take more of a bend than the remainder of the bow, thus increasing the speed of recoil and improving cast. Being thinner, they will stand a greater bend and will be less liable to develop a set or string follow. *Lartdarchereie*, referring to bows to be fitted with horn nocks, in which case the tips are formed to a round tapering point, states that the greatest reduction should be within a palm's breadth of the ends, where it should be reduced as much as can safely be done because 'the principal spring comes from the ends.' *Mary Rose* bows were sharply tapered for the last foot, more or less. Ascham's ideal bow was to be both weak enough for easy shooting and quick and fast enough for far casting.

There is as yet been no distinction made between upper and lower limb. Deviating from Ascham's 'round compasse,' *Lartdarcherie* advises that the lower limb be slightly stiffer than the upper. Mediaeval and Renaissance bows had no clearly defined handgrip so when the bow is taken up by the shooter in preparation to shoot, the bow is balanced on the thumb of the bow hand. The bow is balanced in this way, and the point of balance marked. The distance from this point to each nock is measured, the longer measurement denoting the upper limb, which the author of *Lartdarcherie* considered desirable for three reasons:

The first is that one has two fingers under the arrow, and the hand by which it is held should be opposite the centre of the bow. The second reason is that all bows, according to their make, bend and shoot in the direction of their weakest limb, so that when the lower limb is the strongest, the arrow jumps and shoots high and farther. The third reason is that all men who wish to shoot far, must, to do so with the greatest advantage, shoot with the wind and high: but all the same, every one does not know this, and you must know that when a bow is strongest in the lower limb, it corrects this fault of itself.

Some of the *Mary Rose* bows were marked just above the arrow pass with bowyer's marks of identification which also suggest the proper handgrip area. Sometimes archers gripped the bow a little higher or lower for additional range.

Ascham expressed the wish that bowyers would give their bows 'tillerings plentye and heetes conveniente'. The tillerings having been completed, we may consider the less well known 'heetes conveniente'. Other than references to 'tempered yew' bows, we have no further mediaeval information but some modern bowyers have found application of heat to the belly of a bow to give good results that suggest rediscovery. As previously mentioned, one modern bowyer finds that a heat-treated elm bow is as good as, or better than, a yew bow.

Mary Rose bows and other surviving bows have a slight reflex, a bend throughout toward the back. This could be the result of warping, but is likely the intentional result of heat bending. As string follow lessens cast, a reflex increases it. Another problem associated with string follow is stacking, the sharp increase in draw weight in the last inches of draw.

Heat-bent curvatures are put in after the bow has been tillered to bend in an arc. The sharper curvatures are best done by pressing the heated bow in a two-piece form. To retain the string tension on the bent up bow, a straight line from nock to nock should also touch the handgrip of the stave at rest, or the bow may be slightly reflexed. A wooden self bow will not permit the extreme reflex of an oriental composite hornbow.

Heat could be from boiling, steaming or dry heat and must be maintained long enough to heat the wood thoroughly; 240 degrees Fahrenheit (116°C) for more than an hour makes the wood very elastic. It can then be safely bent to shape, clamped in the desired curvature, including recurved tips if desired, and allowed to cool overnight, after which it should hold its shape. Reconditioned bows with string follow have increased draw weight by 5–10lbs with much improvement in arrow speed and cast. A bow may be braced back past a straight line and heat applied to the belly over a charcoal fire to the point of beginning discolouration to increase compression resistance, decrease string follow and set the reflex. Modern bowyers have clamped the stave to form a slight reflex and used a heat gun on the belly of the bow. A bend produced with dry heat will hold better than one produced by steaming. A Saracen treatment for composite flight bows involved heating them over a dull charcoal fire for a half hour until they were warm, not hot. They were then cooled for an hour before shooting. Heating would seem to be a clear benefit both before and after a bow is completed.

All known mediaeval European handbows other than those introduced from Asia are 'self' bows, made from a single stave. We have no indication that bows were backed before the sixteenth century when Sir John Smythe recommended the equipment of a squadron of mounted archers: 'Let their bows be of good yeugh, long, and well nocked and backed,' and again, that military bows were 'backed so they did but seldom breake'. Backing was a way to make use of inferior wood in an era when good yew, a slow growing tree, was increasingly difficult to find. The Kensals of Manchester are thought to have been the first to do this in the sixteenth century. Backing consisted of a thin strip of tough wood such as elm or ash glued to the back of the bow. The bow was bent backwards while glueing so as to place the backing under tension when the bow was allowed to straighten. English bowyers used a device called a backing box for this, a method apparently devised by the bowyer Waring who had learned from the Kensals.

Horn nocks, previously not usual, seem to have become general if not universal in Tudor times. *Lartdarcherie* refers to them as a normal part of a bow and informs us that horn nocks were usually made of cow horn, this being well suited for square and round bows,' but for flight shooting the harder tips of stag antlers were thought to increase sharpness of cast. It states that for all horns the shorter the better, and that they should be large enough to keep the string from touching the wood. The author had tried the silver nocks used by some people, but did not find them satisfactory.

The bow tips should penetrate 1½ inches into the horn nocks. Ascham cautions: 'You must looke that your bowe be well nocked, for feare the sharpnesse of the horne shere asunder the stringe.' As the horn nocks are round, and the notch cut in only on one side as we see in the horn nock from the *Mary Rose*, it must be cut very precisely to hold the string loop, which must fit closely. If horn nocks are used, the bow ends are fully whipped and made round before the horn nocks are glued in place. If horn nocks bored and roughly modelled are soaked in boiling water, they will fit more closely to the wood and can then be glued and polished.

Englishmen were familiar with archery gear from other countries. In 1580 the Museum Tradescantian had collections of bows, arrows and quivers from the New World as well as from India, China, Turkey and Persia, so sinew backing on these bows was known and could have been used. A problem with the backed bows is the possibility of the glue failing in damp weather.

Since bows was given linseed oil treatments as part of periodic maintenance, it is likely that mediaeval bowyers used linseed oil in the finish of 'painted bows' before rubbing with beeswax; Elizabethan furniture was finished in this way. Thickened linseed oil as sold in artists supply stores was probably not used then. It is applied with the hand, rubbing in well, but not wiped with a cloth. It is allowed to dry for at least a week, and is then rubbed down with a coarse woollen cloth when nearly dry.

Cord bindings seem to have been used on bows throughout the Middle Ages, although I have not seen them pictured in a manuscript. They were already used in the Stone Age. (The Meare Heath bow, a long flatbow with both transverse and criss cross leather and sinew bindings found in Somerset, has been radio-carbon dated to 2690 BC.) Their purpose was to compensate for faults in the wood such as a winding twist or to hold down splinters or spills on the back of the bow, and they were also decorative, but they interfere with proper rubbing down of the bow with a waxed cloth. Ascham thought these bindings not worth the trouble of putting on, and felt that the archer might better buy a new bow than resort to this type of reinforcement. His verdict was categorical:

Agayne to swadle a bowe much about wyth bandes, verye seldome doth anye good excepte it be to kepe downe a spel in the backe, otherwyse bandes eyther nede not when the bowe is any thinge worthe, or els boote not when it is marde and past best.

Still, some of the Danish Roman period bows have bindings of several patterns set on in pitch. Thin cord is used, wound or knotted onto the bow.

The handgrip and nock areas are left bare and in one example bands on the limbs are 1cm broad, spaced one centimetre apart. The bare handgrip area is lower than the midpoint of the bow in a preserved example. In one case the cord is put on in reversed half-hitches (see Chapter 8).

With spirals, the bow tips are bare for about a hand's breadth below the nocks. The bands encircle the limbs at both ends and spiral from one end of the bow to the other with a barber pole effect. A criss-cross is actually a double spiral, the bands crossing at back and belly.

Bows made of branches or saplings are made a little differently than those from boles. Being of smaller diameter, the branches are flattened on one side, designated to be the belly, and tapered. The back requires little work except for removal of the bark and working so as to leave all knots and pins, sometimes a considerable number in a branch, raised. As Ascham noted, 'The boughe commonlye is very knottye, and full of pinnes, weake, of small pith, and sone will follow the string.' Short, crude-looking handbows of this type are pictured in manuscripts as carried variously by peasants, ruffians and the devil. One of these bows, the Cambridge bow, was found in England in 1885. It was of yew, made of three quarters of a branch, all knots and pins left raised; it was 4′ 11½″ long and presumably of mediaeval origin. Early wooden crossbows seem also to have been made in this way. Saxton Pope tested a Yaqui Indian bow of this type made of Osage Orange wood that shot his flight arrow 210 yards, the best cast of any aboriginal bow he tested. Longbows made from the bole were valued at 1s 6d while those of bough wood were only 12d.

Bows made from saplings are made similarly to those made from boughs and do not have as many pins. 'Such a bow for the pith of it, is quicke enough of cast, it will plye and bowe farre before it breake, as all other yonge things do.'

As the best yew eventually became depleted in the late Renaissance, shorter pieces, 'billets', were joined together in a double fishtail splice. This splice was additionally 'armed', wrapped with cord, leather or velvet for security, becoming a handgrip. The poorer quality wood became commonly improved by backing.

The most important rule for anyone thinking of making a bow is not to over-bow or underbow. IThe bow at full draw should be just at the limit of the shooter's strength. He should be able to hold it steady at full draw for a second or two and to loose smoothly. A bow matching the archer's strength will give the best results in both distance and accuracy.

12

THE FLETCHER

In a moment of ill-luck
The strong king fell dead.
The gold-mounted arrows
Spared not the foe of thieves

Arnor Jarlascald[29]

Materials

The fletcher's task was to make the shaft or stele of the arrow, to set on the feathers or fletching, and sometimes to affix the arrowheads produced by the arrowsmith. A list of materials for fletchers of the Hundred Years War includes timber, feathers, silk and wax, and an order for military shafts specified 'shafts of seasonable wood, well and cleanly cross-nocked, peeled and varnished'.

The shafts were cut from seasoned timber of more types than were considered suitable for bows. Ascham classified a number of types of wood used in his time as either too heavy or too light for good shafts and found that 'Byrche, Hardbeame, some Ooke and some Ashe, being both strong enough to stand in a bowe and also light enough to fly farre are best for a meane.' He also thought 'cornus [dogwood] very fitte for shaftes.' Aspe (aspen) which he considered too light for a good arrow, was however much used for the long sheaf war arrows, like those found on the *Mary Rose*, and an English statute of 1416 prohibited the use of aspen in the manufacture of clogs for this reason. The clog makers insisted that they used only such wood as was unsuitable for arrows and were allowed to resume production. Ascham thought ash best for war arrows, 'being swifter and heavier, best for shafts' while *Lartdarcherie* considered taper ash arrows fit only for proving armour. Most of these kinds of wood were available locally.

Lartdarcherie advises that arrows for butt or prick shooting should be of aspen seasoned for a year or two and without artificial heat, while flight arrows should be of a stiffer wood such as birch or cherry, adding that the wood should not be much baked. Apparently, heat treatments were used on arrows as well as bows.

Ascham considered 'Brazell, Turkie wood, Fusticke [pistachio] and Sugercheste' to make 'dead, heavy, lumpish shafts' and 'Servistree, Hulder, Blackthorne, Beche, [beech] Elder, Aspe and Salow' as, either through weakness or lightness, making 'hollow, studding, gadding shafts'.

Not everyone agreed with Ascham. Gervase Markham, writing in 1684, apparently preferred heavier shafts: 'the best shaft is of birch, sugarchest or brazel.' Elsewhere Markham writes that 'ewe and horn-beame are best for tackle' and that 'elm and birch are also sufficient for private practice.' 'Tackle' had formerly meant arrows, but by Markham's time, had apparently come to refer to archery gear in general. Since neither yew nor elm were recommended for arrows, it is assumed that these woods are here considered for bows. Yew had however been used for crossbow bolts. Viking arrows were primarily of birch, sometimes ash, and also hazel, pine, fir and willow. The Welsh used birch.

Feathers used by the English fletcher were usually those of the domestic greylag goose, which was Ascham's preference. Their natural colours were white or grey, the preferred feathers being from white ganders according to T. Roberts in *The English Bowman* (1801). Ascham suggests that the cock feather be grey or black as a visual aid in nocking. Manuscript illustrations show that white feathers were sometimes partially dyed red, blue or black, the colour being applied to portions while separated. Ascham comments:

> The old goose feather is stiffe and stronge, good for a wynde, and fittest for a dead shaft; the young goose feather is weak and fyne, best for a swift shaft, and it must be couled at the first sheering, somewhat high, for with shooting it will sattle and faule very much.

Markham, presumably referring to goose, writes that 'the best feathers are gray or white'. Ascham specified the stiff primary feather from an old goose for a dead shaft or the secondary pinion from a younger goose for swiftness, the latter to be cut higher at first. In 1417, a time of military need, six feathers were collected from every goose in 20 southern English counties to supply the yeomen in the Hundred Years War. The feathers used were the three at the tip of each wing. When all geese in the kingdom were plucked for war arrows, most would necessarily have been grey. The 1397 Arundell inventory lists crossnocked grey goose arrows, some with duckbill heads. Geese were regularly plucked alive of down for feather beds as well as the feathers for arrows and quill pens. Some considered the goose feather 'the best feather for the best shooter' but *Lartdarcherie* considered goose fletching only fit for war arrows.

Ascham states that the pinion feather is the best but that the second feather from some birds like the wild 'fenny' geese might be better than the pinion feather from others. The pinion feather is the first one at the tip of the wing, all fletchers using either the first or second pinion feathers.

Swan feathers, a little heavier than goose, were appropriate for a dead shaft; a 1459 inventory of Sir John Fastolf's effects included arrows fletched with swan feathers. Ascham mentions duck as good only for a flight shaft for one shooting.

Peacock feathers were also use for 'dead' shafts, found for example on the arrows of the 'yeman' in *The Canterbury Tales*. Peacocks were kept as decorative domestic fowl even by Norwegian Vikings and made a festive mediaeval dinner, on occasion being served in full plumage. Ascham did not care for peacock fletching, saying that 'the Pecock fether doth seldom kepe up the shaft eyther ryght or level, it is so rough and hevy, so that manye men, which have taken them up for gaynesse, hath layde them downe agayne for profit.' However, some archers chose the feathers for their attractiveness. The pinion feathers of the peacock are of a uniform buff brown colour and seem about the texture of turkey feathers, which have now replaced other types of feathers in modern fletching. Dr Robert Elmer, author of *Target Archery*, who used peacock fletching on occasion, thought it all that could be desired, being stiff, resilient, durable, firm and smooth. Of course he was comparing peacock to turkey feathers.

Still other birds are recorded as being pressed into service for their feathers. Feathers mentioned as fletching in an English will of 1475 bequeathing a sheaf of arrows 'plumatarum cum gruibis nigras,' are 'black crane' feathers. A Scottish poem recommends eagle feathers, which were much prized for fletchings in Asia and are believed to have been used on the arrows found in Nydam Bog. While only feathers were used for fletching handbow arrows, leather was used to fletch sprights, arrows fired from muskets.

Manufacture

Arrows made as copies of Nydam arrows each required 50 minutes work to cut the shaft, 30 minutes to affix the bound four-vane fletching using birch tar, and 15 minutes for painting, gluing and binding the arrowhead that took 25 minutes to make: two hours in all. Mediaeval arrows were commonly sold in bundles or 'sheaves' of two dozen shafts 'steeled or unsteeled', that is to say with or without arrowheads. Some purchasers bought shafts and heads separately and put the heads on themselves. Mediaeval wills sometimes include these items that the owner never got around to assembling.

Ascham comments that a shaft must be 'straight as the grain lyeth' and not simply made straight by the fletcher. Such shafts are less subject to warping or breaking. By preference then, a fletcher would begin with a perfectly straight-grained billet without knots, pins or curls in it, for these were considered to diminish the cast of the arrow. The timber for shafts may have been seasoned in the log to avoid possible warping or may have first been split into ½-inch square staves. The ends were painted to prevent checking.

If intended for war or hunting, sufficient weight for penetration is a necessary consideration which making an arrow. Longbow arrows are heavy enough to achieve this, but short arrows are light unless they are parallel or have heavy heads.

Mary Rose taper shafts with ½-inch maximum diameter, some 30 inches or more in length, and ⁷⁄₁₆-inch cylindrical arrows were to be shot from the bows of more than 100lbs draw weight. Most medieval arrows that have been found, although often tapered, are about this maximum thickness. The British Longbow Archers fraternity specifies a ⅜-inch shaft at least 31½ inches long as a 'standard arrow', to be shot from bows of 70lbs minimum draw weight. Weaker bows would be further weakened by constant use of these heavy arrows.

In modern times few arrows are made in forms other than cylindrical, and the standard length of shaft is 28 inches. An arrow bends under the pressure of the string's return to brace height upon loosing, then straightens. An arrow with the right amount of stiffness for the strength of the bow will straighten out almost as soon as it is loosed and fly without a wobble in flight. Mediaeval and Renaissance arrows, shot from very strong bows, were thicker than those most used by today's bowmen. The thicknesses for arrows that will shoot straight and steady have been found by trial and error for 28-inch cylindrical arrows made of Port Orford cedar.

⁵⁄₁₆ inch	bows of 30–50lbs
1¹⁄₃₂ inch	bows of 45–70lbs
⅜ inch	bows of 70–100lbs
½ inch	war bows of 100–200lbs

These diameters are generally valid for birch but there may be some variation in samples of wood of the same kind. To have the proper suppleness, an arrow shorter than 28 inches should be thinner, a 30-inch one should be thicker. These thicknesses are not valid for crossbows, in which pressure of the string is more nearly in line with the shaft. A crossbow shaft a foot long and more than half an inch thick is far too stiff to fit modern theories of 'spine'.

For arrows of various tapers, the crucial thickness is at the middle of the shaft, the point of greatest stress at the loose. A breasted arrow will be lighter than a parallel one, a taper arrow will be heavier. While a light arrow will generally fly farther, weight distribution is also a factor. Some mediaeval arrows were weighted in the shaftment with piecings of heavier wood, with metal nocks, or with lead to keep the foreshaft up for level flight. Such an arrow will fly farther than a lighter one with the balance point farther forward as the heavier foreshaft will drop first. Once the foreshaft drops, the arrow tends to dive to the ground.

The best way to determine the right thickness is to make several arrows in the general stiffness required and reproduce those that shoot best. As self nocks of much less than ⅜ inch are not advisable, arrows for some weaker modern bows have to be of the parallel type.

The Saracens felt that a set of arrows should be made according to the lay of the wood as it grew, the foreshafts being of the part of the tree that was closest to the ground. A fletcher could easily keep track of this if the ends of the billet were painted in different colours. Ideally, a set of matched arrows should be made from the same log.

The fletcher's first task was to split his timber into shaft blanks slightly larger than the shaft was to be. The blanks could have been split off with a riving knife, the tool with which this type of work was done before the introduction of power saws. The riving knife, or 'froe', was a straight blade about a foot long with a thickened back and a handle at one end, at a right angle to the blade. In use it was held with the handle upright and struck on its back with a wooden-burl mallet, called a froe club, while being twisted by pressure on the handle. It was in fact a wedge to split from the end of a log rather than the side. Froes were most recently used to split off shingles, this being considered an easy job for older people. The split should be straight and flat.

After boards of the proper thickness are split off, these can be split into ½-inch square rods which are then seasoned for three or four years. A chuting board, a board with a v-shaped groove running nearly all its length, is useful for parallel shafts. The groove is deeper at one end than the other to produce the tapered shafts of the *Mary Rose* type arrows. The rods are planed octagonal with a finely set plane, then they are planed round. This can be done with a very sharp reversed flat plane but it is probable that a moulding plane with a groove of the proper size was used. A Saracen writer recorded that an arrow shaft should always be shaved along the grain, never turned on a lathe as that would loosen and tear up the grain. This was certainly true of the slow-speed lathes of that time, and even some used at present. A draw knife or spoke shave with a rounded notch could be used instead for barrelled shafts or others with bulbous nocks.

The craftsman of today, willing to be content with parallel shafts, might make do with birch dowels but these are sawn rather than split. Dowels with perfectly straight grain from end to end should be selected because these would be least likely to warp or break. Nowadays one can order shafts from a professional supplier who can provide a set of matched weight and stiffness.

At this stage piering was done, if desired. Arrows were already made with two point piecing in the Stone Age. Ascham considered that

> … two pointes in peecing be enough, lest the moystnesse of the earth enter to much into the peecing and so louse the glue. Therefore many pointes be more plea-saunte to the eye than profitable for the use.

This may have been a problem with the glues used at the time. For arrows meant to fly far, weight was moved toward the shaftment so 'some use to peece theyr shaftes in the nock with Brasell or Hollye to counterwey with the heade.'

The method of piecing was probably not that different from that used today. The ends of the shaft and piecing to be joined are smoothed with a file in order to clearly see the direction of the grain. Parallel to the reed of the grain a saw cut is made in the softer shaft exactly down the middle for about four inches and the outside of the two wings thus formed are tapered to cause it to bend uniformly. The piecing is cut in a corresponding four-inch wedge, slightly concave, leaving the end the width of the saw cut. The shaft at the bottom of the saw cut is tightly bound with string to prevent splitting. Glue is applied to both slit and wedge, and the wedge jammed tightly into the slit and bound tightly with string. When the glue is dry, the whole is finished like a self shaft.

Four point piecing is a little more complicated. Two saw cuts at right angles to each other are made in the shaft. Then four corresponding right-angled grooves are made in the piecing. Of course the grooves widen toward the end leaving a cross-shaped edge the width of the saw cuts, at the butt. Assembly is as above.

The shafts are now be tapered as desired. If the shaftment tapers to a nock (meaning in this sense the area in which the nock is cut) that is left the maximum size; it is necessary to finish the shaving with spoke shave or drawknife, cutting to a groove made with a rat-tail file about ¾ inch from the end. An alternative was to glue a nock of horn or even cast brass, made with a tang to glue into the end. The silver nocks referred to in the ballad *A Lytel Geste of Robyn Hode* could be sections of silver tubing covering a full nock, or may be tanged castings like the brass ones. These would serve to prevent splitting of the shaft as well as adding a little weight to the shaftment of the arrow, which, as we have seen, was considered desirable by some archers.

Ascham also mentions cross nocks 'for surety of the shaft'. He seems to mean the transverse slit for the horn slips, as in the arrow from Westminster Abbey (see p.63) and the *Mary Rose* arrows. This is advisable if the shaft end is not more than ⅜ inch thick. A piece from the thin edge of cattle horn, naturally slightly tapered, is filed flat and glued into a saw cut 2 inches long, parallel to the end grain of the wood. Leather also works well in place of the horn. The slip is filed flush with the wood. Another possibility is a horn wedge 1-inch long cut from the solid tips of cattle horns or from antlers. This is suited to arrows with thin nocks. The horn, filed to a wedge, is glued into a v-shaped cut in the end of the shaft. The horn should be bare of wood at the nock ends. Final rounding of the shaft is done with a concave dowelling block plane or a scraper with a concave edge, and finished with a piece of 'hurfish' skin, coarse dogfish skin, the mediaeval version of sandpaper.

The foregoing steps being completed, the nock (notch) is cut across the end grain. The nock must be wide enough to accommodate the served bowstring, usually ⅛ inch and from ³⁄₁₆ to ¼ inch deep. Ascham advised a deep nock for war arrows, 'for sure keeping in of the string', and thought 'a shallow and round nock best for pricking'. Making the nocks in a set of arrows not only the proper width but also identical can be a tedious chore if one follows the usual instructions in archery books, first cutting with single or doubled hacksaw blades, then filing with needle files and finally smoothing with sandpaper folded around a metal strip. It did not take much of this to convince one that mediaeval fletchers probably used a coarse needle file or a fine toothed saw of precisely the right thickness for the desired nock. Ascham advised that, like today's archers, the nock should properly fit the string, tight enough to hang on the string but loose enough to be dislodged by a tap. The bottom of the nock should be a little looser than the opening.

The tedious but very important part of arrow making is matching or 'pairing' the bearing arrows. T. Roberts informs us that formerly (before 1800) arrows were commonly paired by being weighed against each other on a stick that was made the beam of a balance. This can be made by cutting grooves around the ends of a dowell of about a foot long and tying on cord loops. The balance point of the dowell is found, at which a third grove is cut for a cord from which the dowell can be suspended. Arrows can be hung from the loops by means of a larkspur knot, and the heaviest shaft shaved down. However the midpoint thicknesses of the arrows must remain identical. The Saracens additionally located the balance points of the shafts. Matched arrows had matched balance points.

The shaft of an arrow is then sandpapered longitudinally followed by dyeing, painting and cresting if desired. Most old illustrations show arrows the natural colour of the wood, and Ascham mentions that some archers liked the appearance of piecings, which would rule out painting or dyeing, but some Viking sources refer to red arrows (before hitting their marks). These would most likely have been dyed rather than painted. T. Roberts gives a recipe used in 1800 for making shafts black, using dye made from logwood.

Cresting, shown in manuscripts and paintings, usually consists of narrow bands of red or black encircling the shaftment, under the feathers or towards the nock and towards the foreshaft, as now, serving to decorate the shaft as well as identify its owner. Remains from a pre-Viking Swedish grave have red bands edged in black. In the Jomsviking Saga, Palnatoki's arrows are easily identified by the gold bands of his cresting and a Viking poem mentions 'gold mounted arrows'. A fifteenth-century English inventory lists a cross-nocked peacock fletched arrow bound in two places with gold. The 1422 Arundell inventory lists 'a broad hooked arrow, the head dagged, peacock feathered and bound in three places with gold', as well as other arrows powdered with red and gold. 'Powdered' meant an overall pattern of equidistant spots. These would not seem to be military arrows.

Pigment ground in linseed oil would have been used, applied with a fine brush. Modern arrowmakers have found that the easiest way to do this is to use masking tape, which is also ideal when applying bands of gilding, (not an option in earlier times). Mediaeval arrow shafts were varnished although bows were not. Mediaeval varnish was based on amber, larch turpentine – which included resin – sandarac and colophony. This finish was meant to prevent warping caused by dampness.

At this point the feathers, or fletching, are put on. *Viridio greco* was used in fletching as early as Edward I's time. *Mary Rose* waxed arrows also show that green colour on the shaftment and feathers were bound with red silk in place of the milkweed fibres of the Roman period. General consensus is that the feathers used on an arrow must be from the same side of the bird, either the right or left wing. However, Ascham suggests having arrows fletched from both wings, as a side wind against the concave side of a feather will disturb the arrow's flight. A section a little longer than the desired fletching is cut from the stiffest part of the feather. Ascham advised

> … that your fethers be not drawen for hastiness, but pared even and streyghte with diligence. The fletcher draweth a fether when he hath but one swappe at it with his knyfe, and then playneth it a lytle, with rubbing it over his knyfe He pareth it when he taketh leysure and hede to make every parte of the ryb apt to stand streight and even on upon the stele.

Drawing the feather is quickest, and is done by taking the top of the feather and pulling downward, stripping the web from the quill in one piece. Trimming the edges of the strip prepares the vane for gluing.

Paring produces better fletching. The feather is laid on its back on a smooth board and the quill is split down the middle with a very sharp knife. The edges are then pared close to the web with the knife held sideways. If paring the remaining pith requires more skill than possessed by the fletcher, the pith is readied by holding the web between two flat, straight edged pieces of wood or metal and rubbing it against a sheet of sandpaper on a table, so that the vane will stand 'straight and even on the stele'.

Ascham noted that there was a difference of opinion as to whether a feather should be 'set on streight or somewhat bowing'. He also thought it necessary for penetration that an arrow spin in flight, and Viking arrows were set at a slight slant to make them spin. It may be that Ascham meant that the 'streight' feathers were to be in line with the axis of the shaft and that 'somewhat bowing' meant a curve in the nock end of the feather like the fletching of the crossbow bolts of the time. In those, fletching of various materials was set in grooves cut into the shaft. Helical fletching was that set on a slight slant to catch the air and cause more spin, placed with the concave side facing forward. Depending on the layout, the feathers are cut to the desired length. If the fletching is to be bound, a portion of the quill must be bare on each end.

Methods of attaching feathers to the shaft have varied through history. Birch tar, was used for binding from the Stone Age until the Viking era; a wax and pitch mixture was used later and found on the *Mary Rose* arrows; animal hide glue was used until the twentieth century, as well as fish glue, isinglass, made from the swim bladders of sturgeon.

Bound fletching was used from the Stone Age to the Tudor period. Originally birch tar of the proper consistency, perhaps with pine resin added, served as the base; later sealing wax was used. Heated until liquid, it was applied to the intended fletching area and allowed to cool. The feathers were tied in position over the bare quills at the ends with a thread and the barbs of the feathers were pulled the wrong way so they stood up. The thread was then wound in a spiral through the feather and bound. The positions of the feathers could then be adjusted either helical, 'streight or somewhat bowing' and the barbs smoothed back together. Ascham advises 'nearly straight on'. The fletched area was then carefully heated to make the pitch fluid without damaging the feathers, thus fusing the tar, feathers and wrapping together. In the Welsh language, the common word for fletching was '*bon-cawiad*,' 'bon' meaning the butt end and 'cawiad' meaning a winding around. In Tudor England, birch tar gave way to wax, similar to the recipe used for sealing wax which, until the sixteenth century, was made up of beeswax, resin or pitch, and pigment, often vermillion or verdigris.

Another adhesive, animal glue, becomes liquid when heated and tacky before drying so that the feathers can simply be pressed into place. The entire shaftment is first sized with hot glue, wiped clean with the fingers but not with a cloth, and left to dry overnight. The prepared feathers can be made to stay straight by placing them between the folds of a hot steaming blanket with a flat weight on top until they are soft. Glue is spread on the pith of the quill and stuck in place, the concave side of the feather facing slightly forward. The first feather placed is the cock feather at a right angle to the slit of the nock. The two remaining shaft feathers are likewise put in place. Some *Mary Rose* arrow shafts have small marks that could have been left by pins holding the ends of the vanes in position.

When cool, the feathers are cut to the desired style with a very sharp round knife used with a template to hold the web firmly against a cutting board; alternatively they are burned to shape with a red hot rod. Ascham cautioned that a 'younge goose fether must be couled at the first sheering somewhat hye' because it would settle with use, and could later get its final trim.

Thread binding was wound to the bare ends with the help of a pointed instrument separating the barbs, and adjusted in place before final wrapping. Modern fletchers sometimes use model cement applied between the feathers and on the end bindings. To prevent damage to the binding it is necessary to add glue over the binding, especially on the side that runs on the bow. If the feathers are not bound, some kind of jig will be needed to hold the vanes pressed against the shaft until the cement or glue is dry. An unbound helical fletch may require a commercial jig. Today the feathers can best be trimmed with masking tape on one side to hold the barbs in position for shearing to the edge of a stiff template of the desired shape.

The shafts are now ready for the arrowheads. These are affixed by the fletcher with sealing wax, which, since it can be softened by reheating, allows precise aligning of the point with the axis of the stele. Analysis of *Mary Rose* arrows suggests fish glue was used. Viking and Saxon socketed arrowheads were additionally secured by a pin through socket and shaft. Flat blades such as broadheads are put on in line with the nock (across the grain). Tanged arrowheads are glued into a drilled hole and the shaft end strengthened by a copper or brass wire binding. Socketed arrows are set 'full on or close on', either with the foreshaft cut into a cone to fit the socket or with an edge cut in the top of the cone to make the opening of the arrowhead socket flush with the shaft, a typical cone being ⅞ inch.

13

THE STRINGER

Nec habeo, nec careo, nec curo (I have neither property, want, nor care)

Motto of the Stringers[30]

They shot so well in that tyde,
Theyr stringes wer of silke ful sure,
That they kept the stretes on every side
That batayle did long endure.

The Ballad of Adam Bell

Materials

Bowstrings were variously made first of linen flax and later of silk or hemp, though some crossbow strings were made of sinew. In *Le Livre de Chasse* Gaston de Foix tersely declared that 'the string must ever be of silk.' Silk, the finest, strongest and most costly material came by the Silk Road through Rome or to Khazar trading posts in Viking Scandinavia; this notwithstanding, Viking bowstrings were normally made of linen. The Saracens preferred raw silk, the strongest natural fibre in the world. *Roi Modus* explains:

> The string should be of silk and nothing else for three reasons; because it is strong and endures a long time without breaking; because when the threads thereof are properly united together and well set on, it is so stiff and hard; that it will drive an arrow or bolt farther, and strike a heavier blow than any string made of flax or hemp: because it can be made of whatever strength and thickness the shooter pleaseth.

Lartdarcherie recommends strings of raw undyed silk and the fifteenth-century manuscript *La Fachon de Tirer de L'arc a Main* found them especially suitable for

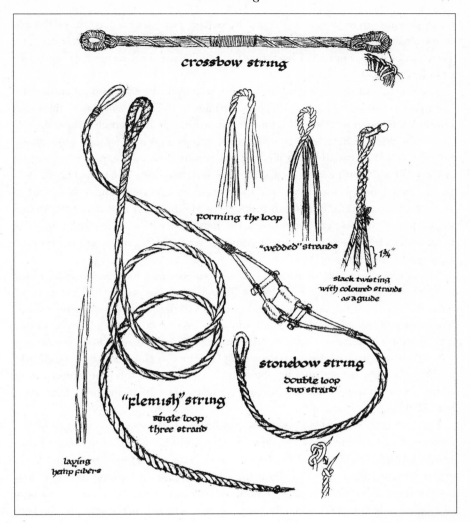

crossbow string

forming the loop

"wedded" strands

slack twisting
with coloured strands
as a guide

1¾"

stonebow string
double loop
two strand

"flemish" string
single loop
three strand

laying
hemp fibers

flight shooting. In general *La Fachon* recommends carefully picked and well chosen female hemp, the coarse male hemp being worthless for this purpose. Stringers bought the hemp and made it into thread, which they then made into bowstrings. In England hemp was used from the mid-fifteenth century and well chosen English hemp, 'not 'tubbed' hemp nor Colleyn [possibly Cologne] hemp' was specified in 1499. English military archers were supplied with hemp strings for their yew bows. John Smythe in *Certaine Discourses Military* writes: 'and the strings being made of verie good hempe, with a kind of water glewe to resist wet and moisture; and the same strings being by the archers themselves with fine threed well whipt, did also verie seldome breake.'

Surprisingly, although Chinese and Japanese stringers could easily obtain silk, they also made bowstrings of hemp. Today, 10lb hemp cord made in China is ideal for making strings. In deference to the guilds, Ascham expresses no personal preference. 'Now what a stringe oughte to be made on, whether of good hemp as they do nowe a days, or of flax, or of silke, I leave that to the judgement of stringers, of whom we must buy them.'

The formula of the glue used on Flemish strings in the nineteenth century was lost upon the death of the last longbow stringer in Belgium who knew the secret but took it to his grave. However, a thin solution of hoof glue, which is more flexible than hide glue, has been used to stiffen bow strings. This may be the 'water-glewe' referred to by Smythe above. As it is not waterproof, this could explain the need for archers to keep their bowstrings dry. Mediaeval archers were concerned about their bowstrings getting wet so they coiled the strings and kept them under their helmets to protect them. Elizabethan gun proponents claimed that rain made the strings slack and the Genoese crossbowmen at the Battle of Poitiers were said to have had this problem, but linen and hemp are stronger wet than dry, and excessive dryness is a danger to bowstrings.

The composition of the gum and the 'water-glewe' may have been similar to the mixture used on bowstring loops by the Turks, the silk bowstrings themselves being wound directly off the cocoon around two pegs to the thickness 'of a goose quill', like the double loop bowstring. The loops were tied into the ends of this skein by a special knot. The recipe is given by Kani, author of an old Turkish book on archery: 5 parts beeswax, 10 parts resin, 20 parts fish glue. The fish glue could be used by itself if it had the right properties. Like the other ingredients the fish glue would also be waterproofing if it were isinglass. A finish was applied to the main body of the string but not the loops or rat-tail.

The fifteenth-century Hastings manuscript advises that arming points made of 'fine twine like that used to make crossbow stringes, must be 'wexid with cordeweneris coode, so they would neither recche nor breke.' The 'coode,' used by leatherworkers to prevent stretching or breaking, may have been used on bow strings. It may have differed from 'sowters code'. Coode or code was made up of two or more of the ingredients pine pitch, rosin, beeswax and oil. Wax was not always included but Drayton's poem talks of 'well waxed strings'.

Manfacture

Originally archers made their own strings and some were also made by the archer's female relatives who could use their distaffs to advantage in spinning and twisting the strands. Women's hair might be used in emergencies, but after guilds came into being, most bowstrings were made by Longbow Stringers, and Stringers who made the strings for smallbows, stonebows, and crossbows.

Mediaeval bowstrings were mostly of the single loop type, now known as the 'Flemish' string. The Parisian *Lartdarcherie* of 1515 refers to the single loop string tightly twisted of three strands of fibre or thread, the loop to be as small as possible and stretched with a stone weight. Ascham describes this type as consisting of a tightly twisted main portion with a reinforced rat-tail at the lower end and a reinforced loop at the upper end. The lower end is affixed to the lower nock by a timber hitch that Ascham calls 'the bending' or perhaps in some cases by a series of half hitches, as with Viking bows. The Viking bow found at Susaaen had two holes in the bow tip in addition to a nock, and a Swiss wood sculpture of 1600 shows a string without loops or reinforcement bound through holes in the bow tips. Some Native Americans used a similar method and Japanese traditional archery uses bowstrings cut from a ball of uniform string tied at one nock by the same timber hitch used by the early Europeans.

Crossbow strings of sinew or thread were made as double loop strings, which may also have been used on handbows as pictured in the *Luttrell Psalter*. No ancient bowstrings have been preserved, even in the Danish bog finds.

Bowstrings throughout the world have commonly been about ⅛ inch in thickness, and the *Mary Rose* arrows have nocks ⅛ inch wide. The string must of course be strong enough not to break in use. Beyond that, mediaeval bowstrings were made thinner for distance shooting, thicker for slower but more dependable short range shooting. Thick strings are easier on the bow, absorbing some of the shock of the release. Let us consider the making of the 'Flemish' string of linen thread, as it was made by archers no longer able to get hempen ones from Belgium at the end of the nineteenth century. As the motto of the Stringers cited at the start of this chapter suggests, little equipment is needed.

Flax bowstrings had been used at least from the time of Edward I and into the Renaissance. Because flax has short fibres, it is best used in the form of thread. For the modern stringer, Barbour's linen shoe thread made in Ireland has been found convenient in sizes #10 or #12. If another size must be used, it should be tested for strength by tying the end to the hook of a spring scale and noting the reading when the thread is pulled to the breaking point. #10 thread breaks at about 10.5lbs. Thirty strands make a string that, whipped, nicely fits a ⅛-inch nock and is strong enough for a 50lb bow. Today's rule is to make the string of a strength three times the draw weight of the bow to allow for the stress of arrow release or for possible uneven tension of threads.

Lartdarcherie specifies a three-strand string, which is more nearly round than a two strand one, allowing a proper fit for each nocking. Three skeins of 10 strands each are cut, 15 inches longer than the length of the bow between nocks and six strands a foot long. The ends are laid flat and scraped with a knife to taper them, then, with the skein held including the short strands, the threads are pulled out to form 8 inches of even taper, with care taken to ensure that the threads are parallel. 3–10 additional threads 8 inches long are laid in each skein, likewise tapered, to reinforce the nock, and the skein ends are waxed heavily for about 20 inches. At this point a coloured thread the length of each skein is added as a tracer, to aid in getting an even twist.

All three ends are held in parallel and close together with the thumb and forefinger of the left hand eleven inches from the free ends which point right, and are twisted three inches. This is done by taking the skein farthest away with the thumb and forefinger of the right hand, and twisting hard clockwise while bringing it across the other two skeins and tucking it under the left thumb. When three inches are got, the little rope is bent into a loop. The short ends are waxed point together with the corresponding long ones middle one first, and the rope is twisted until the ends of the short strands are twisted in. A temporary piece of thread is tied around this to prevent untwisting. If the loop is to be used with a round bow tip or horn nock with a side notch it will have to fit more closely as *Lartdarcherie* suggests, especially if the string is of silk, because it will stretch considerably with use. This must be allowed for or the loop will not remain in place.

The loop is hung on a hook or nail, and the strands are combed out, first with the fingers, then with a coarse comb. The three strands are waxed to the end. Beeswax or a mixture of beeswax and resin was used by mediaeval archers; three parts wax to one part resin has been found satisfactory by modern stringers. No thread is allowed to cross another. Each strand is rolled between thumb and forefinger to get it round and then twisted clockwise. If the tracer thread is used it is easy to see if the twist is the same in all three strands. The three strands are lined up parallel, and twelve inches from the end another three 12-inch threads are laid in each strand to begin another rope, the 'bending'. Once laid, the end is tied with an overhand or a wall knot. The loop is put back on the hook, the string given a good pull, each strand twisted tightly, then the three are twisted together counter-clockwise to form a thin rope. The string is now be set on a bow to stretch it, and a temporary thread tied where the end emerges from the timber hitch. Linen stretches very little.

A piece of thin leather is folded over the string and rubbed briskly to smooth the string and melt the wax into the fibers. After removal from the bow, the end beyond the bend can be untwisted, the strands tapered by cutting threads at intervals, retwisted and tied off. *Lartdarcherie* suggests an inspection:

> And if you wish to know if a string is good, untwist the middle of it, and if the three strands are separate and distinct, it is a good one, provided always that when the string is twisted up again, it is hard and firm, for the harder it is, the better it will be.

A tightly twisted string stretches more than a slack twisted string. This does not give maximum cast, but reduces risk of breakage with a powerful bow.

A double loop string such as a crossbow string is made by winding a thread around two pegs until it reaches the desired thickness, then tying the two ends of the thread. The distance between the pegs is crucial as there is no way to alter the length of the completed string except by twisting the entire string, which is sometimes impractical. In the past, crossbow strings had extra looped skeins added as reinforcement at the loops. These skeins were securely whipped to the string at both ends by a series of half hitches, the whipping thread then bound to form the loop and spiralled down the tautened string to the middle, at which point it was closely whipped in a long enough section to prevent chafing of the string against the tiller.

While linen strings are good and serviceable, I have found silk strings so much stronger and more pleasant to work with, that I would prefer to make them exclusively if silk were more readily available. They are stronger not only because silk has a greater tensile strength for its size and weight than linen, hemp, or any other natural fibre, but also because the smooth threads may be more effectively combed out to get equal tension and because the individual thread that may be under greater tension will stretch a little more rather than break. One must buy strong thread such as is used by shoemakers, and test its breaking point on the spring scale to determine the minimum number of threads necessary. The bowstring is made much as a linen one, but if thin and made for a strong bow, should have enough extra reinforcing threads at loop and tail to avoid unduly marking the bow and the loop must be made small enough to take stretching into account, about the size of a pencil for a sidenock on a slim tipped bow. It is also necessary to allow for string stretch which can be as much as 25 per cent. Simply form the string shorter but with a longer area of reinforcement in the tail. After a short period of use the string will have done its stretching and will retain its length. Then the part of the tail past the bending can be untwisted, shortened, tapered and retwisted. The drawback of silk strings, for some, is their noise. A thin string on a powerful bow twangs like a harp.

The string is now complete except for whipping. This was done by the archer rather than the stringer and will be described in Part II.

14

THE ARROWSMITH

Bow of yew Essrakin,
Feather from the eagle of Lochtreig,
Yellow wax of Balenageloun,
And a head from the smith Mac Peteran.[31]

The heade makers of Englande shoulde make theyr arrow heades more harder
pointed than they be.

Roger Ascham, *Toxophilus*

The arrowsmith was a blacksmith specialised in making arrowheads. The process
was not markedly different from the making of tools like socketed chisels or tanged
knives. They got their share of complaints for sub-standard products; Henry IV reg-
istered an official one that arrowsmiths were 'to the great jeopardy and deceit of
the people' making arrowheads of inferior metal. He required that arrowheads and
quarrels be 'well boiled and brazed and hardened at the points with steel', as well as
marked with the maker's mark. Ascham found that the situation had not been permanently corrected in his time. Still, the arrowsmiths got some good marks too. One
historian wrote that their arrowheads 'were so sharp and strong that no armour could
repel them'.

Tools and weapons of the mediaeval period were commonly made of iron or low
carbon steel with a hard high-carbon steel edge or point hammer-welded to the
blade in various ways. In addition to being cheaper, this gave a very hard edge or
point without the blade being brittle. In England, then as in the nineteenth century
and even today, the steel of highest repute was made in Sheffield. On the continent,
Germany was especially noted for the production of steel, which was exported, along
with finished armour. The Vikings tended to use the sandwich method of a layer of
steel welded between two layers of iron.

Steel before the industrial revolution was different from that which we use today.
Iron at that time was from surface ore that might contain a great deal of manganese

and was purer in iron content. It was smelted as well as worked with charcoal heat, from which it absorbed carbon. Many people in isolated huts in wooded areas made their living from the production of charcoal. Present-day Japanese swordsmiths have combed the isolated villages in their countryside to find iron pots that were made in the old way as the last source of metal suitable for the superlative sword blades of the old kind.

Modern analysis of the steel in some mediaeval arrowheads has found surprisingly excellent quality. An English type 16, was found to have a hardened steel tip with a carbon content of about 0.35 per cent and with a very fine grained, tough microstructure. The rest of the head was of softer mild steel. Forging and heat treatments had been done with considerable skill, resulting in an arrowhead that combines both toughness and hardness. These were much favoured for war arrows in the thirteenth and fourteenth centuries and later. A Dr Brewer examined a swallowtail hunting broadhead and found a similar fine grained microstructure. The quality of these randomly chosen arrowheads is such that, using today's materials and skills, it may not be possible to make copies suitable for testing.

Arrowheads were made either socketed or tanged, the earlier tanged ones being simpler to make. A tanged hunting head without barbs can be made by heating the steel red hot, hammering it on the anvil to suitable thickness, and cutting it to shape with a chisel. Then the hard steel is hammer welded to the point, the blade beveled and packed, and the head allowed to cool, after which it may be filed to its finished shape, hardened and tempered. An expert smith could do a decently finished job without filing on some kinds of arrowheads. Packing is done at a heat of 'sunrise red' with a light hammer. The edges are turned from side to side and hammered until all red disappears. This aligns the molecules and compresses the edge. Hardening is done by heating the steel to 'cherry red' and quenching in water or oil.

High carbon steel will now be hard and brittle and must be tempered. The surface of the steel at the point is emeried or polished bright. Then the piece is evenly heated until the desired colour appears on the bright surface. The colour progresses from pale straw yellow to brown to blue, each colour indicating a further softening. When the desired colour is reached, the steel is again quenched to stop the process. Hunting heads are tempered to a blue colour, also used in saws. The steel has then a balance of hardness and flexibility so that the arrowhead can be filed to sharpen it and it will hold an edge well, but won't break easily. War arrows for use against plate armor were better tempered only to a light yellow, harder but necessarily more brittle. The narrow but thick bodkins and the short triangular ones, compensate for brittleness.

Sockets, used on most arrowheads, are made by hammering the metal into a fan shape which is hammered around the conical end of a rod called a bick or using forming tongs, one side being a cone, the other side flat to hold the socket in place for forming. The edges that come together may be scarfed and hammer welded, but were often left unsealed. Sockets on Saxon and Viking arrowheads were ⅜ inch outside diameter, while later ones were ½ inch. Low carbon steel is relatively easy to hammer weld, but high carbon steel forms the points and edges of some mediaeval arrowheads. Welding the components together must have required skill as the two steels weld best at different temperatures.

Other methods of producing sockets may have been used as well. White hot steel is very plastic so another method would have been to make the socket separately, slit the point, and hammer-weld it to the blade. The socket being completed, the blade is formed. The flat leaf shaped blades used by Saxon and Viking hunters were easy to make. If intended for war, they could be made with a raised central rib to help penetrate some armour without the points curling on impact.

Triangular bodkin heads required a steel block with a tapered v-shaped groove to accommodate two sides of the head while the third was being hammered. Square points could simply be drawn down using the fin side of a hammer, and smoothed.

Crossbow quarrels were so called because of their square points. In 1256, 25,000 quarrels were produced at St Briavels in Gloucestershire. Quarrels examined were not hardened. Such bodkin points as have been examined were not well hardened. even when steel was present. Some bodkin points may have been for practice shooting, especially at the wooden disc targets called 'rounds'. Some were probably case hardened. Packed in a mixture of ground bone and charcoal or a combination of leather, hooves, salt and urine. inside a well-sealed box, the whole was heated to a high temperature for a length of time. This carbonised the surface making it harder, black, and more resistant to rust. This process is described by Theophilus, a twelfth-century German monk, as being used to finish iron spurs. Some steel arrowheads were been coated with copper, either to prevent rusting or in the hope of causing poisonous wounds. Steel can be coated with copper by dipping in a mild sulphuric acid solution in which copper had previously been dissolved.

15

THE ARBALASTIER

Again they lept and went forth until they came within shot;
then they shot fiercely with their crossbows.

Froissart's Chronicles[32]

A shadow covers all the sky around.
So dark the cloud of arrows which ascends.
The breath and sweat, combined with dust, compound
A turbid mist which over all impends.

Ludovico Ariosto, *Orlando Furioso*[33]

The specialised making of crossbows in England dates from at least as early as 1205, at which time the Constable of Northampton received orders from King John to retain one Peter the Saracen and another with him to make crossbows and to allow them ninepence a day. In 1226 Roger, King Henry III's crossbowman, was recorded as buying glue and bark (cortice), to cover the King's crossbows.

English crossbow makers were known by the French term '*arbalastier*', and were distinct from bowyers. Eventually crossbow makers had their own district of London for their shops, and a popinjay target to test their crossbows. In Switzerland, cross-bow makers were exempted from watch duty on the town walls and, if foreigners, were automatically granted citizenship, but had to join the army when they were called to duty.

An early type of crossbow mechanism was one in which the string rested in a groove in the tiller and was released by an upward moving pin. Crossbows of this kind were still used in Norwegian whale hunts until the introduction of harpoon guns. One composite crossbow in the Swiss National Museum has a tiller with this type of mechanism, its only metal part being the iron stirrup.

In the twelfth century a revolving nut replaced the hole and peg tiller, and laths came to be made of wood, horn and sinew. By far the most difficult and exacting job in making a crossbow was making the composite lath, the type used most extensively throughout the Middle Ages. A 1358 list of materials for making 25 crossbows included 25 pieces of yew, 25 staples, 25 crossbow nuts, 25 stirrups, 25 keys (trigger levers), 12lbs of hempen string, 1lb of wax, ½lb of resinous pitch, 4lbs of tallow, some charcoal, 4lbs of glue, 4lbs of ox sinew shredded out like lint, 1lb of varnish and 12 ram's horns.

A core was first formed of flat strips of horn, or sometimes of whalebone. These were cut on both sides with longitudinal grooves forming a zig-zag surface. This was probably done with a plane having the edge of the blade appropriately cut. The strips were glued together to form a solid rod, the grooves on adjacent strips fitting into each other. Butted ends were located at various points to avoid unnecessary weakening of the rod, which could be made as long as desired. It was to run the length of the bow, which for hand-held crossbows was usually 27–29 inches. A strip of yew or oak was then glued to the belly side of the rod, the two surfaces being grooved as above.

Now the resultant core was covered on back and sides with shredded sinew saturated with glue laid lengthwise, more thickly on the back. This was shaped with a slight taper toward the tips and nocks were made in the ends, sometimes double nocks, the outside pair in this case for the bastard string that was used to bend the bow far enough to get the working string on. These bows were much too short and powerful to bend up like hand bows; some late mediaeval crossbows had draw weights up to 1000lbs. Now, an additional thin layer of sinew might be applied, this time encircling the bow, to help hold everything together. Great care had to be taken to be sure that the bend in both limbs was precisely identical, as this was crucial to proper functioning of the weapon.

With so much glue involved there had to be a protection against dampness, and the bow was waterproofed by covering with cherry or birch bark and/or a pig intestine stretched over the bow like a sausage casing and waterproofed with varnish. The bark was applied so that the dimension of the bark that formed the circumference of the tree was placed longitudinally on the bow. In this way it was less likely to crack when the bow was bent. If two pieces were necessary, a further strip was wrapped around the middle to cover the ends. These bows were often painted, a common pattern being small yellow dots on a black background. The designs appear to have been printed on, as more elaborate designs show duplication

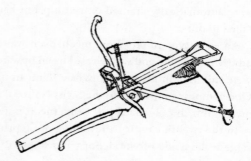

Crossbow with 'goat's foot lever'.

of the same error on both limbs. In thickness the completed bows measured 2–2¼ inches wide and about 1½ inches thick at the middle, with little taper and having a flat belly and rounded back. A wood and horn core that I measured was ⅞ inch x 1³⁄₁₆ inches.

The stock, or 'tiller' as it was called, was made of wood. Any hard wood such as pear, walnut or oak was suitable, but the tiller had to be heavy enough to compensate for the shock of release and was matched to the strength of the bow for steadiness. The tiller was completed by affixing the nut, made from the base of an elk antler, ivory, or sometimes iron. The key and stirrup were made of iron by a blacksmith. Also of iron were the pin to fasten the key into the stock, and a small insert for the nut, for the end of the key to bear against.

The nut was placed in an opening in the top of the tiller and held in place by an iron pin though its centre, by cord passing through its centre and bound around the tiller, or by a bearing of bone or brass let into the tiller. Since less than half of the nut remained above the surface of the tiller the bearing could hold it in place. In any case it had to revolve freely and easily. The key was then pinned in place to engage with the nut. Sometimes the nut was notched to accommodate the vertically flattened butt of a bolt, which should not fit too tightly. A grooved nut had to be wider, and the tiller also had to be wider at the point of the opening to retain strength. Forward of the nut, the tiller was grooved for the arrow bolt. An alternative permitting visibility of the mark at greater distances was the placing of a notched bridge at the forward end of the tiller, the tiller then being grooved only immediately forward of the nut. To reduce friction of the bowstring against the tiller on release, the tiller forward of the nut might be covered with a strip of bone. Another means of reducing friction was to narrow the top of the tiller from the nut to the point of string height.

The tiller being completed, the bow was bound to it with linen or hemp cord through a transverse hole in the tiller. The end of the tiller was either flat or recessed to take the bow, which usually had a flat, smooth belly. The iron stirrup was also bound in place with the same binding, or separately with leather bands. First the cord was passed around the bow and through the hole in the tiller a number of times, then passed between binding and tiller to tighten it further. Renaissance Spanish documents inform us that it was essential for the bow to bend evenly and be perfectly centred at right angles to the tiller.

As described earlier, while bolts for hunting into the fifteenth century were like short arrows with feather fletching, bolts for the later military crossbows were of wood, yew or ash, up to ¾ inch thick and from 12–18 inches in length. Bolts, like arrows, were fitted with a variety of heads. Those headed with the square armour piercing heads were called 'quarrels'. In 1232 a king's 'quarreler' was contracted to produce 100 quarrels per day. Crossbow strings were always of the double loop type, sometimes of sinew, more often of hempen thread whipped in the loop and spirally wrapped.

As guns became popular, their manufacture fell to the lot of the crossbow makers, who eventually became exclusively gunsmiths.

16

SUNDRY GEAR

Paid to Scawsby for Bowys, Arrowys, shafts, brode hedds, bracer, and shooting glove for my Ladye Anne, 33s.4d.

The Privy Purse of Henry VIII[34]

They say that the softer the tunic the better do they withstand the blows of arrows and swords ...

Dominic Mancini

To obtain his bows and arrows, the archer required the services of the four types of craftsmen discussed in the previous chapters. For additional gear he had to turn to other guilds. The main articles he required were the shooting glove, bracer, bow-case and quiver. According to period and preference, some archers used none or only some of these items, some used all.

The shooting glove, of gauntlet style, was made by a 'glover' or 'cordwaiiner'. The London Company of Glovers was formed in 1349 in which year the price of a pair of sheepskin gloves was fixed at a penny. Other leathers used in gloves were pigskin, buckskin, doeskin or cordovan morocco goat, Usually the rougher sorts were used by hunters and archers. Elizabethan gloves were made similarly to those of today but stitched seams were turned inward, the opening where the thumb was sewn in was oval, there were no decorative welts on the back of the hand, and a gauntlet cuff covered most of the forearm. Ascham tells us quite a bit about the shooting glove, saying: 'A shooting glove is chieflye to save a mans fingers from hurtinge, that he may be able to beare the sharpe stringe to the uttermoste of his strength.' Many archers used only one glove for the drawing hand but for comfort some also used one on the bowhand, especially if they used a squarish bow and tended to grip it tightly. Two leather mittens, both left handed, were found on the *Mary Rose* but no shooting glove was found.

An early mention of a shooting glove is from 1461–2.when the Duke of Clarence was given a shooting glove, a quiver and bowstrings. In Tudor England, Henry VIII

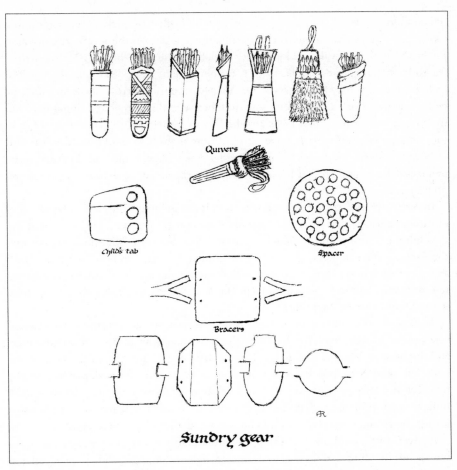

Quivers

Child's tab

Spacer

Bracers

Sundry gear

European quivers were typically cylindrical or tapered to hold arrows with fletching exposed; box-like quivers were a variant. Oriental quivers expanded at the bottom, holding arrows point-upward so that the archer could choose the type of arrowhead, and quivers for crossbows were often made this way. A badger fur covering was popular. A cloth arrow bag for crossbow bolts, however, had the fletching uppermost as a spacer was used, and damage to the fletching could be avoided. The cloth covered the fletching when not in use. The spacer shown, like those on the *Mary Rose*, holds a sheaf of 24 longbow arrows. Bracers, usually of leather, were also made of horn, silver, or even ivory. The rectangular bracer shown is the usual type found on the *Mary Rose*.

bought one for Anne Boleyn (see quote above) and a shooting glove and bracer were recommended for military archers.

Ascham mentions several particulars in which the glove was adapted to the practice of archery. It was to have a lining of soft wool such as 'scarlet' (a fine wool cloth) to prevent the leather being damaged by perspiration. (Because scarlet was so frequently dyed with the prized cochineal stain derived from the lac beetle, the term 'scarlet' came to be applied to the colour.) The inner surfaces of the glove's first three fingers, which hold the string, were to be reinforced with leather of thickness corresponding to the pressure of each finger on the string, the thickest on the forefinger, and ring finger, the thinnest on the middle finger. Suitable leather for this purpose was a thin, tough leather without a tendency to form permanent ridges, like horsehide. If the archer was troubled by his fingers being pinched against the arrow nock, Ascham suggested the insertion of a strip of goose quill between the leather and lining between the fingers where the arrow nock touched, or even better, a roll of leather set in at the juncture of the first two fingers to hold them apart. A similar feature is found on some modern shooting tabs, and a leather three-finger child's tab, believed to be mediaeval, has been found. It has a deeper slit for the arrow nock to fit the mediaeval finger placement.

In order that the string might glide smoothly off the fingers Ascham advised using ointment, perhaps that of virgin wax and deer suet (kidney fat). He also noted the possibility of cutting off the fingertips of the glove for a smoother loose. According the Ascham, the gauntlet cuff should have a purse in which to keep fine linen cloth and wax to rub down the bow, however this was not a universal requirement; a shooting gauntlet of soft material without a pocket may be seen in a Swiss statuette of 1600 in the Swiss National Museum.

Ascham writes: 'Little is to be said of the bracer. A bracer serveth for two causes, one to save his arm from the strype of the stringe, and his doublet from wearinge, and the other is, that the strynge glydynge sharpelye and quicklye of the bracer, may make the sharper shoote.' Bracers were made of various materials depending on the finances and taste of the archer. More expensive ones were of silver or ivory (the hollow portion of an elephant's tusk was sometimes used), cheaper ones of horn or leather. Ivory and horn bracers could be decorated with engraved designs.

A silversmith could inscribe the outline of a bracer on silver sheet and cut it out with a saw. Bending it to the shape of the arm, lightly doming it with a horn mallet in a shallow depression in a piece of hardwood and drilling the holes for attachment to a strap would complete his work except for ornamental engraving and polishing. One bracer of horn and eleven of leather were found on the *Mary Rose*. Tooled designs on these were of the royal arms, Tudor roses, or castles and pomegranates for Catherine of Aragon. One had a stamped design.

In *The Art of Archery*, Gervase Markham notes three possibilities for leather bracers:

1. Spanish leather, smooth side up
2. Spanish leather, flesh side up
3. hard, stiff, smoothe bend leather.

The latter he considered the least desirable form of bracer. The frontispiece to his book shows a cavalier with a bracer in the form of a loose cuff, the edges tied together by several ribbons. An English fifteenth-century bracer, now in the British museum is of black bend leather. It is deeply tooled or carved with the rose and crown emblem of Lancaster and the motto 'I.H.S. Helpe,' and the background is gilded. It has been claimed that it was left by Henry VI at Boulton Hall in Yorkshire.

Ascham suggests that the bracer have no 'nayles' (studs) or buckles and be fastened by laces without *agglettes* (metal tips) so as to avoid damage to the bow or string. Known examples are however fastened with buckled straps and the illustration of the archers from the *Luttrell Psalter* shows studs as decoration.

Apart from making some forms of bracer, leatherworkers were also called upon to provide the archer with a pouch (especially if the latter did not have one in his shooting glove). A 'fine, short, close compact pouch' worn at the belt was recommended to carry maintenance gear such as a file, stone, Hurfish skin, a cloth to wipe shafts clean, and spare strings.

The craft of the Horner was also sometimes called upon by archers for their bracers. Horners generally made spoons, combs etc. from the horns of cattle and sheep as well as from antlers. Ordinarily, cattle horns had the ends removed and were split down the middle and pressed flat after boiling, but a bracer could be cut from the convex side of the whole horn and drilled for attachments. The horner could also provide slips for arrow nock reinforcement cut from the thin edges of the horn. The solid ends of the horn could be formed into horn bowtips, wedges for arrow nocks, or blunt arrowheads turned on a lathe as well as whistling heads. Horn bowtips, partly hollow to begin with, and thin, had to fit well. In the case of the *Mary Rose* bows, an opening of 12mm was be bored out with an auger shaped to match the coned bowtip.

The bowcase, 'a saveguard for the bowe,' was needed to protect the bow from dampness, dents and scratches and was in the form of a tube just wide enough to contain the bow. neither too loosely nor too tightly. Ascham recommended wool bowcases in preference to leather ones because leather would attract dampness, though he approved of large leather cases designed to hold three or four wool cased bows ordinarily brought to practice sessions. Wool produced before the Industrial Revolution retained much of its natural oil like some wool yarn that is used at present for Irish knit fisherman's sweaters, and therefore shed water. Markham and Drayton mention bowcases of canvas, which in those days was linen, a highly absorbent fibre if not specially treated. Ascham also refers to a kind of narrow upright wooden cabinet in which cased bows were stored standing. These cabinets later became known as 'Aschams' in England.

Quivers for arrows were of various forms and were not universally used. There were cylindrical quivers as well as tapered ones, the narrow bottom being for the arrowheads. Attached to the belt at the top, these were carried at either the right or left shoulder, or at the right hip, as pictured on the Bayeux Tapestry and in various other representations up to the end of the Renaissance. Alternatively, straps attached at top and midpoint and at the belt enabled the quiver to be hung at the hip on a slant for convenient walking and withdrawing of arrows. A cylindrical quiver found at Nydam was cut out of timber, and of round section and others have been found in Viking graves of both men and women. An expedition sent by Arnulf, King of the West Franks, encountered Viking raiders who formed a defensive circle, 'then making a great noise with their quivers, according to their custom they raised a shout to Heaven, and joined battle.'

Quivers expanding at the bottom, originally used by Asiatic horse archers, were

Archer's bracer of black bend leather deeply carved with the royal Rose and Crown and the motto 'I.H.S. Helpe'. The depressed background is gilded. It was said to have been left at Bolton Hall in Yorkshire by a follower of Henry VII in the fifteenth century and is now in the British Museum. The strap is missing. (The Trustees of the British Museum/Art Resource, NY)

most commonly used with arrows for short handbows or crossbows. Points were usually upward so the archer could easily select the type of arrowhead desired. Renaissance bolt quivers of this type had wooden parts in their base, in the leather covered wooden opening, and in the lid with which they were sometimes fitted. Some were covered with badger fur. Some quivers were of rectangular section, made of stiff leather. A partially preserved Alemannic quiver of this type with stitched edges may be seen in the Swiss National Museum. Another, shown in a fifteenth-century Spanish painting is black and seems to be tooled in a plant motif. An English account of 1480 lists red leather arrow cases costing 9d and belts of 2d each, while Henry VIII had 200 arrow cases of red leather 'with girdeles' at Calais as well as two personal ones. The Elizabethan archer was to have 'one sheaf of arrows, with a case of leather, defensible against the rain'.

Certain archer's items were specifically military. Before the Battle of Agincourt, Henry V ordered that each English archer was to provide himself with a square or round pole or staff, six feet in length, of sufficient thickness and sharpened at each end to be set in the earth against cavalry attack. In the reign of Henry VI, the Earl of Shrewsbury ordered eleven-foot stakes to be used in pairs, carried slung over the archer's shoulder, one before, one behind. Clearly after Agincourt, these had become a standard defensive weapon. In 1529 a blacksmith supplied 5000 archer's stakes 'ready garnished with heads, sockets, rings and staples', and with pointed ends. To drive in the stakes without blunting the points, leaden mauls were used. With a five-foot wooden handle, the ends of the head bound with iron straps, the maul also served as a weapon and was carried slung at the archer's back. In 1531 the English 'fought with bow, sword and buckler, celata (salade) and a two pronged iron stake'. These were used from 1520 up to Elizabethan times, and the remains of such stakes were found on the sunken *Mary Rose*.

Another sundry item, known primarily from the *Mary Rose*, is the leather spacer, a thick 6-inch leather disc punched with 24 holes for a sheaf of arrows. Other spacers had a short slit on one side of each hole. These discs may have been used to prevent the crushing of the fletching of arrows stored in wooden chests and some were found at battle stations on deck. These shafts, bound at the foreshaft with a leather strip, were held below the fletching by the spacer. As an arrowhead wider than the shaft would not pass through the hole, and pulling the shaftment through could damage the fletching, the spacers would probably have been used with bodkin points only. Stitching holes are visible at the edge of a *Mary Rose* spacer suggesting that it was sewn in a bag. A 1557 inventory lists 'a long bowe, one quiver, one arrow bagge and a sheaf of arrows'. Manuscript illustrations show varied types of arrow bags. Some were open at the fletching end only, some open at both ends. Others are in a closed cone shape, implying the spacer in this case to be at the nocks of the arrows, which were covered. A fourteenth-century illustration of armoured crossbowmen shows their bolts, which would in this case have narrow bodkin heads, carried in a white cloth bag hung at the belt. Unlike the usual crossbow quivers that held the points upward, here the fletching is upward, exposed by the loosened upper part of the bag that would normally protect the fletching. The spacer would be sewn in place below this upper part. We don't know what prevented the boltheads from piercing the bottom of the bag.

Once made and set in order, the bows, arrows, strings and other gear became the responsibility of the archers.

PART II

THE ARCHERS

A Yeman hadde he, and servantz namo
At that tyme, for hym liste ride soo;
And he was clad in cote and hood of grene,
A sheef of pecok arwes bright and kene
Under his belt he bar ful thriftily.
Wel koude he dresse his takel yemanly,
Hise arwes drouped noght with fetheres lowe
And in his hand he baar a myghty bowe.
A not-heed hadde he, with a broun visage,
Of woodecraft wel koude he al the usage.
Upon his arm he baar a gay bracer,
And by his syde a swerd and a bokeler,
And on that oother syde a gay daggere
Harneised wel, and sharpe as point of spere
A Cristophere on his brest of silver sheene,
An horn he bar, the bawdryk was of grene.
A forster was he, soothly, as I gesse.

CANTERBURY TALES
Geoffrey Chaucer

The yeoman from *The Knight's Tale*. A woodcut version from a
printed sixteenth century edition of Chaucer's *The Canterbury
Tales*. The print was later used to illustrate Robin Hood ballads.
(University of Glasgow Library, Special Collections)

INTRODUCTION

Lord, how hastely the soldioures buckled their headlines, how quickly the archers bent their bowes and frushed their feathers, how redele ye byllmen shoke their bylles and proved their staves, ready to approche and joine when the terrible trumpet should sound the bluddy blast to victorie or death.

Sir John Beaumont, *Bosworth Field*

Throughout the Middle Ages, handbows were used in hunting and warfare in Europe. Charlemagne, countering attacks by Viking, Saracen and Avar archers, armed his cavalrymen with a bow and a quiver of arrows in addition to a lance, longsword and short sword. Footmen were to provide themselves with a yew bow with an extra string and twelve arrows besides a spear, shield and scramasax (a single-edged long knife or sword). From the tenth century onwards, tradesmen and other commoners formed militia groups or fraternal associations of archers in France and Flanders. A Norwegian law of the mid-eleventh century, the time of Harald Hardrada's raid on York, required every warrior on a longship to be armed with sword, spear, broadaxe and shield. Additionally, each thwart, with two oarsmen each, was to be equipped with a bow and 24 arrows, 720 arrows for a longship of 60 oars.

In the late eleventh century, crossbows came into fashion. Popularised by Richard the Lionheart, they were used across Europe by the thirteenth century (despite papal disapproval, see p.53) and as late as 1281 crossbowmen were paid twice as much as archers. However, traditional bows remained more popular in England; as Villani observed (see p.66), an archer could shoot three arrows for each crossbow bolt. Henry II encouraged archery and on an expedition to Wales, was struck in the chest by a Welsh arrow where his armour was strongest and the arrow rebounded. Frightened at the power of the shot, he exclaimed that it must have been from an English bow.

The English army effectively used mercenary Welsh archers in the early Scottish wars not because Welsh were better archers but because feudal levys of Englishmen could only be used locally and the men had to be released at harvest time. It was only later that the majority of the archers were English. In 1252 Henry III's Assize of Arms required all fit Englishmen to have in their possession a bow and four arrows. Those with a higher income were required also to have a sword and buckler and a dagger. In 1264, the year of the defeat of Henry III by Montfort's rebels at Lewes, Writs of Array summoned knights and tenants to London to form a militia. The most promising men were organised in units of 20s and 100s. Archers were to supply their own weapons with '30 or 24 arrows at least'.

At the outset of the Hundred Years War England could not field the numbers of men-at-arms that France could, so it was necessary to arm the common people inexpensively and the feudal levy system was abandoned in favour of indentured contracts, forming a paid army. Rather than pikes, spears or crossbows, longbows were chosen as the chief infantry weapon despite the need for intensive training, and practice was made compulsory. Archers, now each with an issued yew livery bow and a sheaf of 24 arrows, or a double sheaf, far outnumbered other soldiery. Crossbowmen generally played a minor role in the English army, although Edward III hired 625 Gascon crossbowmen with 70,000 bolts.

Because of the importance of archery in warfare, learning to shoot in mediaeval England was regulated by statutes, the number of which increased in the later Middle Ages, especially under Henry VIII who wished to restore archery to its former effectiveness, and his statutes could be considered attempts to legally reinstate what had been common practice before the waning of archery. During the centuries of compulsory archery practice in England, various sports such as football, hockey, tennis, handball, coursing and cockfighting – along with the resultant gambling – were prohibited to eliminate distraction from the serious business of archery. The bowman, as we know from Ascham, frequently brought several longbows to the compulsory practice sessions. They would be of varying lengths and strengths for use at various distances. His arrows too, would be suited to different purposes. Archery practice was a serious matter; Henry I (reigned 1100–1135) ordained that an archer having shouted 'Stand fast!' was not be responsible for the death of someone between himself and the butts.

English statutes were fiercely protective of English archery talent and equipment. In the fourteenth century archers were forbidden to leave England without royal licence and foreigners were not permitted to practise archery, or export bows and arrows, under pain of forfeiture, and in default of paying such fines as might be imposed on them, imprisonment.

The Scots seem to have originally used short bows but James I of Scotland (reigned 1406–1437) was raised in England and there learned to shoot the longbow; he was apparently exempt from the law that prohibited foreigners from archery practice. On his return to Scotland in 1424, he enacted legislation requiring butts to be constructed, especially near parish churches, and requiring all males from the age of twelve years to practise archery on holidays. Non-compliance was punishable by a fine. His successor James II specified the practice season as being from Easter to Allhallowmas (Halloween), requiring that each man had to shoot at least six shots on pain of a fine of two pence to be paid as drink money to those present. Howver, Roger Ascham considered that this attempt to promote archery in Scotland had been a lost cause from the beginning:

When James Stewart, first king of that name, commanded under pain of a great forfeit that every Scot should learn to shoot, neither the love of their country, the fear of their enemies, the avoiding of punishment nor the receiving of any profit that might come of it could make them to be good archers, which they be unapt thereunto by God's providence and nature.

Perhaps the Scots were never the equals of the English as military archers, although Textor, Rector of the University of Paris, and author of *Officina* had pronounced them good archers, much to Ascham's disgust. Bows were much used by the Highlanders, especially in hunting. Scottish military archers were employed by French and Burgundian rulers and Ascham's contemporary, Taylor, the Water Poet, wrote that 'The Highlanders, or red shanked men of Scotland, be exceeding good archers.' Forests such as Ettrick and Jedburgh were known for archers, and apparently they were thought a threat, because a law remains in force that a Scotsman with a bow and arrow within the gates of York may be killed without penalty.

The French attempted to promote military archery in the latter part of the Hundred Years War. *Ordonnances* called for units of 100 *lances*, each lance to consist of a knight accompanied by two archers and other personnel. In 1444 every parish was obliged to furnish an archer in order to raise 4000 of them, so there would seem to have been no group practice. The French, 'to the intent that they should become good archers, granted unto all who became perfect in that weapon, great priveleges [sic] and rewards so that the English longbow was practised in the greatest part of France for years.' Amongst those rewards was exemption from taxes, which alone should have been sufficient incentive to make a marksman of every Frenchman. This corps of *Francs-Archiers* seems to have distinguished itself little during its relatively brief history, although it was a *Francs-Archier* who ended the military career of John, Lord Talbot, England's greatest commander. Archers from Picardy seem to have had the best reputation. French crossbowmen still retained their importance and all infantry came under the command of the Grand Master of the Crossbowmen, while in cities elsewhere in Europe (Germany, Switzerland and the Netherlands) crossbowmen were organised in guilds under the patronage of St Sebastian, going to war as a group.

An obvious incentive for the archer to practise diligently was the knowledge that his choice in war was victory or death. Fleeing the fight could mean beheading by one's own comrades. Capture too would often mean death for any prisoner not worth a ransom until the Wars of the Roses, when the generally accepted rules of combat changed.

Queen Elizabeth officially ended military archery in England and the Scottish King James VI sent his bowyer to take advantage of the bargains on surplus bows. John Taylor wrote that Highlanders were armed with 'long bowes and forked arrows, swords and targets, harquebuses, muskets, durks and Loquhabor axes'. As late as 1688, arrows flew in a Scottish clan battle. The last recorded use of English archery in war was by the Royalist forces during the Civil War in 1642.

17

SOURCES ON SHOOTING

All they schot a bowthe agen,
The screffes men and he;
Off the marke he welde not fayle,
He cleffed the preke on thre.

Robin Hood and the Potter

The great and ancient defence of this realm hath stood by the archers and shooters
in long bows.

From an Act of 1487

Our major sources for the knowledge of shooting technique in mediaeval and
Renaissance times are books written in France and England, already quoted in this
book. *The Book of King Modus and Queen Racio* (often referred to as *Roi Modus*) was
published in France, probably Normandy, in the fourteenth century during the
Hundred Years War. It is a book on hunting and gives details on the use of the longbow in hunting situations.

Roi Modus tells us that for hunting, the bow (a longbow) should be weak and gentle
for hunting from a hide, a place of stationary concealment. A bow of 60lbs draw
weight would be 'weak and gentle' by mediaeval standards but is nowadays considered
quite powerful enough for elk or moose hunting. *Roi Modus* advises that shooting too
strong a bow compels the archer to incline his body forward, thus exposing himself
to his quarry. The arrowhead should not be too heavy and the feathers cropped short
and low unless it is a heavy shaft. The bow is held in the left hand and drawn with the
right. The feathers are to run flat on the bow (cock feather up) for accurate shooting.
The arrow is drawn with three fingers, the nock being held between the forefinger
and the next thereto. The hunter should raise the bow perpendicularly holding the
drawing hand with the arrow nocked directly before his face. He should very silently
and cautiously extend his arms, and draw his bow softly so that the arrow may be
pulled up to its head before the game come near. The bow being weak and gentle

he may hold it drawn for a reasonable space. The bowstring should be pulled to the right ear. The game is followed with the bow. The arrow is drawn and redrawn for an instant in order to take aim and is let fly with a sharp and steady loose. Technique is here much influenced by the need to remain unheard and unseen. The draw to the ear was used in longbow shooting until at least 1841, as George Agar Hansard stated in *The Book of Archery*.

However, for 'shooting at view' or at beasts in chase, a much stronger bow could be used because of the greater distance and because the hunter would have no occasion to hold the arrow drawn up, even for an instant. For a flight shot he might extend his arms more fully, still drawing to the ear, and drawing and redrawing his arrow for an instant in order to take aim.

The later *Le Livre de Chasse*, another book on hunting by Count Gaston de Foix repeated much of *Roi Modus*. The concealed archers should nock their arrows and bring their arms into shooting position as soon as they hear that the hounds are slipped, so as to be able to shoot before the deer can take warning. They are to shoot either before or after the deer has passed their position as a hurried broadside shot could pass completely through the animal and wound a hunter opposite.

La Fachon de Tirer de L'arc a Main, written on vellum in the fifteenth century in the Picard dialect, deals with archery as preparation for war and as a sport. It was printed in Paris in 1515 as *Lartdarcherie*.

Roger Ascham's *Toxophilus* was published in 1535 at the tail end of the Middle Ages under the patronage of Henry VIII, and was England's first book on archery, or indeed on any sport. Clergy were exempt from compulsory archery practice and Ascham, being a scholar (he was tutor to the young Elizabeth I), was technically included among the clergy, but practised archery for reasons of health. *Toxophilus* is, alas, not a complete book. Ascham avoided discussing the manufacture of gear so as not to trespass on the guilds' monopoly. Also, the book was written to instruct people already familiar with the archery of his time, and for that reason, parts of it are difficult to interpret for the modern reader without a knowledge of archery and the terminology of the period. A later book, *Country Contentments* by Gervase Markham, almost duplicated Ascham but made a few additional comments.

Today's interest in mediaeval archery is focused on the great war bow, a very strong version of the longbow. As the mastery of such a bow requires many years of hard practise and greatly developed strength, hunting weight bows are more appropriate for most people today. These instructions for the use of archery in hunting lead us to the way of shooting at marks with a longbow as described in *Lartdarcherie* and *Toxophilus*, which describe the longbow shooting ideal.

18

LEARNING TO SHOOT

In my tyme, my poore father was so dilligent to teach me to Shoote as to learn any
other thynge; and so I thynke other menne dyd theyr children. He taught me how
to draw, how to lay my bodye in my bowe, and not to draw wyth strength of armes
as other nacions do but wyth strength of bodye. I had my bowes bought me according to my age and strength; as I increased in them, so my bowes were made bigger
and bigger: For menne shall never Shoote well unless they be brought up in it.

Hugh Latimer, Bishop of Worcester, 1540[35]

We wish that every young Roman of free condition should learn the use of the bow
and should be constantly provided with that weapon.

Maurice. Emperor of the East, *Strategicon*

Learning to shoot began early for Mediaeval English boys, who had to be provided
with a suitable bow and two arrows by the age of seven by his parent or guardian who
had the responsibility of teaching him to shoot. (It was not uncommon for children
to complete their growing years in households other than those of their parents.)
Henry VIII specified beginning archery training at the age of six. Six-year-olds in
Chester were required to learn to shoot and to shoot on Sundays and holidays as well.
Practice was contined into adulthood; King Edward III decreed that all able-bodied
males should practise archery as formerly in their games'.

An important function of the instructor in teaching proper form was to see that
the pupil drew to the exact length of the arrow so that he might not be tempted to
look at the arrowhead, which Ascham was not alone in considering an archer's worst
fault. 'Yf he learn to shoote by himself he is a frayde to pull the shaft through the
bowe and therefore looketh always at hys shafte' though the shooter could check his
own length of draw by feel if he were using, instead of standard piles, bulky blunts or
the shouldered piles called silver spoon heads that seem to have been a new innovation in Ascham's time. As a boy, Ascham learned shooting under the guardianship of
Sir Humphrey Wingfield along with other children brought up in his house:

And when they should playe, he would go with them himself into the fielde, and see them shoote, and he that shoote fayrest should have the best bowe and shaftes, and he that shoote ill favouredly, should be mocked of his fellowes, til he shot better.

Dominic Mancini, a Venetian visitor, wrote:

It is the particular delight of this race that on holidays their youths should fight up and down the streets clashing on their shields with blunted swords or stout staves in place of swords. When they are older they go out into the fields with bows and arrows and even the women are not inexperienced at hunting with these weapons.

The enthusiasm of a young boy was stimulated by the archery contests and Robin Hood plays of the May games, in which the parts were frequently played by archers. A nostalgic archer reminisced: 'Myselfe remembreth of a childe, in contreye native mine A Maygame was, of Robin Hood, and of his traine, that time, to traine up young men, stripplings, and eche other younger childe, in shooting.'

A boy would be given successively stronger bows as soon as he was able to manage them. For the beginner, Ascham suggested a bow well under the shooter's strength and the arrows a bit longer than he aould fully draw to avoid a possible overdraw. These might later be cut shorter once his draw length had been established. Commonly, draw length increases after a period of shooting, as does the thickness of the string.

In the Middle Ages, a powerful bow was necessary to propel the heavy war arrows to the long distances shot up to the time of the Tudors, when bows were of more than 100lbs draw weight, although by 1800 a bow of 60lbs was considered strong. Saracen archers in training practised daily and changed bows every few days. This may not be necessary for the modern archer in training, but for significant improvement, frequent practising *is* necessary.

A mediaeval archer's final bow, after his muscles had been developed by the use of increasingly strong bows, was to be of the archer's own strength, but allowing some leeway. Such a bow allows not only the greatest accuracy but also the best penetration of arrows. In recent years much has been said about overbowing while underbowing seems no longer to be recognised. But amongst causes for not shooting straight Ascham recommends 'a bowe either too strong or els too weak'. In the nineteenth centry Horace A. Ford also pointed out that underbowing is as detrimental to good shooting as overbowing is and noted that even for flight shooting, the bow must be one that the bowman can both draw and one he can master. A full-grown healthy man should with regular practice be able to work up to a bow of 80lbs draw weight. In the twentieth century Howard Hill used strong bows to gain flat trajectory and hard striking power. His bows drew 70lbs for everyday shooting, 85lbs for hunting and well over 100lbs for elephant hunting. Mediaeval archers used bows under their strength only when training and for certain kinds of hunting and the war bows from the *Mary Rose* seem nearly all to have drawn in excess of 100lbs.

Some English longbowmen practised every day, the passing of which dedication was lamented by John Stow in his 1603 book *A Survey of London*. Neade felt that daily practice by an accomplished archer for one month, or three times weekly for two months, was sufficient training for shooting in line in military situations.

While yew has always been considered to be the best bow wood, no one under 17 below a certain income was permitted to own a yew bow as they were needed for war. From the age of 17 a mediaeval man had to provide himself with bows and four arrows (one law specified 12 arrows), the old Assize of Arms requirement reintroduced by Henry VIII, and with the exception of barons and clergymen, every male subject of the King 'not lame, decrepit nor maimed, nor having any other lawful or reasonable cause or impediment' was required to practise on all holidays and Sundays with the longbow until the age of 60, the limit of legal obligation for military service. Pastimes and games other than archery were prohibited. Edward IV's requirement for Englishmen in Ireland to practise from the beginning of March until the end of July was dictated by military necessity, summer campaigns needing archers already in form. Butts had to be provided in every community, usually near the church so that practice could begin immediately after services.

Until the age of 24, the young man was forbidden to 'shoote at any standinge prick excepte it be a Rover whereat he shall chaunge at every shoote his marke.' This was to develop skill in hitting marks at varying distances with the first arrow. After the age of 24, he was not permitted to shoot at any mark of less than eleven score 'with anye prickshafte or fleight', these lighter arrows being meant for longer distances rather than impact.

19

SHOOTING TECHNIQUE

Drawing to the ear he prayseth greatly, whereby men shoot both stronger and longer. Drawing therefore to the eare is better than to drawe to the breste. Holding must not be longe, for it both putteth a bowe in jeopardy and also marreth a man's shoote.

Roger Ascham, *Toxophilus*[36]

For in those daies the yeomen had their lims at libertie, sith their hosen were then fastened with one point, and their jackes long and easie to shoot in; so that they might draw bowes of great strength and shoot arrows of a yard long, beside the head.

William Harrison, *Description of Britain*[37]

Then the English archers stept forward one pace and let fly their arrows so wholly and so thick that it seemed snow. When the Genoways felt the arrows piercing through heads, arms and breasts, many of them cast down their cross-bows and did cut their strings and returned discomfited.

Froissart's Chronicles[38]

Ascham tells us that hitting the mark comes from shooting fair, which is shooting in proper form, keeping length, which is shooting to the distance of the mark, and shooting straight, which is controlling the direction of the arrow flight on a horizontal plane. The act of shooting was divided by Acham into five partitions: standing, nocking, drawing, holding and loosing. Ascham's prerequisites for a good archer were:

Clear sight, steadily directed toward the mark.
Proper judgment, to determine the distance of the ground.
Knowing how to take advantage of a side wind.
Being well acquainted with what compass his arrows will require in their flight.
Courage. Whoever shoots with even a little trepidation is sure to shoot badly.

This first part of this chapter does not deal with the matter of aiming (shooting straight), which should not be considered before one has mastered shooting fair and keeping length. The act of shooting has to become an automatic reflex action, as if arrows are not consistently released with the same power and steadiness, attempts to compensate for previous misses will only result in confusion. The famous modern archer Howard Hill did not permit his students the use of a target for the first three weeks of instruction, during which time the arrows were shot into a backstop of straw bales. Likewise in times past, mastery of an archer's final bow was considered necessary before he even attempted to hit a mark, while the crossbowman had only to master the smooth squeezing of the trigger key. This is why a crossbowman could be trained so much more quickly than a longbowman.

In learning to shoot, a bracer to protect the bow arm and a shooting glove are very helpful although either or both can be dispensed with. Ascham found that correct technique and a high strung bow would eliminate the need for a bracer and he knew many good archers that did not use one, but in 1571 boys attending school at Harrow were required to have a bow, three shafts, bowstrings and a bracer. No mention is made of finger protection, which indeed seldom appears in manuscript illustrations. Nowadays, French popinjay shooters draw their powerful bows bare-handed, serving the bowstring with butcher's twine to a thickness of three times the usual ⅛ inch string. My fingers are relatively soft, but I have shot barehanded with a thin stringed 90lb bow with minimal discomfort using the shooting style described herein. A butcher to whom I was giving lessons shot barehanded for two hours the first time he used a bow (which drew some 35lbs) and experienced no soreness in fingers toughened by tying off roasts.

The descriptions of shooting at marks with a strong longbow in *Lartdarcherie* and *Toxophilus* have few contradictions and we may consider them together to represent the manner of shooting in the two centuries in which the longbowman made his mark in European history. Because of cultural interchange some Saracen writings of the period are also helpful.

Shooting Fair

Standing

Mediaeval form was to hold the bow in the left hand and the string in the right as most archers do today. However it has been found that people who have switched hands after beginning the practice of archery have experienced little difficulty in the changeover and in some cases have even found their shooting improved. Perhaps military archers were encouraged to shoot right-handed to avoid problems when shooting in close formation.

In settling himself to shoot, the bowman takes one pace forward with his bow-hand foot. In nearly all mediaeval illustrations this foot points at the mark as it does in fencing. The rear foot being set at a comfortable angle, the weight may be either distributed evenly on both feet as was evidently Ascham's preference for 'fair and

1 John Gower draws
a yew smallbow with
horn nocks and a green
painted back, as suggested
by *Livre de Chasse* for a
hunting bow. The arrows
are of parallel form
headed with bearded
broadheads. They seem to
have tanged horn nocks
like the brass ones from
pre-Viking Scandinavia
and are fletched with
peacock feathers on a
dark shaftment, perhaps
birch tar. The usual spiral
binding is not visible.
(From John Gower's
book *Vox Clamantis*,
*c.*1400. Glasgow
University Library/the
Bridgeman Art Library)

2 William the Conqueror's Norman lancers charge through the line of archers who have rained arrows on the Saxon defenders at Senlac Hill in 1066. A man-at-arms carries all his arrows in his bow hand. The archers have both hip and shoulder quivers and all draw to the breast. These are clearly smallbows. (Bayeux Tapestry, Bridgeman Art Library)

3 A surgeon extracts a swallowtail broadhead. (Library of Trinity College, Cambridge)

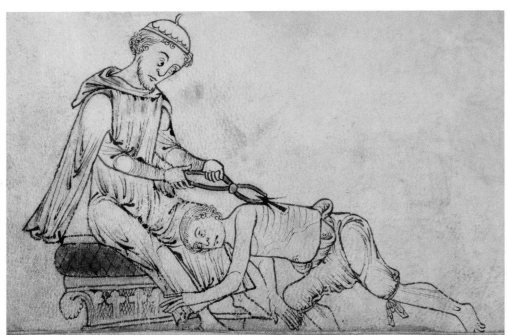

4 A woman with a smallbow shooting at view, looses at a deer pursued by her greyhound. Early fourteenth century. (HIP/Art Resource NY)

5 An Ottoman Turk horse archer turns in the saddle to deliver a parting shot. Turks were the most formidable opponents faced by the Crusaders in *Outremer.* (Ottoman miniature, fifteenth century. Topkapi Palace Museum, Istanbul. Erich Lessing/Art Resource, NY)

6 A fourteenth-century nobleman accompanied by a servant aims a blunt bird bolt. His hip quiver contains two more bolts and a cocking hook hangs from his belt. (Der Kol von Nüssen, *Manessa Codex*, Heidelberg University Library)

7 The author drawing a self-made longbow of Viking type, bow tips steam-bent towards the shooter.

Below, left to right

8 The arms, crest and livery colours of the Bowyers' guild. The white charge is the 'flote' *(*float) with a blade like a combination of a plane and a file of the type still called a float file. These arms are the only heraldic application of this bowyers' tool.

9 The arms crest and livery colours of the Fletcher's guild.

CRECY
POITIERS AGINCOURT

Arms of
The Worshipful Company of Bowyers
of London

Arms granted 1488 ..

Livery colours: white and black

TRUE AND SURE

Arms of
The Worshipful Company of Fletchers
of London

Arms granted 1467
Crest granted 1486

Livery colours: blue and yellow

10 A longbow
archer examines
a blunt arrow for
butt shooting.
(*Luttrell Psalter*, the
British Library)

11 Antoine, the Bastard of Burgundy, holds a tapered arrow with swine back fletching. One vane has two red stripes. Fletchings were sometimes coloured in various styles. (Musées Royaux des Beaux-Artes, Brussels, Belgium; Scala/Art Resource, NY)

12 A man attempts to draw a very short bow with both hands and using his feet as described by Sigurd the Crusader. (*Luttrell Psalter*, the British Library)

13 St Sebastian, here shown as a king, holds a taper arrow with enlarged nock and square fletch, possibly of peacock wing feathers. The black shaftment suggests use of coode or birch tar, which had fallen out of English use by Richard II's reign, or it may be black sealing wax. (From the Wilton Diptych, The National Gallery)

14 The Battle of Aljubarotta in 1385 resulted in Portugal's independence from Castille. The victory was aided by a contingent of 100 English archers against numerically superior Castillian and French forces. All the archers are pictured with yew smallbows where we would expect longbows. Arrows are shown with long 'tryangel' fletching with red binding at the ends of the quills. (Wavrin's *Chronique D'Angleterre*, the British Library)

15 A fourteenth-century archer bends up his bow. Tucked in his girdle is a single arrow with a large hunting broadhead, and short 'tryangel' fletching bound with red thread and bulbous nock. His long tunic is tucked up for unimpeded movement. (*Luttrell Psalter*, the British Library)

16 A scene from a thirteenth-century illuminated Bible shows a crossbowman besieging a castle. (The Morgan (Maciejowski) Bible, the Pierpont Morgan Library)

17 Archers practising at the butts, one of whom has a bow with following tips. The arrows are butt shafts with enlarged nocks, swine back fletching and blunt heads. Two archers wear small round bracers. Bowstrings appear to be double looped. Paper was not yet known in Europe and the mark is probably cloth sewn to a hoop. (*Luttrell Psalter*, the British Library)

18 A bow and stable hunt. Green-clad nobles loose their arrows at deer that are driven towards them by dogs, both greyhounds and brachets. Two men use the smallbows recommended by Gaston de Foix for hunting, while a third man aims a crossbow. From his girdle hang a quiver of arrows and a belt hook. All arrows are tipped with very large swallowtail broadheads, also as recommended by the Count de Foix. (*Le Livre de Chasse,* Bibliothèque nationale de France)

19 King Charles VII of France at his devotions accompanied by his Scottish archer bodyguard, liveried as described by de Coussy. Every third man carries a glaive, the next a sword and shield, and the next carries a longbow, *c.*1449. (Erich lessing/Art Resource, NY)

20 A model showing the Black Prince's green and white liveried archers defending his banner at Crecy. One has just loosed an arrow, one is at full draw, another is nocking and a fourth is selecting an arrow stuck in the ground. (Marco Venturi)

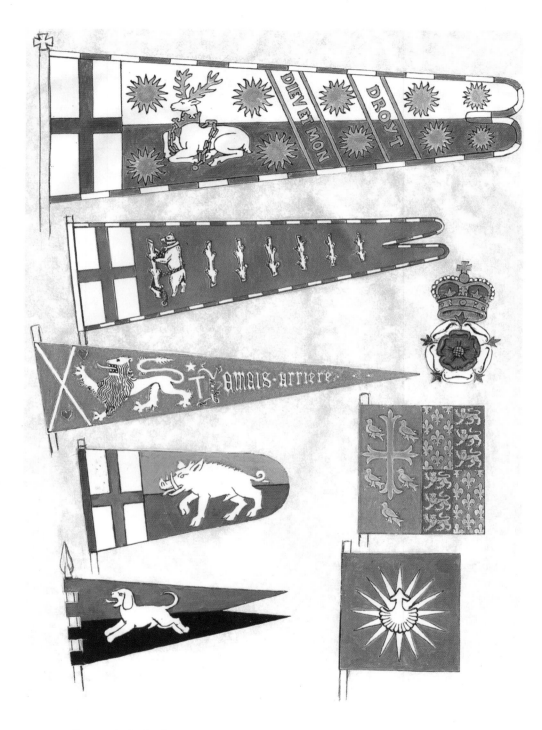

21 Counterclockwise from top: Standard of King Richard II with lodged hart badge; standard of the Earl of Warwick with ragged staff badge; standard of the Earl Douglas with heart badge; guidon of King Richard III with white boar badge; pennon of Lord Talbot with Talbot courant badge; badge banner of the Earl Rivers with scallop shell with rays; banner of King Richard II (no similarity to his standard); Tudor crowned Tudor Rose badge for guardsmen.

22 A crossbowman cocks his crossbow using a belt hook. (*Luttrell Psalter*, the British Library)

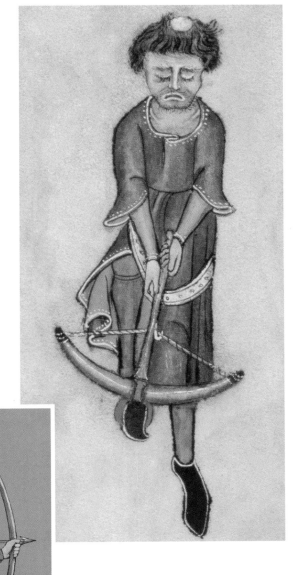

23 An archer in the greenwood shooting at view. He holds a leafy twig between his teeth to mask telltale facial glare. Some poachers blackened their faces for that reason. (Author)

24 St Edmund refused to cooperate with Viking attackers and was tied to a tree and used for target practice. The bows are shown with tips bent toward the archer like the Viking bows from Ballinderry ans Schleswig. (Pierpont Morgan Library, NY)

comely' shooting. Alternatively, more weight may be on the rear foot, rear leg bent, front leg straight. This latter may be the stand that Ascham thought looked as though the archer was pulling on a rope. It is a solid stance, especially good on uneven ground and is used in karate. The book *Saracen Archery* specifies that the feet in this sort of stand should be a forearm's distance apart and the left heel should point at the right instep with knees slightly bent. Earlier English practice included little bend at the waist but with the upper body inclined slightly forward rather than the bolt upright posture of Victorian bowmen. *Lartdarcherie* gives the odd instruction that only the toe of the forward foot should touch the ground, the heel to be brought down at the loose without moving the foot. This is theoretically to make the archer's side to turn toward the butt to give a good impetus to the arrow.

The mediaeval bow had no clearly defined handgrip of any kind and was gripped on the waxed bare wood. The bow should be taken up 'even in the middes', the middle being located by balancing the horizontal bow on the thumb of the hand, according to *Lartdarcherie*. For butt shooting it should be balanced exactly. Archers sometimes gripped higher or lower for distance shooting, and one aspect of the Flemish style of shooting was that the arrow pass was at the middle of the bow with the bowhand grip below. This does give increased cast but it is stressful for the bow and Ascham lists this as one of the reasons for breakage.

> When you have taken good footing, then must you loke at your shaft, that no earth, nor weete be left upon it, for so should it leese the lengthe You must loke at the head also, least it should have any stripe at the last shot.

Archers at practice usually tucked their two or three arrows under their belts. Some used quivers hung at their right side, their sword being at their left. Arrows of ten fists are too long to be readily drawn from a quiver in a single motion; *Lartdarcherie* advises that the archer should therefore draw an arrow from his quiver in two motions, first pulling it halfway out by the nock, then taking it by the middle to set it in the bow. *Lartdarcherie* differs from Ascham only in giving the shooting sequence as first nocking, then taking a stand.

Nocking

Gervase Markham says to 'bring the shaft under the string and over the bow.' The arrow is laid 'streight overthwart' the horizontal bow and rotated to bring the cock feather, the one at a right angle to the nock, upwards. The English archer nocked by sight while the Saracen archer nocked by feel.

The arrow held by its middle may be pressed back onto the string or it may be held in place by the forefinger of the bow hand.while the nock, held by thumb and forefinger of the right hand, is pushed forward over the string with the thumb and pulled back onto the string. The latter, which avoids fumbling, is my preference. If the arrow is nocked ⅛ inch higher than a right angle to the string it will shoot as well, and this is the preference of many modern bowmen, but it should not be nocked lower. The arrow rests on the knuckle of the bow hand.

A number of manuscript illustrations, including one in the *Luttrell Psalter*, show the arrow as having been nocked on the shafthand side of the bow, the arrow resting either on the thumb or between two fingers. Whether these illustrations, some looking very realistic, show an actual method or are a product of ignorance on the part of the artist, I cannot say. It is certainly a general rule that arrows drawn with the fingers are laid on the bowhand side of the bow and arrows drawn with the thumb are laid on the shafthand side, as in these cases rotation of the string due to pressure from the draw will keep the arrow against the side of the bow.

Drawing

Many late mediaeval manuscripts portray a two-finger draw. This may illustrate a Flemish style by the Flemish artists who did the illustrations. Editions of John Gower's book *Vox Clamantis* from the late fourteenth century show two versions of an illustration of the author aiming an arrow at a representation of the world. In one, he draws a longbow with three fingers, while in the other he draws a smallbow with two fingers. We learn from Ascham and *Roi Modus* and from the warning of the English commanders at Agincourt that archers captured by the French were to have three fingers cut off, that both French and English archers drew longbows with three fingers. The instructions given below are for shooting long arrows in longbows with a draw to the ear in the mediaeval manner. The three drawing fingers are placed on the string, as in modern usage with the arrow nock between forefinger and middle finger. Ascham:

> When a man shooteth, the might of his shoote lyeth on the formooste fynger and on the ringman, for the myddle finger which is the longest, lyke a lubber starteth back and beareth no weight of the string in a maner at all … and for sure loosyng the foremost finger is most apte because it holdeth best and for that purpose nature hath as a man would saye yocked it with the thoumbe.

Lartdarcherie also says to hold the string on the second joint of the first finger and the first joint of the third finger so, this placement of the fingers was probably internationally standard in the fifteenth and sixteenth centuries. I personally find that this makes for better accuracy than when attempting to keep even pressure on all three fingers.

Lartdarcherie states that the hand by which the arrow is held should be opposite the centre of the bow. The actual drawing can be done in two ways; some draw with the bow hand raised and some with it low down. The latter

> … is good for butt and target [clout?] shooting and is a more natural way of shooting than with the bow hand high, besides which it assists the loose, and also because the arm, not being raised so high is, in cases of necessity, less exposed.

In drawing from the low position, a six-foot bow would of course be held more or less horizontally. Before commencing the draw, the forefinger and middle finger must be held far enough apart that the fingers will not be pinched between arrow and string at full draw and loose. The shooting glove sometimes had a roll of leather between these fingers to keep them apart, as do some modern shooting tabs. Ascham advised that the arrow nock should grip the string, but not too tightly, as also advised in modern practice.

The bow hand grips the bow with no bend at the wrist, whether loosely or tightly being an individual choice, so that the arrow rests on the bowhand knuckle. The elbow is turned outwards, not down. During the draw the pressure of the bow should come against the ball of the thumb. In drawing a powerful bow gripped on the bare wood, pressure against a bone would be painful enough to disturb concentration.

At this point the vision should be focused on the mark (not looking at the arrow), both eyes open, and they should remain so until the arrow is in flight, not looking. The elbow of the drawing should remain close to the body in order to make use of the powerful body muscles during the draw, the arm muscles being used as little as possible. From the nocking position the drawing hand moves directly to the ear and the bow hand moves to nearly full extension of the bow arm, while, as Ascham advised, the bow swivels to a vertical position. In this action the bow arm is not held rigid but presses forward into the bow as the drawing arm pulls back. As instinctive shooters have a tendency to loose in the instant the arrow is pointed at the mark, it is best to not point the arrow before the draw is complete. That the drawing hand passed close to the cheek is seen by Ascham's observation of one archer who wore a leather cheek bracer to keep from scratching himself. Some modern 'instinctive' archers, including Howard Hill and Fred Asbell, kept the bow arm straight throughout the draw while raising it into position and that also works very well.

Roi Modus says to draw the arrow fully, just as Shakespeare's Richard III shouts 'Draw archers, draw your arrows to the head!' English boys learning shooting had someone to tell them when they were at full draw. Without this training, it is difficult to determine this without looking at the arrow. However the arrow of ten fists length as described in Part I should be long enough to be fully drawn without risk of over drawing.

When using a longbow, at full draw the thumb of the drawing hand, which may remain in contact with the forefinger as a check, lightly touches the back of the earlobe. The arrow will be at the right of the line of vision, allowing a clear view of the mark. In the draw to the ear, the forearm of the drawing hand may be held in line, both in a vertical and horizontal plane, with the arrow. This long draw, mechanically strong and steady, minimises variations in the loose, and a long arrow flies more steadily than a shorter one.

There is one problem with this draw. If the bowman draws close to his face at full stretch and is quite erect, the string may be impeded by the chest and adjustments in posture are helpful to clear it. Roberts' 1801 book *The English Bowman* advises a forward inclination of the head and upper part of the body, 'not from the waist, not stooping, nor yet standing fair upright'. The reader who has seen photographs of

Howard Hill will be familiar with the posture, which is also seen in mediaeval manuscripts. It should not be excessive. *London's Artillery* notes: 'A great many archers bend
the body very considerably from the waist, but this is most highly objectionable on
every account.' A warning must likewise be given against bending the head too much
forward. 'The string, in recoiling, will every now and then give the unfortunate archer
such a merciless rap on the nose as effectively to cure him of the fault.'

The draw to the ear was known to the East Roman Empire; it may have been
learned from the Huns and was practised by Byzantine 'cataphracti'. It can be used
with longbows that are long enough to tolerate that length of draw. Saracens, who
drew with the thumb and also drew to the ear said that, seen from the side, the
forearm of the shaft hand, the arrow, the shoulders and the bow arm should all be
in a straight line, 'like a paper rule', but some European manuscript illustrations
show the elbow of the bow arm raised, which is acceptable if it naturally occurs. If
shooting slightly upwards or downwards, the entire torso should be inclined insofar
as practical, rather than raising or lowering the bow hand. This is the position of
full draw and loose. The draw was sometimes made with the bow arm extended,
especially in hunting, in order to avoid telltale movement. It is a less powerful draw,
not as well suited to a longbow. Redrawing, that is nearly completing the draw,
relaxing the draw a few inches, then coming to full draw, is an option of which
Ascham approved.

As mentioned above, Saracens drew the bow with the thumb rather than the fingers. This grip, or lock as they called it, is an effective way to draw, that permits use
of a powerful bow and a clean loose. Few archers shot with the bare hand, and a
thumb ring was used, the string being taken on its upper edge, at the crease of the
first thumb joint. The thumb joint was then bent and covered by the forefinger which
rested one-third on the skin and two-thirds on the nail. A Saracen writer described
the Slav (Aqd As-Saqalibah) draw in which the shooter put his three middle fingers
on the string and extended the index finger along the shaft of the arrow. The thumb
was not used and the bow was held vertically. The slavs were reported to have used
fingerguards of gold, silver, iron and copper.

When shooting longer arrows to considerable distances with the bow hand elevated, the draw is made to the point of the shoulder or 'to the right pap' (nipple) as
advised by *Lartdarcherie*, which also says that a good archer should preferably draw
ten palm breadths of arrow, although many good archers have a shorter draw and
some a longer one. An alternative is to draw to the centre of the collarbone as seen
in some manuscripts.

For prick shooting, roving or flight shooting when considerably elevation was
required, the archer drew to the breast or to the point of the shoulder, depending on
the length of the arrow. Clothyard arrows might be used in these situations. This kind
of shooting is described in a poem in Richard Nichols' *London's Artillery* of 1616.

> A youth of clean compacted limb
> Who, with a comely grace in his left hand
> Holding his bow, did take a steadfast stand,

Setting his left leg somewhat forth before,
His arrow with his right hand nocking sure.
Then with his left hand, little above his sight
Stretching his arm out with an easy strength,
to draw an arrow of a yard in length ...

It is odd that with so many written references to drawing to the ear, that we should find so few manuscript illustrations showing archers shooting in this way. Many illustrations, from periods in which we know the draw to the ear was used, show men shooting longbows at level marks drawing to the breast. This was done when shooting at roving marks. Short handbows, small bows, are shown being used in this way, the arrows being too short for the draw to the ear. These bows are also occasionally shown being drawn to the chin or cheek, especially when shooting downwards, and are usually drawn with two fingers rather than three. The two-finger draw is suitable for weaker bows as these bows generally were. The archer has a little more control at the loose and there is not such a tendency for the fingers to get pinched against the arrow.

Modern archers often draw to the chin or cheek, as drawing to the ear means that the right eye is not over the arrow. Modern shooters who sight along the shaft would find this a distinct disadvantage for aiming. Howard Hill drew to the cheek and, in addition to his slightly hunched posture, canted the bow to bring the tail of the arrow under his eye. Some bowmen in Roberts' time, drawing to the ear, canted their bows also. And while *Roi Modus* says to keep the bow perpendicular, Ascham caustically commented on some archers he observed: 'an other waggeth the upper end of his bow one way, the nether end an other way'. In drawing to the ear the bowstring will not permit much canting of the bow and we shall learn that if the bowman is aiming instinctively, it is really of no importance whether the arrow is under the eye or not.

In the *Luttrell Psalter*, a man is shown preparing to shoot in a manner that modern flight shooters call 'free style', lying on his back, his feet against the bow middle, and drawing with both hands. This is a method by which a man can shoot in a bow that would otherwise be beyond his strength, but accuracy is out of the question.

Some archers deviated from the straightforward classical shooting style and Ascham, an incurable purist, commented on variations he observed at the butts. He considered them perversions, lumping them together with facial grimaces and the like, but apparently some archers in Ascham's time, as well as archers in other times and places, found them of value.

The interrupted draw

The draw is made to the cheek a few inches short of full draw, and held while the archer takes aim (Ascham knew some good archers who, much to his disapproval, glanced at the shaft at this point, then concentrated on the mark). Then the draw is completed and the arrow loosed. This method is recommended in at least two mediaeval Saracen books on archery and was seen in use by Horace A. Ford in the nineteenth century, though he advocated a continuous draw. It is similar to the drawing and re-drawing noted in *Roi Modus* and *Toxophilus* in which the full draw is relaxed a few inches to take aim, then again fully drawn and loosed. An instinctive shooter drawing in one smooth motion may have the tendency to loose the arrow as soon as it is pointed at the mark, before full draw is reached. The interrupted draw is a cure for this habit.

The downward draw

The bow arm is raised vertically and the arrow drawn downward to the ear, bringing the draw to within a few inches of the arrowhead. The draw is completed by bringing the stiffened bow-arm down into shooting position like a lever. This sort of draw was used by Native American and perhaps by the Mongols. Flemish popinjay shooters claim it is easier to draw an arrow pointed upwards. Again, the downward draw helps correct the problem of a premature loose.

The upward draw

The draw is commenced with the arrow pointing slightly downwards at the ground. The hands move directly to final position. This was used in the Japanese Heki, or military draw.

The low draw

The archer first draws to the breast 'as if he would shoot at a roving mark,' then raises to the ear. This seems to make it easier to draw a powerful bow.

The high draw

The hands are raised to eye level or above, then brought down to hold position, the bow hand in a movement Korean archers call 'going over the hill'. The high draw is clearly shown in Spanish and Burgundian manuscripts and was part of the old Japanese Heki. It was also used by Liangulu archers of Kenya. It makes drawing a powerful bow easier and completes full draw before the arrow is pointed at the mark.

Holding

The hold is the pause upon completing the draw. 'It must be so lytle that it may be perceyued better in a man's mynd when it is done, than seene with a man's eyes when it is in doing.' Saracens held for not longer than the count of three. However brief, this pause is essential for good shooting, but the longer the hold, the greater the strain for the bowman, and the greater the difficulty of taking steady aim and loosing cleanly, in addition to the disturbance of shooting rhythm. Also, the bow is placed in jeopardy by an overlong hold and loses power for the cast. This loss is greatest in the first three seconds and continues more slowly, bringing the bow closer to its breaking point. For these reasons it is important that the hold not only be brief, but of equal duration at each shot.

The described hold position is strong, the weakest part being the bow arm and shoulder. During the hold, all muscles not necessary to retain the position should

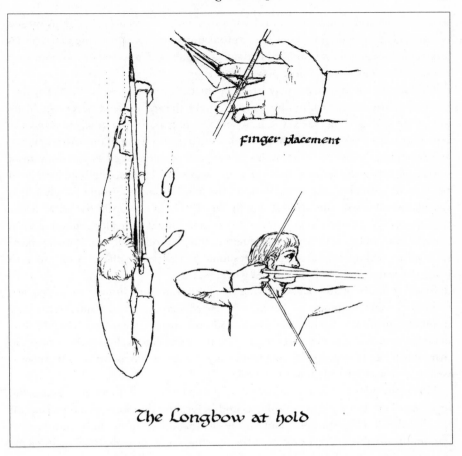

finger placement

The Longbow at hold

be relaxed, the back and shoulder muscles, the 'strength of body' doing nearly all the holding. Relaxing the muscles of the drawing arm will automatically bring the fore-arm into line with the arrow.

Loosing

Without a good loose the shot will fail and a good loose has never been easy to attain. It must be 'quick and hard, yet soft and gentle'. The loose is accomplished by the coordinating of the opening of the drawing hand with a backward push of the elbow or a pressing together of the shoulder blades, and a forward pressing with the bow hand.

The opening of the drawing hand is tricky. The forefinger and middle finger are held forcibly apart and cannot simply be relaxed to get rid of the string. I do not suppose anyone using the deep grip would try that more than once. The fingers must actually be opened out straight but this must be done smoothly, without a jerk. When done properly, the result is a clean sharp loose, without creep or drag. This should occasionally be practised without finger protection to be sure the string is clearing is jerky and uncontrolled, but the string must not be allowed to creep or move forward as this will cause the shot to lose power.

On loosing, the bowstring may strike the bracer or the arrow may strike against the bow. With a high strung bow properly held, the string need never touch the bracer, but with a string braced to a palm and two fingers, it is practically unavoidable, especially toward the wrist. The arrow strikes the bow as a result of the arrow bending and whipping back to straightness due to the push of the released string, and is most noticeable when the arrow is too stiff. If the arrows are striking the bow hard, hold the bow so as to bring the string more to the left. The arrows should be released as freely as possible so if the string strikes the bracer a hard blow, or if the arrow leaves the bow with a definite clacking sound, correction should be made. If shooting form is not at fault, hold the bow at arm's length in the position of loosing. If the problem is the string striking the bracer, the bow should be gripped on the next shot so as to bring the string slightly to the right of where you see it.

Pressing the bow, also called driving the shot, is not much done today but was formerly much recommended. Saracen writers advised that the pressure on the bow should be greatest at the loose, and one modern instructor likewise advised his students to 'punch the target in the face.' The movement both directs the arrow and sharpens the loose. A powerful bow will in any case move when loosed and it may as well move toward the target as to one side.

The Saracen loose was accomplished by straightening the finger and thumb, the forefinger being straightened a split second before the thumb, to avoid tearing off the thumbnail. The arrow was laid on the shafthand side of the bow, and shot off the thumb, the forefinger, or off both the forefinger and the thumb below the nails, the pads of the tips of these digits being pressed together. The latter alternative was considered best.

Footwork

Ascham wrote of certain of his fellow shooters that 'Summe stampe forward, and summe leape backwarde,' but such footwork is not noted among the English bowmen. However *Lartdarcherie* makes the claim that loosing depends on the step and gives three variations.

One step: step forward with the bowhand foot and bring back the drawing arm pushing out the bow and arrow and step back with the other foot. A long and sharp step straightens the arm.

Two step: step back with the rear foot so that on bringing the front foot down, sufficient impetus is given for the loose.

Three step: the front foot is moved forward, the bow thrust forward as the back foot is brought back so that at the loose, one can step forward with the front foot.

Such movements would seem to make it difficult to hit a mark although a co-ordinated forward movement or thrust can add ten yards or more to the distance shot. Perhaps something has been lost in translation from mediaeval Picard dialect. In the latter two the motive seems to be to get a forward movement at the moment of loosing, as modern flight shooters rock back and forth several times to add a little extra momentum to the arrow, and *Lartdarcherie* does deal with flight shooting.

Forehand and Underhand

Reference to forehand and underhand shooting are found in *Toxophilus*, in Shakespeare and a Robin Hood ballad. It is clear that everyone knew what these terms meant, but they are no longer used. Ascham tells us:

> Taper fashion is fit for them which shote under hande because they shoot with a soft lowse, and stresses not a shaft muche where the weight of a bow lyeth as you may perceyue by the weringe of every shaft.
>
> Agayne the bygge brested shafte [barreled or breasted] is fytie for hym, which shoteth right afore him, or els the brest being weke shoulde neuer withstande that strong pithy kynde of shootynge, thus the underhand must haue a small breste, to go clene awaye oute of the bowe, the forehande muste haue a bigge breste to bere the great myghte of the bowe.

He says elsewhere that 'a big breasted shaft for him that shoteth under hand will hobble' and a little breasted shaft 'for him that shoteth above the hand will start' and these shafts are therefore unfit in these cases.

In Shakespeare's *Henry IV Part II*, a character muses: 'Shallow … John a Gaunt loved him well and betted much money on his head. Dead! A' would have clapped i' the clout at twelve score; and carried you a fore hand shaft a fourteen and fourteen and a half that it would have done a man's heart good to see.' Dropping an arrow into a clout (see p.165) at 240 yards is not bad; clouts/pricks are no longer even shot at from that distance anymore. But fourteen is only 280 yards and the minimum range at which an archer was permitted to use such an arrow was 220 yards. Elizabethan archers shot considerably farther than that, so it may be that flight arrows were not considered as forehand shafts, and that forehand shooting implies the use of heavier prick shafts. The Robin Hood ballad describing a shooting competition tells us that 'Loxly puld forth a broad arrow. He shot it underhand.'

Forehand shooting seems to mean shooting straight ahead, apparently the same as shooting above the hand, and we know that taper shafts were used in drawing to the breast for far shooting. We might conclude that shooting underhand means drawing to the ear in point blank level shooting, while a forehand shot, one above the hand, means shooting long distances with a heavier arrow apparently with a stronger bow or a longer draw.

Later Publications

In 1684 Gervase Markham published *The Art of Archery* which was almost a direct plagiarism of *Toxophilus* with some additional material. During Cromwell's time archery nearly died out, even as a sport, but was revived with the Restoration. Markham then published a book called *Country Contentment* in which he advised that the archer should

> … stand faire comely and upright with his body; his left foot a convenient stride before his right; both his hammes stiffe; his left arme holding his bowe in the midst stretcht strait out; and his right arme with his first three fingers and his thumb drawing the string to his right care; the nock of his arrow resting between his for-finger and long finger of his right hand; and the steale of his arrow before the feathers, upon the middle knuckle of his for-finger on his left hand. He shall draw his arrow up close to the (arrow) head, and deliver it on the instant without hanging on the string.

I don't suppose Markham meant touching the thumb to the string, but probably to touch it to the tip of the forefinger. The forefinger of the bow hand is here held bent with the fingertip touching the back of the bow to bring the middle knuckle into position. This minor variation, first coming to our attention in these instructions, continued in use for over a century. Markham also advises extending the bow-arm before beginning to draw, which also seems a new innovation.

Keeping Length

> Now schall y wet an thou be god,
> And polle het op to they nere.
> So god me helpe, seyde the prowde potter,
> Thys ys bot ryght weke gere.
>
> *Robin Hood and the Potter*[39]
>
> Now if you mark the weather dilligently,
> keep your standing exactly,
> hold and nock truly,
> and keep your elevation correctly,
> you will never miss your length.
>
> Roger Ascham, *Toxophilus*

Keeping length means shooting with such cast and elevation as to bring the mark into the arrow's trajectory (parabola), which should be mastered before attempting to hit a specific point on a mark (shooting straight, see below). It is much easier to shoot without deviation to either side than to shoot to a correct elevation, especially at longer distances. This is because of the trajectory of the arrow, because the distance to the mark may seem greater or less than it actually is, and because of variances of wind or weather (dampness will cause a loss of length). Because these factors have more importance at the longer distances, and mediaeval archers shot at marks at much greater distances than we do today, much emphasis was placed on keeping a length.

If one's arrows are as nearly identical as possible, if one's length of draw is always the same, if the loose is always of the same sharpness, and the holding always occupies the same interval of time, then the arrow will always be loosed with the same force and therefore velocity. For this reason the five partitions of shooting should have been mastered before learning to keep a length.

The next step is learning to keep the correct elevation by familiarity with the capabilities of one's artillery and by practice in shooting to various distances. Ascham wrote: 'A perfyte archer must firste learn the sure flyte of his shaftes, that he may be boulde alwayes, to trust them...' At this time the shooter should observe the flight of the arrow not only to learn its trajectory, but also to note any deviations from smooth flight. An arrow that does not fly truly has as its cause a crooked shaft, or one too weak or too strong for the bow, or faulty feathering. An arrow wavering or tumbling from improper feathering loses in velocity and striking force. On the shooter's part, if the shaft hand has been thrown to the side when loosing, if there was a jerky loose, or the arrow was nocked to high or too low, the cause should be determined and corrected.

That much attention was paid to true flight is evident by the varied descriptive words for deviant arrows in the literature of the Middle Ages. A 'scudding arrow' was one that skimmed upon the wind, a 'wagging arrow', also called a staggering or 'hobbling arrow' was one with a wagging tail. A 'gadding arrow' was one that flew erratically, a 'starting arrow' was one that jumped from its true course.

Maximum distance, as for flight shooting, is achieved by shooting upward at an elevation of about 45 degrees. For this purpose an open field is needed, at least 300 yards long, although in the Middle Ages more than 400 yards were needed. Arrows shot at this distance, unless they land in high grass, are not hard to find, as they stick into the ground nearly upright. The archer should know the maximum length of which his artillery is capable.

Another important distance to be familiar with is the length at which, rather than a true arc, and for some distance, trajectory is slight. The shooter must hold high on uphill marks, low on downhill ones. As the degree of elevation is dependent on the distance to the mark, it is important to have the maximum depth perception afforded by keeping both eyes open. Optical illusion can mislead a shooter as to the true length. 'You must take heed also, if ever you shoote when one of the markes, or both, stands a little short of a high wall, for there you may be easely begyled.' In shooting across a ravine, the distance is also deceptive.

A litle wynd on a moistye day stoppeth a shaft more than a good whyskynge wynde in a cleare day. Yea, and I have seene when there hath bene no wynde at all, the ayre so mistye and thicke, that both markes have been wonderful great, meaning that one must elevate as though they were farther away than they really are.

Any wind must be taken into consideration. The shooter must be alert for the situation of wind blowing in one direction at his position and in another, perhaps opposite direction, at a distant mark. In clout/prick shooting (see p.165) he must consider the frequently greater wind speed at higher levels.

Archers used to pluck grass and toss it up to determine wind speed and direction. A light breeze will carry the arrow with it to some extent, depending on the size of feathers and weight of the arrow. The heavier an arrow, the better it will 'stand in a wind' or retain its course. Ordinarily the archer with the wind at his back will find his arrows flying farther, and if shooting into the wind, they will fall short. However, in some cases an archer with a strong wind at his back may also find his arrows falling short because of the wind catching the fletching and throwing the shaftment of the arrow forward, causing the arrow to dive to the ground. Compensations of elevation are again based on experience and a ready-made cure for this is to use a 'deade' heavy shaft.

A side wind is less of a problem in keeping a length but one of the major problems for shooting straight. The archer must know how to compensate for a side wind by directing his arrow to the proper degree upwind, the technique that American soldiers used to call 'Kentucky windage'. A side wind will also push the shaftment to the side, but the rudder effect of the fletching will drive the arrow upwind somewhat, so the deviation may be less than one would expect. If broadheads are used, they may also be caught by the wind, as well as the fletching.

Shooting Straight

> Having a mans eye alwayes on his marke,
> is the only way to shoote streight.
>
> Roger Ascham, *Toxophilus*

If the would-be archer has thoroughly learned the previous partitions to the point that shooting has become a reflex action requiring no thought and has mastered the keeping of a length and become thoroughly familiar with the behaviour of his artillery, then he can consider shooting at a mark.

These preliminaries are important because to have to consciously pay attention to one's technique would distract the attention from aiming. The second or so that full draw is held in mediaeval shooting is not enough time for a shift of concentration or even a change of focus of the vision from arrowpoint to mark. For this reason and also because if one is not yet shooting consistently, making compensations in order to hit the mark can become very confusing. If the first arrow is shot with a dead loose and fails short, the bowman raising elevation and shooting with a sharper loose on the next arrow will overshoot the mark, and so on. The bowman who can curb his impatience to hit a mark before he has mastered the use of his artillery will learn to hit his mark with accuracy sooner than one who attempts to hit a mark from his first shot.

The 'mark' is anything at which one shoots, such as the pin or spot in the middle a the target (not simply at the target). Directing the arrow is called 'aiming' or 'marking'. Making a successful hit is called 'making the mark'. An unsuccessful arrow has 'failed of the mark'.

If the modern archer, as Ascham advised, shoots without the use of sights and without sighting on the arrowpoint or down the arrow and concentrates his vision on the mark, then he is aiming instinctively. Instinctive aiming, often incorrectly called instinctive shooting, is practised by few archers at the present time. It involves aiming by 'feel' or intuition without using sight marks, or sighting down the arrow or using the point of the arrow as a sight. There is no estimation of distances in feet or yards; with practice the bow hand learns to point at the precise spot the archer wishes to hit. He lines up the arrow and looses, in much the same way as he would throw a stone or dart, or drive a golf ball.

Instinctive aiming is a surprisingly emotional topic today in archery circles. Many modern bare bow (no sights) shooters, particularly bowhunters, call themselves instinctive shooters when they are really using the arrow to aim with in one way or another. When this is pointed out to them, they angrily maintain that there is no such thing as purely instinctive aiming and that every bowman visually uses his arrow for aiming whether he is aware of it or not. Otherwise he could not hit anything.

However Ascham makes it clear beyond any doubt that no visual use of the arrow should be made when aiming, intentionally or unintentionally. He considered looking at the arrowhead while shooting to be the worst fault – and had a cure:

> If a man will leave to loke at his shaft, and learne to loke at his marke, he may use this waye, which a good shooter told me ones that he did. Let him take his bow on the night and shoot at two lights, and there he shall be compelled to looke alwayes at his marke, and never at his shafte: this thinge, ones or twice used, will cause him to forsake loking at his shafte. Yet let him take hede of setting his shafte in the bow.

Markham suggests a black mark between two paper lanterns at night, in order to make the bow and arrow invisible to the archer, forcing him to focus on his target. Eugen Herrigel in his book *Zen in the Art of Archery* describes an event during his own laborious process of learning traditional Japanese archery prior to the Second World War; in response to Herrigel's insistence that the shooter must use some kind of visual relationship between the tip of the arrow and target, his instructor told him to come to the practice hall at night, which was brightly lit:

> The Master told me to put a taper, long and thin as a knitting needle, in the sand in front of the target, but not to switch on the light in the target-stand. It was so dark that I could not even see its outlines, and if the tiny flame of the taper had not been there, I might perhaps have guessed the position of the target, though I could not have made it out with any precision. The Master 'danced' the ceremony. His first arrow shot out of dazzling brightness into deep night. I knew from the sound that it had hit the target. The second arrow was a hit, too. When I switched on the light

in the target stand, I discovered to my amazement that the first arrow was lodged full in the middle of the black, while the second arrow had splintered the butt of the first and plowed through the shaft before embedding itself beside it.

Today there are hunters and other archers such as G. Fred Asbel who do not look at the arrow, who loose without a noticeable hold, and who aim by intense and exclusive concentration on the tiny point the arrow is to hit.

Mediaeval English texts repeatedly stress keeping both eyes open and looking at the mark. The accomplished archer had only to look and shoot, and little time was lost between seeing the mark and putting an arrow into it. There is a big difference between shooting at a stationary target at a known and familiar distance, and shooting at a running or flying animal or charging horseman at an estimated and changing distance, or shooting arrows in high trajectory. In instinctive aiming, each shot is independent of other shots and the first shot at a mark is likely to be the best.

There is little to be said about how one should learn instinctive aiming except that one should eliminate distractions in order to concentrate more fully on the mark. Beginning practice should again be with a bow well under the shooter's strength at a distance that arrow trajectory is not involved. One should avoid any problems in case of missed shots by having a backstop of ample size and one that won't cause breakage of arrows. It is preferable to follow the mediaeval practice of shooting only two or three arrows at a time rather than the conventional five or six of present usage because the bowman takes each shot more seriously and hits are better. One should not shoot twice at the same marks from the same position. In learning instinctive rifle shooting, small objects are thrown into the air as marks. They are tossed up from a position slightly behind and to the right of the shooter. If a modern archer wishes to try this, one needs an open field and a blunt arrow with fletching that will keep it from flying far. Today's 'flu–flu' arrows are suitable for this purpose.

Some medieval archers may have used Howard Hill's 'split-vision' method. The vision is fixed on the mark, but the arrow is seen by peripheral vision without shifting focus, and is used in aiming. This would seem to divide concentration, but Hill certainly got incredible results with it. He used a draw in which the position of the drawing hand was established by touching the third finger of the drawing hand to the cheek against a back tooth. He canted his bow and cocked his head to bring the tail of the arrow under his right eye. While Hill pointed out that the instinctive method does not enable the shooter to make corrections on a second shot, some of his shots at moving targets – such as flying arrows – can only be explained by instinctive aiming.

In the case of moving marks, the technique is what Howard Hill called a crossing shot. The shooter beginning from a point behind the mark swings his bow in the direction the mark is moving, but at greater speed. When his aim has passed to a point in front of the mark at which he estimates the mark will arrive at the same instant the arrow will, he looses. Unlike the gunner, the archer who misses in such situations can readily see why he failed of his mark.

The point-of-aim method should also be mentioned here. This is a recent method of present-day longbow shooters. It was developed in the last century for use in such competitions as the 166 arrow York Round at measured distances, and can be very accurate. The shooter does not look at the target but instead he lines up his arrowhead with a point predetermined by experiment which, when sighted on, will result in the arrow hitting the bullseye. The position of hold is such that the shooter can sight along the arrow, the draw being made to the centre or the side of the chin. Some medieval manuscripts possibly show bowmen shooting with this sort of draw. The shooter can make compensations with successive arrows. However, for use in one-shot situations, at unknown distances or against moving targets, its value is negligible.

Ascham mentions a shooter who had left his gear between the marks and supposed that he had done this as an aid in shooting straight. He says that men continue the fault of looking at the arrowhead because it is so helpful in keeping a length. These comments imply use of one of the two methods described above, which Ascham clearly regarded as cheating.

Sight Marks

Several bows found in Denmark, from both Roman and early Viking periods, have one or two transverse lines cut on them that seem to be sight marks. These marks in each case are on one of the limbs near the middle of the bow. The longbow from Susaaen has one 70cm from one end and 115cm from the other, the bow being 185cm long. Whether these marks are on the upper or lower limb is difficult to determine as with most mediaeval bows it is not always easy to decide which is which. If on the upper limb they would be used as an aid in aiming up to point blank range which might be about 50 yards if the bow was drawn to the ear. If the marks were on the lower limb, they would be for determining the degree of elevation for a long shot. The use of sight marks implies that the arrow pass and the nocking point must be fixed. On the ancient bows there is no indication of how this might have been done and the manner of using the sight marks remains a matter of speculation.

Will Thompson, one of the first American hunting archers, wrote in 1879 of the bowsight as having a degenerating effect. He had tried it and while there was no question about its use producing higher scores, he felt that it spoiled the archer. There is little doubt that Ascham would have felt the same.

Shooting with the Crossbow

The crossbow can be effectively shot at close range with considerably less practice than the longbow requires. Due to its mechanical nature, the only aspects requiring skill are aiming and loosing, as with firearms. One modern crossbow champion finds it the same as small calibre rifle shooting, in which he also won a championship. As powerful mediaeval crossbows were difficult to bend up, some were fitted with a slack string. Others had the lath made with double nocks, enabling the use of a bastard string, permitting a stronger shot with lath and string under tension.

To shoot, the first step is cocking. With the two-foot crossbow, the type without a stirrup, the crossbowman would place both feet on the bow close to the tiller and pull up the string with both hands. This was the type used by Saracens in the time of Saladin. With the one-foot type, the right foot is placed in the stirrup and the string is grasped with both hands, pulled up while straightening the leg, and engaged in the notch or the nut. The one-foot crossbow with the stirrup was also used with the belt-hook. This was a single or double iron hook attached to a loose heavy belt. A variation used a cord with single or double pulleys. The hook was slipped over the middle of the string, enabling the leg to be used with greater effect. For horsemen, the belt was worn baldric fashion across the shoulder. The Saracen 'Jarkh', a crossbow of 'Frankish' (European) type, was such a crossbow. It could be cocked by a horseman at full gallop. By these methods a crossbowman could cock a crossbow of up to 400–500lbs draw weight.

The stirrup continued in use as long as crossbows were generally used in Europe, but towards the end of the Middle Ages more sophisticated methods were developed to cock the more powerful crossbows that were coming into use. The 'gaffle', or 'goat's foot lever', did not require the use of a stirrup but worked against pins protruding from the tiller. This device, first used in the fourteenth century, was ideal for a mounted crossbowman and could cock a crossbow of 500–600lbs draw weight. The double crank windlass first used in the late fourteenth century could manage draw weights approaching 1000lbs. It was also used with the great wall crossbow 'ad turnum'. A fifteenth-century device, the 'cranequin', consisted of a cogwheel mounted on the tiller and engaging a ratchet bar hooked on the string, the cogwheel being turned by a nine-inch crank to engage the string in the nut.

The crossbow is raised to chest level held in the left hand, which grips the tiller just in front of the nut and key section. A bolt is laid in the groove with its butt end against the nut or in the notch of the nut, if any. The right hand is transferred to the butt end of the tiller with the thumb over the tiller butt, fingertips around the key. The crossbow, unless a very large one shot from a rest, is not supported except by the two hands. Mediaeval crossbows were not made with rifle stocks. (In fourteenth-century Swiss shooting competitions held in Basel, contestants were seated on a three-legged stool and rules forbade the key or tiller touching chest or shoulder.) The crossbowman cocks his head over the tiller, sights over his thumb and squeezes off the shot.

Like the longbowmen, crossbowmen sometimes shot their bolts in a high arc to drop them onto the enemy from above. Aiming becomes difficult at longer ranges because the crossbow covers the mark when elevated. For shooting downward, as in defence of a castle rampart, a spring clip holding the nock end of the bolt in place was necessary.

Crossbows continued in use after the introduction of handguns, and indeed most now found in museums were made after the fifteenth century.

PREPARATION AND MAINTENANCE OF GEAR

Then they bent theyre good yewe bowes,
And looked theyr stringes were round.
The market-place of mery Carlyll,
They beset in that stounde.

The Ballad of Adam Bell[40]

'O pedlar, pedlar, what is in thy pack?
Come speedilie and tell it to me.'
'Ive several suits of the gay green silks,
And silken bow-strings two or three.'

The Bold Pedlar and Robin Hood[41]

The archers in these stages shot so wholly together that none durst appear at their
defence without they were well pavised.

Froissart's Chronicles[42]

The Bow

Ascham placed great importance on the rubbing down of the bow with a waxed
woollen cloth, a practice that fell into disuse along with the old archery,

When you have brought your bow to such a pointe, as I spake of, then you must
have a harden or wullen cloth waxed. Wherewith everye daye you must rubbe and
chafe your bowe, till it shyne and glitter withal. Which thinge shall cause it both to
be cleane, well favoured, goodlye of coloure, and shall also bringe, as it were, a cruste
over it, that is to say, shall make it everye where on the outsyde, so slipperye and hard,

that neyther anye weete or weather can enter to hurt it; nor yet any freat or pynche, be able to byte upon it: but that you shal do it great wrong before you breake it. This must be done oftentimes but specially when you come from shootynge.

In his 1590 book Smythe tells us that archers 'did temper with fire a convenient quantity of wax, rosin and fine tallow, and rubbing their bows with very little of it,' and also that bows were to be rubbed with linseed oil, about once a year, but sparingly, especially with yew which is more absorbent than other woods. A square of coarse woollen cloth can be prepared by melting a bit of the wax in a flat pan and laying the cloth on it.

Before shooting, the bow handle was given an additional application of wax so that the bow wouldn't turn in the hand in use. This use of beeswax to gain a purchase on something rather than spitting on the palms appears also as part of a pluck-buffet game in *The Romance of Richard Coeur de Lion* summarised in Child's ballads: Richard is betrayed to the King of Almayne (Germany) by a minstrel to whom he had given a cold reception and is put in prison. The King's son, held to be the strongest man in the land, visits the prisoner and proposes to him an exchange of blows, the old game of pluck-buffet. The prince gives Richard a clout that makes fire spring from his eyes and goes off laughing, ordering Richard to be well fed, so that he may have no excuse for returning a feeble blow when he takes his turn. The next day when the prince comes for his payment, Richard, who has waxed his hand by way of preparation, delivers a blow which breaks the young champion's cheek bone and fells him dead. People in mediaeval times clearly had many uses for beeswax.

The bow should be unbent (the string removed) when not in use. Some archers unbent their bows when walking or running from one butt to another. This was considered extreme, although the distance between butts in mediaeval times could be considerable. At any rate the bow must be unbent overnight. There is no need to pass the upper loop over the end of the bow except when setting on a new string (see below).

The bow should be stored and transported in a bow case and stored hanging on the wall or lying, never leaning. As mentioned previously, in Ascham's time bows were stored standing on end in narrow upright wooden bowcases that later became known as 'Aschams'.

The String

In preparation for shooting, the archer must choose, prepare, and affix a string to the bow. The thickness of the string varied according to its use.

Great stringes and little stringes be for divers purposes the great string is more surer for the bowe, more stable to prick withall, but slower for the cast. The little string is clean contrarye, not so sure, therefore to be taken heede of, lest with long taryinge on, it break your bowe, more fit to shoote farre, than apt to prick neare. Therefore

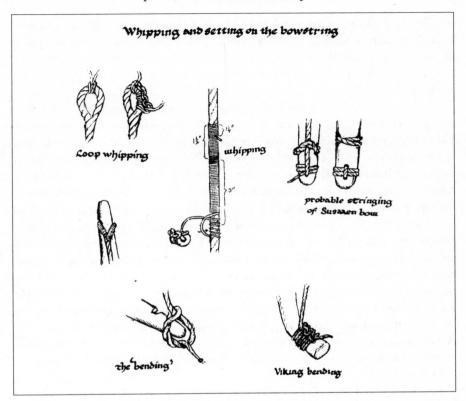

Whipping and setting on the bowstring, the archer's task. The Viking bow having no lower nock, the bowstring is bound with a series of hitches.

when you know the nature of both bigge and little you must fit your bowe according to the occasion of your shootinge.

For flight shooting a thin string at a low brace height gave the farthest cast but a thicker string gave greater accuracy. A noted Saracen warrior's arrows penetrated any armour that his foes could devise. A perplexed erstwhile enemy rented a room in the warrior's house after cessation of hostilities and his wife revealed that the secret was a heavy arrowhead and a thick string.

A new string must be adjusted as to length and whipped. A double loop string can be only minimally adjusted by twisting tighter to shorten and untwisting to lengthen. In the case of a single loop string, *Lartdarcherie* advises the loop to be first placed in the upper nock and stretch the string down the bow. At three finger widths from the lower nock make a timber hitch with 'as few turns as possible', making sure that the timber hitch can be made in the reinforced tail. Ascham calls this knot the 'bending' and cautions the archer to form it with more than one wrap. The end of the rattail projects toward the end of the bow. The string must be so positioned that it will be centred on the braced bow: 'You must mark also to set your string streight on or els the one end shall wrieth contrarye to the other and so break your bowe.'On Viking bows there was no lower nock and the string was tied off, probably in a series of half hitches just below a bend near the bow tip. Archers, especially military ones, always had a couple of 'redie whipt and fitted strings ready to clap on the bow'.

The method of bending the bow to fix the upper loop in its nock, now called bracing, has undergone changes. Nowadays, the step-through method is usual. Formerly, a common method was to rest the lower bowtip against the ground to the left, belly up. The left hand presses down on the middle of the bow while the fingers of the right hand pressing against the upper limb slide the loop into the upper nock. More recently, this method has been reversed with the lower bowtip placed against the instep of the left foot, and the left hand pulling up on the handgrip, probably to avoid damaging fancy horn bowtips, but a few bowmen in Horace A. Ford's time (1822–1880) still used the older method, which is pictured in *Froissart's Chronicles* and in the fourteenth-century *Tickhill Psaltery*. The bowhand being already in position, the archer can nock and shoot instantly. This method is much easier with the nocks cut in only one side as with most mediaeval and Renaissance bows, the upper left and lower right sides as seen from the belly side. If the bowtips extend past the nock as with early self longbows, the heel of the hand presses against the tip while the downward pointing fingers pull the loop to the nock. To release the string, the archer twists the loop clockwise so that the V portion of the loop can easily pass over the nock.

Another method was called 'treading the bow'. The archer presses down the bow's middle with his foot, thus freeing both hands, one pulling up the bowtip, the other adjusting the loop. Variations of bow treading given by Elmer consist of resting the upper tip against a tree and the lower tip against the ground, or resting the bow horizontally between two logs while pressing down with the foot. These variations would be a poor way to treat a bow.

Some archers bent the bow by holding it upright with the lower end against the ground, belly toward the archer who presses against the middle with the knee while pulling on the upper bowtip with one hand and setting the loop with the other. This method is shown in a painting in Ingham church, in a Belgian manuscript and mentioned in mediaeval Scandinavian poetry; 'He bent the bow before his knee.' Bending up a very strong war bow by the above methods is difficult. Some *Mary Rose* bows show grooves of two nocks in one bow tip which may indicate the use of a stringer or 'bastard string'. This is a longer string tied at the lower nock, the loop in the outer groove. The archer places a foot on the string and pulls up on the bow handle with one hand, setting the loop of his string into the inner groove with the other hand.

Having bent the bow, the bowman checks for desired string height. How much bend to have in a bow is the bowman's choice. The space between bow and string of a palm and two fingers as recommended in *Roi Modus* is about the minimum. Its use in hunting is to reduce strain on a bow that is bent for long periods of time. Each inch added to string height strains the bow about as much as three inches of draw. A low string height also gives maximum cast to the arrow. *Lartdarcherie* advises a little less than half a foot, with more or less depending on string follow or reflex. Ascham writes: 'The onlye commodotie of a low strung bow is fast and farre shootynge.' Ascham suggests a greater string height, pointing out that the high strung bow is more easily drawn, 'being half drawen before', shoots more accurately, and does not cause damage to the fletching which is clear of the bow during the draw. It is easier on the bow at the loose, and reduces the need for a bracer.

It is best by my judgemente to give the bowe so much bent that the strynge neede never touche a mannes arme, and so a man neede no bracer as I know manye good archers, whyche occupye none. So let your bow have a good bigge bende, a shaftment and two fingers at the least.

The shaftment, the part of the arrow to which the feathers are attached, was also the measure of the fist and outstretched thumb, the measurement that is nowadays called a fistmele and is now the standard longbow string height. One of the *Mary Rose* bows had apparently been bent up and the remaining curvature matches this string height. This is already a 'good bigge bend', almost the same as the length of a hand specified in an edition of *Le Livre de Chasse*.

The new string having been adjusted to provide the desired bend, it should be waxed. A lump of plain beeswax can be used, and some modern bowmen have melted it together with resin and suet like the mixture Smythe suggested for use on bows. The waxed string is rubbed briskly with a folded square of thin leather to work the wax into the fibres and to round the string.

Six or seven arrows should be shot to stretch and set a linen or hemp string, more to stretch a silk string. The string height must then be readjusted and the string is, as Smythe tells us, whipped by the archers themselves with fine thread. The whipping, or serving, is to prevent chafing of the string, to make it the proper size for the arrow nock, and to permit the arrow to slip off readily. It also helps keep the string round and makes it thicker, easier on the fingers at the loose. Ascham felt that the nock should be just tight enough to hold the string, not more, and that rule remains today. If the loosed string comes out of contact with the arrow at the loose, the bow could be irreparably damaged.

For the modern archer, silk embroidery thread, size D, is about the right thickness for this purpose, traditional colours being green, white or red. Linen thread may also be used. We first determine at what point the arrow nock will come against the string. Mediaeval bows had no clearly marked handgrip. *Lartdarcherie* tells us that the archer preparing to shoot balances the bow on the thumb of his bowhand, then grips the bow. The arrow being nocked at a right angle to the string, the point of contact can be marked. The archer might consider the possibility of nocking higher or lower for a long shot as was sometimes done.

The string is then marked about an inch and a half above the nocking point and several inches below it. Markham specifies the width of four fingers. Tie a heavy cord or leather thong through the hole of the spool and around it to prevent the thread from unwinding by itself. Pass the end of the thread between strands of the string at the upper point pointing right, and begin winding the thread around the string and the end of the thread. After about six turns, pull the end tight and cut it off, being careful not to cut anything else. Continue winding until you reach a point ¼ inch above the lower point. Now make a large loop and bring the end up to the end of your winding and continue the winding over the thread ¼ inch to complete the serving. Pull the end up tight and cut it close to the whipping. The whipping should be firm but not so tight as to cut into the string.

Nock the arrow again. If it fits too loosely, you will have to add more whipping at the nocking point. The proper fit for the nock, as also given by Ascham, is that the arrow should hang from the string but be dislodged by a slight tap or the string. In T. Roberts' time, in 1800, the whipping at the nocking point was of a different colour than the rest. In a short section like this, the ends of the thread should be threaded on a needle and passed through the string, or they will not hold well. This may have been an ancient practice, but I suspect that mediaeval whippings were of one colour, without bumps. As Smythe advised, the upper loop should be whipped as well, a good yard and a half or two yards of thread being needed. Start it with a larkspur knot in the middle of the loop and finish one side at a time as shown. The whipping is now waxed as the string was, and the string is ready for use. Since a mediaeval archer would never have been without spare strings, he would prepare two or three more at this time. A string must be immediately discarded as soon as it shows signs of wear, separation of fibres or uneven stretching. If it breaks during the draw, it can cause the destruction of the bow, as Ascham points out. Military archers kept spare strings under their helmets to protect them from the rain.

Arrows

Arrows also required looking after. Ascham suggested that the archer buy overlong arrows and cut them to his own draw length after trying them out, and we know from John Smythe that military archers cut their sheaf arrows shorter when they found them too long. However, they were not to be too short, as at full draw the shouldering of the pile or the barbs should touch, or nearly touch, the bow hand. It was poorly thought of for archers in the heat of battle to loose arrows less than fully drawn.

Some archers, to shift the balance point of the arrow toward the nock, drilled a hole just in front of the nock and filled it with lead. This helped to keep the arrow level in flight, but if too much lead was used, the arrow flew sideways.

Arrows that have become bent had to be bent straight. The heated arrow was held in both hands and bent in the opposite direction of the bend. The check for straightness was visual, looking down the shaft. A stubborn bend could usually be corrected by heating the bent portion quite hot and holding in position until it cools. Loose feathers had to be reglued or rebound, and 'hard wax' or sealing wax was used to reaffix socketed heads.

Archers used files to sharpen broadheads or to even a bent or broken point to centre it precisely. A piece of dogfish or hurfish skin was used to remove dirt from point and foreshaft when wiping with a cloth would not suffice. Ascham recommends checking arrows for dirt or moisture or damage to the heads before shooting.

Sundry Gear

If a shooting glove was used, it was not powdered to lubricate it as is done today, but greased. Ascham recommends deer suet (kidney fat). T. Roberts' contemporaries in 1801 used a mixture of suet and white wax carried in a greasepot attached to the belt.

Transporting Gear

A modern archer unaccustomed to carrying a longbow and arrows may find it awkward if there are any obstructions to avoid, especially indoors or in the woods. The bow can be carried horizontally across the shoulder as one would carry a beam. In mediaeval times the longbow was sometimes used as a staff, the bending being protected by extended bowtips, and Lapp bows were even used as ski poles. Archers of Hawkwood's 'White Company' carried their longbows on their backs and Ascham writes of an archer with a bow on his back and arrows under his girdle. A manuscript illustration shows a soldier carrying a ready bent short bow in this way, the string across his chest from left shoulder to right hip. However, it is uncomfortable to carry a bow in this way if it has a low brace height.

As illustrated in the Bayeux Tapestry, some Norman archers carried their arrows in hip quivers with the buckled belt put over the head and the quiver slung behind the right or left shoulder to keep the arrows out of the way when walking. A Saxon illustration shows an archer holding the belt lower to keep it off his throat. Arrows carried in this way tend to rattle and alert enemy or game so the quiver would usually be carried on the right hip when shooting was imminent. An alternative hip quiver suspended the quiver from the belt aslant, arrow nocks forward, by thongs fastened at the midpoint and opening. With a longer thong, the slanting quiver could be carried baldric fashion at hip level. This quiver made walking easier and arrow rattling could be avoided by holding them still with the right hand. In Asian-type hip quivers, also used in Europe, short arrows or crossbow bolts were often carried point upwards so the fletching was protected and the hunter could easily select one of his variety of arrowheads.

Not everyone used quivers, especially with long arrows; an arrow approaching a yard in length is awkward to get out of a full length quiver. Often arrows were stuck through the belt or girdle at the right side. Because of the curvature of the body, the shaftmonds of the arrows were spread fanwise and wouldn't rub against each other. Usually they were carried with the points forward. In the case of broadheads, this was not very safe and the points were sometimes pointed to the rear, which was not as protective of the fletching. This was practical for up to a half dozen arrows. Also used was a baldric with a buckled strap holding the arrows under the arm or a bundle of arrows tied in a thong at the belt.

Rather than using a quiver, hunters might have an arrow ready nocked on the string of the braced bow, held in position by the thumb or the forefinger of the bow hand. A hunter carrying a bow in this way had to keep the arrowhead pointed away from himself. Men have died in the woods because they stumbled and drove a razor sharp broadhead through their leg. An extra arrow or two might be held in the bow hand along with the bow.

The bowman's preparation of his gear is now complete. However I would add some advice valid in any age, partly learned through bitter experience, on care of the bow.

Keep the bow unbent when not in use.
Don't let anyone else use or draw your bow.
Wax and rub down both bow and string after bracing.
Don't release the drawn string without an arrow on it.
Draw the bow in gradual increments, especially on cold or damp days.
Don't hold the bow at full draw for more than two or three seconds.
Never draw the bow beyond full draw.

21

MOUNTED ARCHERS

[The Mongols'] arms are bows and arrows and swords and axes, but they rely most on their bows, for they are excellent archers; the best that are known in the world.

Marco Polo, *Description of the World*[43]

Rode Kon the young through copse and woods,
birds he snared, used bow and arrow.

Rigsthula[44]

The nomad herdsmen of the steppes – Huns, Avars, Magyars and Mongols – were bred to the saddle and with their short composite hornbows were superb horse archers. European armies also had mounted archers. Doninic Mancini observed the arrival of Richard III's archers:

There were horsemen among them. Not that they are accustomed to fighting on horseback, but because they use horses to carry them to the scene of the engagement, so as to arrive fresher ... Therefore they will ride any sort of horse, even pack horses. On reaching the field of battle the horses are abandoned. They all fight under the same conditions so that no one should retain hope of fleeing.

The military purpose of mounted archers was to have a more mobile group of bowmen, either to be shifted quickly from one part of a battlefield to another or to be able to keep up with mounted knights and men-at-arms on the march. Having to wait a few hours for archer infantry to catch up could prove frustrating or fatal. Units of archers were usually either all on foot or all mounted.

Horse archers either dismounted and formed ranks on foot as usual or they shot from horseback. In the latter case the effective range of their arrows was reduced to 60 yards, at least according to Smythe. In his time longbowmen and crossbowmen were no longer mounted, but old men could still remember when they were. At the Battle of Crecy, mounted archers attacked the flank of the Duke of Normandy's troops. Mounted archers were much used in the later part of the Hundred Years War, and Scottish mounted archers were employed by both the French kings and the Burgundian army of Charles the Bold.

Some modern historians have declared that a longbow cannot be used from the saddle, but in practice this is nonsense. While it is true that a longbow, unless canted, cannot be readily shifted from one side of a horse to the other, or shot over its rump as readily as the Tartars and Saracens used their short hornbows, it is also true that European war horses since Roman times were 'apt and schooled to wheel in circles round' clockwise, or to pass to the right of an individual enemy when charging, thus keeping the riders shield and lance point or bow arm toward the enemy. The usability of longbows from horseback has been amply demonstrated in our own times. Howard Hill once shot a running bison dead from the back of a galloping cow-pony with a single arrow from his six-foot longbow (the incident is on film). Similarly Japanese archers regularly practise the samurai sport of *Yabusame,* in which arrows are shot at targets out of very long bows from horses at full gallop.

However, it may be that European horse archers sometimes used shorter bows. An Elizabethan picture shows a group of military archers; one is mounted, and his bow is markedly shorter than those held by the infantrymen. Similarly, Tartar archers on foot used much larger bows than the horsemen. Similarly the Bayeux Tapestry shows a Norman archer with a short bow taking aim from a galloping horse at a group of fleeing Saxons.

In hunting, there was a different reason for shooting from horseback. Deer approached by a lone horseman do not so readily recognise him as a human being, especially if they do not get a scent. *Roi Modus* specifies that the bow should be weak and that the archer should position himself so that he may draw the bow to shoot behind him, supporting himself in his left stirrup, which should be a little shorter than the other.

Crossbowmen were also mounted, perhaps more commonly than were archers with handbows. Crossbows are convenient to shoot with from horseback and may be discharged in any direction the rider can turn. Cocking them is the tricky part. *Saracen Archery* describes the method for the 'Frankish' type of one-foot crossbow that Saracens called a 'jarkh'. The rider was equipped with a leather drawing strap of 'broad Frankish style' worn baldric fashion across the shoulder and having a drawing claw with a double hook. At full gallop a good rider could hook the claw onto the string, setting one foot into the stirrup of the crossbow, stretching his leg against the pull of the strap and engaging the string in the nut. The flattened end of the bolt was then set into the notch of the nut. I think it safe to assume that this method, as well as the crossbow type, was adopted from the Europeans. This is probably the method used by Richard the Lionheart and two companions in his pursuit of Saracen horsemen at Jaffa.

Later, the goat's foot lever or gaffle was developed, making the strap and stirrup no longer necessary, and the crossbow could be cocked while held level. An Italian fifteenth-century painting, 'The Battle of San Romano' by Paolo Uccello in the new realistic style shows a tumultuous battle scene with lancers and swordsmen.

Two mounted crossbowmen are shown, wearing caps and without armour. They are holding their crossbows at the ready, bolt upright. Their right hands hold the tiller butt and key, their left hands hold the forward part of the tiller with their thumbs holding the bolt in position. Smythe, in whose time old men could remember the use of crossbows and longbows on horseback, recommended the use of crossbowmen on horseback:

I would they should have crossbows of two pound and a half of the best sort, with crooked gaffles hanging at their strong girdles after the manner of Germans, that they might on horseback bend their crossbows the more easily and readily, with four-and-twenty quarrels in a case well and fitly set at their saddle pommels.

22

ACCURACY OF MEDIAEVAL SHOOTING

Often they did practice with their great bows ... sending the arrows unerringly to
any mark set of them.

Conquest of Granada[45]

'Full fifteen score your mark shall be
'Full fifteen score shall stand.'
'I lay my bow,' said Clifton then,
'We cleave the willow wand.'

Robin Hood and Queen Katherine[46]

While peoples who still use the bow for hunting today (such as Amazonian tribes as
opposed to those who hunt for sport) can often shoot with amazing accuracy at short
range, they often seem to have no conception of making a mark at over 50 yards.
Today, not many bowmen except for the few who occasionally try clout/prick shooting (see p.165) ever attempt to make a mark at more than 100 yards, but in times past,
Saracens, Mongolian nomads and English longbowmen made a speciality of this art
for use in warfare. It is a common misconception that mediaeval military archery was
confined to the 'firing' of unaimed barrages on the off chance that some arrows might
hit something. Unfortunately, mediaeval sources seldom supply the precise documen-
tation we would like, but there are some records that convey an idea of the quality of
shooting at that time.

One such example is the admittedly almost unbelievable tale of the death of the
Norman Earl Hugh the Proud at the hand of the Viking King Magnus Barefoot in
Wales in 1098. The incident is related in Giraldus' *Journey Through Wales*, in the writings of Simeon of Durham and also in the Icelandic *Heimskringla*. Hugh, the Norman
Earl of Shrewsbury, was on campaign with Hugh, Earl of Chester to conquer and
subjugate the Welsh. Their tactics included blinding, the cutting off of hands and feet,
and emasculation of Welsh prisoners. Unfortunately for them, Magnus set forth to
expand his domain at the same time.

According to Giraldus Cambrensis, writing in the twelfth century, some Viking pirates from the Orkneys made their way into one of the island ports in their long-ships. When he heard of their approach, the Earl, who was on a mettlesome horse, dashed wildly into the sea to attack them. Magnus, who was in command of the expedition, stood on the prow of the leading ship and shot an arrow at the Earl, who was completely clad in iron from the top of his head to the soles of his feet, all except for his eyes. At that time the Normans were still wearing the kind of armour pictured on the Bayeux Tapestry: a hauberk and coif of linked iron rings, covering the chin and topped by a conical helmet with a sometimes quite long and broad nasal piece, and leg coverings of mail for the men of rank. The arrow struck his right eye and penetrated his brain so that he fell dead into the sea. In his pride Magnus is said to have shouted: '*Leit Loupe*,' which is Danish for 'Let him leap.' Giraldus refers to Magnus speaking Danish specifically, although Magnus was in fact the king of Norway. However, according to Giraldus, from that moment onwards the Normans lost their control of Anglesey.

The Norse account of the same event is contained in Sturlason's *Heimskringla*, apparently with the assumption that Magnus had fought the local Welshmen rather than Normans.

Afterwards King Magnus sailed with his army to Wales, and when he came to the Menai Straits an army came against him from Wales; two jarls, Hugh the Proud and Hugh the Stocky were in command of it and they straightway came to battle. It was a hard fight. King Magnus shot with a bow, but Hugh the Proud was clad in a brynie [hauberk] so that nothing of him was bare except his eyes alone. King Magnus and a man from Halogaland standing near the king both shot arrows at Hugh; they both shot at the same time. One arrow fell on the nose guard of the helm and it was pushed out to the side by it, but the other shot fell on the jarl's eye and flew cross-wise through his head; this shot is ascribed to the king. Hugh the jarl fell there, and afterwards the Welshmen fled; they had lost many men. Bjorn Cripplehand quoth;

In Menai Straits where the spears
The leader brought about
Sang and the arrows flew
A death shot for Hugh the Proud

Ironically, one chronicler reports that amongst the Vikings was the Saxon man Harold, son of King Harold Godwinson, who had been shot in the eye by a Norman archer according to one possible reading of the Bayeux Tapestry.

There were also good archers amongst the bowmen and crossbowmen serving under Richard the Lionheart during the Third Crusade. It was written of the siege of Messina that 'no man could look out of doors but he would have an arrow in his eye before he could shut it.' This may be the period of origin of the earliest Robin Hood ballads (see Chapter 23 for details of contest shooting in the ballads). Robin Hood's shooting, being the only mediaeval shooting most people have heard of, bears the brunt of modern debunking. At its most extreme are comments that the feats of Robin Hood were quite impossible, but in fact modern archers surpass them regularly. Little that is extraordinary is reported in the ballads, the one really difficult shot being the splitting of an arrow that had already hit a wand at 100 yards. In consideration of Robin's shots reported as misses, this shot was a lucky one, and lucky shots do occur, although mostly for excellent archers.

In *The Ballad of Adam Bell* William of Cloudesle is credited with a hit on a wand at 400 paces with his first arrow.which is rather more extraordinary, and with splitting an apple on his son's head (this as everyone knows occurs in other stories) at 120 paces. The king in the ballad thought these shots impossible, so they were more than could be expected from most archer.

The 'record' for a hit at the greatest distance comes from Russia. An inscription supposedly cut on stone on the order of Chinghiz Khan to commemorate an exceptional shot by one of his Mongol archers reads:

> At one of the great games Nadom organised on the Onon River in the beginning of the thirteenth century, Mergen Yessunkl hit the target from a distance of more than 550 yards.

'Mergen' is a title designating a champion archer. The stone is now in the Academy of Sciences in Leningrad. While the feat is clearly impressive, it would be helpful to know the size of the target to put it into context.

During the Hundred Years War, the apogee of longbow skill, most archery took place in massed formations so we do not have many instances of individual skill, but there are many instances of men-at-arms removing a helmet or raising a visor for an instant and not living long enough to lower it again.

During the Wars of the Roses, Conway Castle was held by the Yorkist faction. In 1461 Lancastrians were observing the castle from across the river when a Yorkist archer, Llewellyn of Nanau, doubtless a Welshman, put an arrow through one of the Lancastrians about half a mile away, around twice the normal crossbow range. In the year of Bosworth, Earl Rivers led an English force to Spain to assist Spanish Christian kings against the Moors. A Spanish chronicler noted that the Englishmen were skilful archers who could hit any mark set before them. In the ballad *Sir Andrew Barton*, an English ship is manned with gunners and 100 bowmen, for an expedition against Barton, a Scottish privateer who had been plundering English and Portuguese merchant ships. The real expedition was in 1511.

> My lord called then a bow-man rare,
> Whose active hands had gained fame,
> A gentleman born in Yorkshire,
> And William Horsley was his name.

The commander designates Horsley to be the head of the 100 bowmen, upon which Horsley says:

If you my lord, have chosen me
Of a hundred men to be the head,
Upon the main-mast I'll hanged be,
If twelve-score I miss one shillings breadth.

Quite a boast indeed, a guaranteed hit at 240 yards within a 2½ inch diameter. Of course this is a ballad.

However, more tangible evidence is found in a letter of Giovanni Mihiel from England to his native Venice in 1557. It is a military intelligence report on English archers, sent to the Council of Ten, the Venetian equivalent of the CIA, and therefore we may infer that its content is reasonably accurate.

> ... there are few among them, even those who are moderately practised, who will not undertake at a convenient distance, either aiming point blank or in the air (as they generally do that the arrow may fly farther), to hit within an inch and a half [*un mezzo palma*] of the mark.

For the powerful bows of that period, point blank range would be in excess of 50 yards. Aiming in the air implies a length in excess of 100 yards. It is unfortunate that Mihiel is not more precise about distances, but he does make it clear that it made little difference in the accuracy of the English archer whether he had to elevate or not. This kind of shooting is possible only with the use of instinctive aiming (see p. 141).

Another example of archery accuracy comes from accounts of the tournament held at the Field of the Cloth of Gold. There stood a group of archers clad in the Kendal green of English foresters, with hunting horns suspended at their sides from studded baldrics. One of their number, a muscular man well over six feet in height, stepped forth. Taking an arrow from under his girdle, he nocked it to his great longbow of red Venetian yew and loosed at the mark 240 yards away. Spectators gasped as his arrows repeatedly struck the white. Crossbowmen of the king's guard were unable to better these hits.

The man was in fact Henry VIII himself, personally demonstrating the power of English archery at the request of the French king. The French were impressed. One wrote of him: 'a marvellous good archer and strong'. Congratulated by the French ambassador on his good shooting, Henry less than tactfully replied, 'Good for a Frenchman.' Henry later established the 220 yard length as the minimum at which archers could use a prick shaft or flight in practice. He did not always win his shooting competitions however; his household accounts contain a number of entries concerning the payment of lost wagers.

Sir John Smythe, determined to promote military archery, set his Essex militia to archery practice as late as 1587, a year before the Spanish Armada set sail. One day at Chelmsford he set up sticks with pieces of paper tied to the tops as marks. Smythe reported that his archers, shooting at lengths of up to twelve score yards, had hit them all down or struck them aside. However, despite Smythe's efforts, no archers faced the Spanish sailors of the Armada.

Despite Queen Elizabeth's abolition of archery for the 'Trayned Bandes', some bowmen remained until the 1620s. Practising at least once a week, a competent bowman was expected to put more than six arrows a minute into a three-foot target.

Crossbowmen could also shoot with considerable accuracy. In fifteenth century Tyrol, two brothers, the knights Hans and Ulrich of Frundsberg, lived in neighbouring castles, but there was bad blood between them. At a window in his castle, Hans was killed by a crossbow bolt shot by Ulrich from his castle, 450–500 yards away. During the reign of Charles II, In 1661, 400 archers put on a display in Hyde Park and some 'shot near twenty-score yards within the compass of a hat with their crossbows' to the amazement of the spectators.

Modern crossbowmen using 'new and improved' weapons with elaborate gun-stocks and shooting from a rest, equal this accuracy – but at 100 yards rather than nearly 400.

23

MARKS AND SHOOTING GAMES

Three marks are there to shoot at: butts, pricks, or rovers. The butt is a level mark and therefore would have a strong arrow with a very broad feather. The prick is a mark of some compass, yet most certain in the distance, therefore would have nimble strong arrows with a middle feather, all of one weight: and the flying rover is a mark uncertain, sometimes long, sometimes short, and therefore must have arrows lighter or heavier, according unto the distance of place.

Gervase Markham, *Country Contentments*, 1615[47]

A ryght good arowe he shall have,
The shaft of sylver whyte,
The hede and the feders of ryche rede golde,
In Englond is none lyke.

A Lytel Geste of Robyn Hode[48]

The accuracy of a bowman is determined in part by the type of mark he is accustomed to. The prototype of the modern target painted with rings in bright colours originated in the seventeenth century, and was therefore not used in the Middle Ages. Dr Pope wrote of Ishi, a Native American from the California hinterland; 'I have seen him kill ground squirrels at 40 yards; yet at the same distance he might miss a four foot target. He explained this by saying that the target was too large and the brightly coloured rings diverted the attention.' Other Indians have reacted in a similar fashion. Conversely, the shooter whose experience has been confined to such a target, would have great difficulty in hitting a ground squirrel. In his book *The Witchery of Archery*, Maurice Thompson wrote:

If you begin your practice for the purpose of learning to shoot wild game …you must not use a target at all. One who is trained to aim at a large graduated target, either with a gun or bow, can rarely shoot well at game, for, after all, a bowman's skill is scarcely worthy of admiration if it is confined to a fixed range.

Thompson, a Confederate survivor of the US Civil War, learned to use archery in hunting situations in the true manner of a mediaeval yeoman.

In the present century, field targets offer some correction to this situation. These are small squares of cardboard with a central aiming spot and a few concentric circles as hairlines rather than bands. They are black on white paper or white on black paper and are much like those used in the late Middle Ages. Instinctive shooting requires, above all, concentrated focus on a very small area.

Mediaeval marks were usually set up in pairs, except for the Popinjay (see below). The distance to the mark was called the 'length'. Except for hoyles and roving marks in field shooting, lengths were measured in score with a line. A score is an interval of 20, and 20 yards is a convenient length for a measuring line in distances pertaining to archery, long enough to measure the distance quickly but not so long as to stretch excessively. Units of measurement were yards, also called 'clothyards' or 'ells', paces or rods. Yards, standardised during the reigns of King Richard I and King John, were of three feet as they are today. In 1602 Richard Carew considered a pace to equal a yard. However, mediaeval paces, Roman paces, were normally measured between successive positions of the same foot. A 1495 source states: 'The pace conteyneth fyve fete' though later military paces were between two and a half and three feet. A rod, perch or rood was a trimmed sapling of as long as 5.5 yards used to control yoked oxen but varied by locality. The northern rod of 7′ 6″ may have been the rod of the Robin Hood ballads.

As the reader may have noted, Middle English words (just as in modern English) sometimes have more than one distinct meaning, such as nock and bending, or two words may mean the same thing, like shaft and stele. In brief old references to shooting at marks, it is sometimes unclear exactly what is being referred to. A prick originally was any sharp stick intended to be stuck into anything, for example, a pudding prick used to puncture a pudding to allow the steam to escape during cooking. Markham refers to a prick as a mark of some compass as a separate category from butt shooting, the prick being the stick planted as a mark. Nowadays this is classified as clout shooting and old references use the same term, but clout is a Middle English word for cloth, which could also refer to the cloth stretched on a frame for a mark in near shooting, through which a prick, or pin, was thrust. Ascham, however, refers to the raising of the drawing hand to prick height in level shooting, and to such shooting as pricking. The word butt ordinarily refers to the backstop, usually of earth or clay, to which the mark was affixed, however, butts were also called pricks. Barrows in Yorkshire and Shropshire are termed Robin Hood's pricks or butts, and even hazel wands are referred to as butts in *The Ballad of Adam Bell*, perhaps humorously, and are also referred to as pricks.

Having confused the reader sufficiently, we will consider butts as those upright earthen backstops used in level shooting, to which marks were pinned, pricks or clouts as the marks on which an arrow is dropped, and wands as upright sticks at various lengths.

Butts

In 1275 the Winchester Statute ordered butts to be kept up in all places. Again in 1466 Edward I decreed that butts should be erected in every township. As we have seen, Edward IV extended that to Ireland and decreed that Irishmen and Englishmen within the Pale between the ages of 16 and 60 were to shoot on all holy days, with daily practice from 1 March to the end of July, thus being ready for summer military campaigns when there was grass for the horses.

The butts were mounds of earth and turf erected in opposed pairs at the ends of a field, and should have faced north and south to avoid shooters having to shoot against the sun. Ascham refers to a 12 score mark and a pair of fifteenth-century butts were 'thirteen score tailors yards measured with a line' apart. Their purpose was to stop arrows and provide a surface to affix the marks. An account of 1583 lists materials for their construction, including posts, rails, turf and nails and 'two barres for the Butts with staplest iron work thereto'. This was presumably to form the internal structure. The account also refers to ditching before the butts. In T. Roberts' day (1801) butts were 9 feet deep, 7 feet high, 4 feet at the base, and 16 inches wide at the top. They were wedge-shaped and tapered somewhat toward the summit. In his 1840 *The Book of Archery* George Agar Hansard writes that turf from a heath common or turbary was preferred because its fibres made it more tough and adhesive than common turf.

The mark shot at was often a black wooden pin, also called a 'prick', stuck into the butt through the centre of a white cloth, sometimes with a central painted black spot, stretched on a small hoop. This was called a 'blanc' or 'white' and was about a span wide, a span being the length covered by the outstretched hand between thumb and finger tips.

The *Luttrell Psalter* shows a butt with an affixed white circle, probably cloth sewn on a hoop, with a spot in the middle. When paper came into use, discs or squares of pasteboard were substituted. The traditional height for the centre of a target was and still is the height of a man's heart. The aim of the archer was to 'cleave the pin', but to 'hit the white' was also counted. Butts were for close range, more or less level shooting and were constructed up to 160 yards apart, possibly up to 220 yards.

Mediaeval references to 'the short butts and the long' refer to distances between butts rather than size of the butt itself. Shooters stood at one of a pair of butts and shot at the other, usually with two arrows each. In practice or in competition, the archer, required to have only four arrows, shot not more than three or four arrows at an end. A shooting companion or competitor was called a 'butty'. When everyone had shot, they went to the opposite butt to check hits and retrieve arrows. This was called 'shooting about' or 'shooting at ends' referring to the ends of the field. They then shot back at the butt they had just left, this shooting up and down constituting a double end, or 'twice about'. Three ends, sometimes shot for purposes of determining best two out of three ends for contests, was called shooting 'thrice about'. Mediaeval shooting involved much walking, and grass grew scantily between the butts on English shooting fields. As mentioned previously, Henry I created the law that stated that if someone walking between the butts was killed or wounded by an arrow, the archer was not liable. This statute was re-issued by Henry VIII in more elaborate form.

A type of butt used in the Low Countries that almost certainly dates back to the Middle Ages was a flat wedge-shaped clay will about the size and shape of the English earthen butts. The clay was wetted down before shooting and a square piece of paper with a black spot about 2 inches in diameter was affixed to it by pins through the corners. Eckerman, Goethe's secretary, noted that these butts were to be found at inns in Brabant for the entertainment of the customers, and he tells us that five out of fifteen arrows went into the mark (the black spot) at the distance of 60–80 paces that they usually shot. The clay was smoothed over after use. Turks are supposed to have used similar butts. English butts were also wetted down before use although we do not know if any were faced with clay.

After the Middle Ages, portable backstops came into use, rectangular in shape made of wicker or discs of coiled straw constructed by beehive makers. Butt shooting was the original form of our modern contest archery, although today few bowmen shoot at lengths of more than 100 yards.

The sixteenth-century *Lartdarcherie* recommends the use of a screen in butt shoot- ing 'for it is easier to learn to shoot by shooting under the screen, than in any other way.' The screen was to ensure that a level shot was made. It was to be 'placed across the range, halfway between the butts, the bottom edge being one foot above the ground for every ten paces there is between the butts.' So butts 100 yards apart would have a screen ten feet off the ground and 'the bottom edge should have bells on it so that even if the feather of an arrow should touch it, one may know it by hearing the bells ring.' The screen was to be at least 'half an aune' in height to be sure that an arrow would not pass over it unnoticed. This would require a shot with a less than five foot rise in trajectory.

In a variation of butt shooting. Henry VIII practised or shot competitive games at the rounds in his park behind Hampton Court, The Yeoman of his Bows who was custodian of the King's archery gear when it was not in use, had made the 'rounds', wooden discs set up on stakes. These had come into use in the fourteenth century. Some, about two feet wide, were pictured painted white with a black central disc about a hand span wide. Similar targets were sometimes square. It is likely that the arrows used here were headed with bodkin points to stick in the wood. Some bodkins were made of steel too soft to be useful in warfare. The wooden discs also became called 'targets' because of their resemblance to the similar sized wooden shields called by that name. Unlike the smaller buckler that was held by the fist, the 'target,' or 'targe', was held by a strap around the forearm and a second strap to grasp. Later targets were painted in coloured rings and the word 'target' replaced the word 'mark'.

A survival of continental rounds is found in the *Beursault* shooting of northern France and Belgium, dating from the fifteenth century. The round itself was black and white, suggestive of the width of a man's shoulders, with a heart-sized central disc. Two were placed about 57 yards apart at the ends of an alley of trees or perpendicular wooden walls. Teams shot alternately, only one arrow for each archer.

Pricks

Prick shooting, or clout shooting, was the art of dropping an arrow on a mark from above. Today this is occasionally carried out at 180 to 200 yards. Henry VIII set a minimum of 220 yards for this form of shooting. Maximum range may have been full range of the prick shafts, which were heavier than flight arrows. Markham emphasises that pricks are most certain in the distance, that is, at specified and known ranges. In Roberts' time the clout was 12 inches in diameter. Modem clout shooting uses a rather larger target.

The mark itself was the wooden pin or prick wand thrust through the centre of a white cloth, called the 'clout' or 'blanc' stretched on a hoop or square frame. The clout may have been stuffed with straw, and was laid flat on the ground or at a slight angle so that falling arrows would strike it perpendicularly. The 'chapperon', the French equivalent of the English clout, a cloth, was originally a hood with a cape to cover the shoulders. This could be spread on the ground with a prick holding the hood upright. *Lartdarcherie* gives the distance shot in chapperon shooting as 300 paces, 400 for first class archers. In England it was 8 score (160 yards) for the young developing archers, and 12 score (240 yards) for regular shooting.

As we know, maximum length of flight is attained by an elevation of about 45 degrees. This type of shooting was purely military practice to enable archers in the rear ranks of a formation to readily shoot over the heads of their comrades in order to drop arrows on the enemy from above, while archers in the front ranks could keep length by decreasing elevation. William the Conqueror ordered his archers to shoot in high arc to drop their arrows on Harold's Saxons, who had tied their shields in place before them. Crossbowmen too, shot their bolts in a high arc for the same purpose.

Rovers

Roving, or shooting at rovers was ordinarily shooting over open ground at casually picked marks at varied, unmeasured and often considerable distances. At Finsbury and St George's Fields in London, marks were fixed and at measured distances, but were also called rovers.

Finsbury Field — as a site for archery — was formed in 1498 of the gardens about and beyond the lordship of Fensberry. Several hundred permanent standing marks called stakes were set up at varying distances apart. The stakes were upright wooden beams set in stone bases, often ornamented. Each had a name and was set up at the expense of some important person who wished to gain favour with the public. In 1599 an information sheet, *The Ayme for Finsbury Archers* was printed as a guide to help archers locate the marks giving their names, locations and distances. They ranged from nine to nearly 20 score, close to 400 yards, at a time that archery was considered to be in considerable decline. In 1628 the maximum distance given by the sheet had shrunk to nineteen score, 380 yards. These were not flight shooting records, but distances at which archers using the public grounds commonly tried for hits. The fields were in use until 1791 when they succumbed to the pressures of expanding population.

Roving was practice for estimating distance and for making a mark at varying and unknown lengths. The military archer was to compare the apparent size of men and horses in relation to the elevation of the upper limb of his bow. In competition, the archer whose arrow hit closest to the mark was the winner. The archer selected his bow and arrows as the golfer chooses his golf club. The most distant roving marks were at the maximum possible range of the archer's artillery, and for these shots he would require a long, light, breasted flight arrow with short low fletching, a bow short for the draw length and a thin string at low brace height. He would have to shoot at about a 45 degree elevation. For closer marks he might choose a combination more 'forgiving' of slight errors such as a heavier tapered arrow with longer higher fletching and a longer straight end bow with a thicker string at higher brace height.

According to T. Roberts, writing in his 1801 book *The English Bowman* a short distance version of roving, sometimes at no more than 15 or 20 yards, was called 'hoyle' shooting or 'shooting at hoyles', a hoyle being a natural mark such as a clump of grass. Some modern bowhunters engage in this kind of field shooting, calling it roving. However Drayton's poem *Polyolbion* includes the line, 'At long butts, short and hoyles, each one would cleave the pin,' implying a more formal target was used. Hoyle shooting, with appropriate wagers, was favoured by mediaeval travellers to entertain themselves while making a trip to town down a country road. The shooter whose arrow was closest to the mark was the winner, and got to pick the next mark.

In 1602 Richard Carew wrote of an earlier time in Cornwall when the Cornish archers, using clothyard arrows for long shooting, were

> … well skilled in near shooting and well aimed shooting. The butts made them perfect in the one, and the roving in the other, for the prickes, the first corrupters of archery, through too much preciseness, were formerly little known and little practiced.

Wands and Garlands

Wands and garlands were used as marks where no butts were at hand. For this reason we find them frequently mentioned in the Robin Hood ballads. Wands were cut saplings several feet long, preferably hazel, which is straight and has enough pith to split readily. Wands were set upright in the ground in opposed pairs as the butts were, and were sometimes set up in front of a butt. Present day wands are some 6 inches by 3–6 inches wide.

In *The Ballad of Adam Bell,* William of Cloudesle is said to have found the butts used by the King's Archers too easy to present a challenge and instead used 'butts such as men use in my countree.' He 'set up two hasell roddes, full twenty score between', 400 paces. The King thought this an impossible target. Few modern archers would disagree. Cloudesle cleft one wand with an arrow, then volunteered as an additional test of skill to shoot an apple on his son's head, however reducing the distance to 'syxe score paces' and again made his mark. Hits at these distances would seem no more than lurid fantasy, but serious accounts of the shooting of those times cause one to wonder a little. At any rate, in shooting at wands, an archer could be off a foot or so in his elevation and still make a hit.

Garlands of flowers or leaves were worn as circlets on the head by both men and women during the Maying, the holiday in celebration of spring that took place in early May. Maying festivities in England included Robin Hood plays and archery contests. A garland was a convenient size for a mark and hung on or leaning against a wand gave the options of counting an arrow within the garland as a hit, and a hit on the wand as cleaving the pin.

The Popinjay

The popinjay was the term for a bird at the top of a pole used as a target. In Roman times a live dove was used; by the mediaeval period the real animal had made way for a wooden model, with or without the addition of actual feathers. The word 'popinjay' is the English version of the Spanish word '*papegai*', meaning parrot, and there were wooden popinjays carved and painted to resemble that particular bird. The object was to dislodge the popinjay from its perch on top of the pole, which was often very high; ships' masts were sometimes used. Shooting was almost straight up, with blunt arrows. This type of shooting was practised as early as the thirteenth century on the Continent (the Flemish popinjay, set on a tall mast, was solid and about the size of a sparrow) as well as in Britain, and in fact survives in some places as a kind of public festival.

Popinjay shooting was practised with crossbows as well as handbows. In 1603 John Stow in *A Survey of London* reports: 'The crossbow makers rented Tazel-Close, a place near Moorfields, for the purpose of exercising themselves with that weapon, at the Popinjay.' In 1615 Belgians were shooting at a leather popinjay with crossbows. Popinjay (the Scots called it 'papingo') shooting contests were held in Kilwinning, Scotland as early as 1482. The wooden 'papingo' was stuck on a spike in the end of a beam projecting two or three feet from the 105-foot tower of Kilwinning Abbey. It was made in three parts, the wings attached by iron spikes were 'made louse for shooting af,' so that a light touch could 'ding her doun'. Competitors shot at it perpendicularly, resting the left foot against the base of the tower. The prize was a multicoloured Persian taffeta sash called a 'Benn'. The winner, called the Captain, tied this sash around his waist. The Ancient Society of Kilwinning Archers is the oldest archery club in Britain; besides popinjay shooting, it also shot at 30 yard level butts.

Archery Competitions

Mediaeval shooting matches, even festive ones, were short, simple tests of skill. As in the qualifying tests for Japanese archery, a few shots were thought enough to demonstrate this skill. A 'game' was a contest or portion of a contest determining a winning shot. The best shot at any point in a game was called the 'upshot'. 'In game' meant a contest in progress. A winner could be determined in several ways; by everyone shooting two or three arrows with the arrow closest to the pin taking the prize, by the best two out of three ends, or by continuing to shoot in rotation until the first hit or a specified number of hits in the white. In such a case, shooting order was important and decided by rank, mutual consent, or drawing of lots.

Gambling was as pervasive a part of mediaeval life as it is now, and there were few contests in which no money or other prize was at stake to make it more interesting. Some men, lacking money, played pluck-buffet, the prize in this case being the winner's privilege to strike the loser an open-handed blow on the head with full force.

Prizes at rural fairs for such sports as wrestling or archery could be costly, such as a saddled and bridled horse or butts of ale or wine. A silver arrow was the traditional archery prize; one was awarded by Harrow to the winner of that school's competitions and another by the Lancashire Bowmen. In 1583 gold bows and silver arrows were offered as prizes; these may have been covered with gold and silver leaf as opposed to being made of solid metal. With the development of sport archery, other prizes such as spoons and pieces of plate came to be offered. A cryptic record informs us of a wager 'shott at Fynsbere Field … of six men against six men, and one part had fifteen for three and lost the game.' Apart from physical rewards, contests were also a matter of honour for some; in 1530, Lord Howard, heading a delegation of Henry VIII to the Scottish court, challenged the Scots to an archery competition. Each team was to be of three landed gentlemen and three yeomen. The Scots won!

Major sources of information about mediaeval archery competitions are ballads, especially those concerning Robin Hood. A number of these date from the fourteenth century or earlier and provide good evidence about the nature of mediaeval contests, whatever Robin's own provenance. In the ballad of *Robin Hood and Guy of Gisborne,* Robin and Gisborne cut two summer schroggs (wands) in the forest and set them 'three score rodd apart' with garlands hung on them as 'prickes full neare'. In this match, Gisborne, a bounty hunter and no mean shot, leads off at Robin's insistence. Robin's first arrow misses by an inch, but betters Gisborne's shot. Gisborne's second arrow passes through the garland, but Robin's arrow cleaves the prick wand, ending the contest.

In the ballad of *Robin Hood and the Potter*, a shooting competition at an unspecified distance with a 40-shilling prize is given. The sheriff's men go to the butts with 'bows and bolts'. They shoot, but do not come within a half bow of the mark. Robin, disguised as a potter, borrows a bow from the sheriff that he finds weak, but sets an arrow on the string, takes a bolt from a *quequer* (quiver) and shoots to within a foot of the mark. Everyone shoots again and this time Robin cleaves the prick in three, emerging victorious once again.

The anachronistic ballad of *Robin Hood and Queen Katherine* involves a competition between the King's Archers, and the best archers the Queen can find in the kingdom. She chooses Robin Hood and his outlaws who make their way to London under assumed names as the Queen's Archers. The match takes place at Finsbury Fields, a length of fifteen score being measured out with a line by the King's bow bearer.

Three men are chosen for each team and each shoots one arrow, the three arrows closest to the mark are counted. The King's Archers lead about (shoot first). They win the first game while Robin's men take the second, the tally now being three and three, with the third three points to take the not inconsiderable money, barrels of wine and other prizes. The Queen's ladies cry out 'Woodcock, beware thine eye!' (The Woodcock was proverbial in the Middle Ages as a stupid and foolish creature, the name being applied in mockery. The eye of the bird was used as a mark by hunters using stonebows.) Robin takes advantage of the pause to increase the ante of the wagers. Then, shooting under his hand, Robin hits the mark, his companion Clifton cleaves the willow wood (prick), and Mitch the Miller's son shoots within a finger of the prick. Thus they win the contest and collect the booty.

A Lytel Geste of Robyn Hode is one of the older ballads, and has several shooting contests in it. The fifth fit of the ballad describes a match held at Nottingham. The Sheriff of Nottingham 'did cry a full fair play', a shooting contest with a silver arrow headed and feathered with gold offered to the best shooter at a pair of 'fynly' butts. The butts at Nottingham are described as fair and long, though we are not told the precise length. With six of his men Robin shoots thrice about, slitting the wand each time, as does Gilbert of the White Hand. When they have all shot about, Robin is the winner, but after receiving the silver arrow prize is set upon by the Sheriff's men.

In the seventh fit of the same ballad, Robin arranges a match for the entertainment of his guests, one of them King Edward disguised as an abbot. 'Two yerdes there were up set. Thereto gan they gange.' The King considers these marks too long by 50 paces. On each side is hung a rose garland, and whoever fails put an arrow through the garland has to forfeit his 'tackyl' (arrow), and take a buffet from Robin. Robin shoots twice about, cleaving the wand both times as does Gilbert of the White Hand. Little John and Scathelock miss and are 'smote full sore'. On Robin's last shot he misses by more than three finger widths, and chooses to yield his arrow and take his buffet from the disguised monarch. The King gives him one that stretches him on the ground. In the eighth fit they ride to Nottingham, Robin riding together with the now revealed Edward, the two of them shooting pluck-buffet as partners. Robin is the better shot and this is his chance to get in a few buffets of his own, the King not besting him once.

In the ballad *Robin Hood and the Monk*, Little John does not so lightly take a buffet under other circumstances. Robin, wishing to hear mass after a long absence from church, decides to go to Nottingham with only Little John to bear his bow. Little John tells him to bear his own bow and offers to shoot a penny. That is, shooting at random marks along the road with a penny wagered at each mark. Robin refuses to shoot a penny and offers instead three to one. Then they shoot 'bothe at buske and brome', until Little John has won five shillings. Robin, obviously in a bad mood that day, not only refuses to pay up but strikes John with his hand. Little John draws his sword saying that if Robin were not his master, he would be 'hit ful sore' and leaves Robin to go on alone.

In *Robin Hood and Clifton,* yet another archery competition is described, in which Clifton shoots first and hits a two-inch wand at 100 yards. Robin Hood then makes the celebrated shot that splits Clifton's arrow. Splitting an arrow (not the entire shaft), with a second arrow is not as uncommon as one might suppose, especially at short lengths; some modern indoor archery ranges mount these pairs of arrows, called 'Robin Hoods' on the wall. In the ninteenth century Horace A. Ford, on making a shot, once had an acquaintance, also a shooter, approach and casually offer to split his arrow, which he indeed accomplished. Ford watched the man closely for a time but his subsequent shooting was nothing exceptional.

There is a historical account of a mediaeval contest like those above: The Chester Sheriffs' Breakfast. The city of Chester, which lies on the Welsh border, was famous for its excellent archers, bowyers and its frequent archery meets. Here the Black Prince's archers and Richard III's Cheshire Archers were recruited. Annually on Easter Monday, the two sheriffs held a shooting competition.

> The day previous, the drum soundeth through the city, with a proclamation for all gentlemen, yeomen, and good fellows that will come with their bowes and arrowes, to take part with one sheriff or the other …

Next morning, all being assembled, the sheriffs alternately chose their teams and then alternately shot at a mark twelve score distant, until three shots were won. Then all repaired to Chester's Common Hall, the winning team first, with arrows in their hands, followed by the losing team, all with bows in their hands. Then all took part in a breakfast of calf's head and bacon 'in loving manner'. Also in Chester, a football was formerly given as a prize for excellence in archery. Later, with royal disapproval of sports that distracted from archery practice, the more appropriate prize of a silver arrow was given. Newly married men were required to provide the silver arrow, to be delivered to the Guild of Drapers in front of the mayor.

In the above contest, as in the ballad *Robin Hood and Queen Katherine*, the rule is that members of the two teams shoot alternately until one of the teams accumulates three hits, this being the game. In the Robin Hood ballad this was repeated for best of three games.

In *A Survey of London* John Stow informs us that before his time (1603) it had been customary in London at Bartholomew Tide for the Lord Mayor, with the sheriffs and aldermen, to go to Finsbury Fields, where the citizens were assembled, and shoot at the standard, with broad and flight arrows, for games. Henry VIII was an excellent archer and did much to encourage the practice of archery, both for war and sport. He practised with his archers often and caused sundry matches to be made concerning shooting in the longbow, and to which came many principal archers, who:

... being in game and the upshot given, as all men thought, there was yet one Barlo yet remaining to shoot, being one of the King's Guard, to whom the King very graciously said 'Win them all and thou shalt be Duke over all the Archers.' This Barlo drew his bow, and shooting won the best. Whereat the King greatly rejoiced, commending him for his good Archery, and for that Barlo did dwell in Shoreditch [an outlying part of London], the King named him Duke of Shoreditch.

On this occasion apparently the best hit during the match was the winner, with no system of points or scoring – the 'upshot'.

Henry VIII chartered the Fraternity of St George, one of the oldest shooting clubs, to encourage the practice of arbalest and longbow. The club was later renamed 'The Honourable Artillery Company'. Its members were permitted to practise 'shooting at all sorts of marks and butts, and at the game of the popinjay, and other games, as at fowls and the like'. The King granted the fraternity the renewed privilege that if any of the members 'shooting at a known and accustomed Butt, having first pronounced the word fast, (or stand fast) should happen to kill any person passing between shooter and Butt, he should not suffer or be imprisoned.' The warning shout 'fast!' is still used by archers and was the origin of the expression 'playing fast and loose'. But there was no intent to excuse murder; in 1557 a trumpet was blown between each shot and no one was allowed within 20 yards of the mark.

Other archery clubs or shooters companies began to appear in the early sixteenth century. The Honourable Artillery Company, mentioned above, was granted patent in 1537. The Finsbury Archers and the Lancashire Bowmen appeared at about the same time, and regular shooting matches began to be held. The Finsbury Archers held several scheduled matches each year: the Easter Target, the Whitsun Target and the Eleven-Score Target. Clearly Englishmen still enjoyed archery as a sport. At a two-day meet in Shoreditch in 1583, 3000 active participants, with one arrow each, shot from dawn to nightfall at a 148-yard butt. But by 1600 the loss of common ground had made it very difficult for the general public to find a place to practise long shooting.

The Lancashire Bowmen met weekly, and in 1673 in Yorkshire, held their first shoot for the Silver Arrow, which was the Captain's prize. The target, with four coloured rings in addition to the gold or yellow centre, was the forerunner of the modern target, the inner white now being replaced with blue. This is the earliest recorded use of this type of target. Two dozen arrows were shot, two arrows at an end, at a distance of 100 yards. The first arrow in the gold, or a cutter, an arrow on the line but touching the gold, won the Silver Arrow and the title Captain of the Archers. Any archer heard swearing or cursing was subject to a fine. This 'Antient Scorton Arrow Contest', established by Charles II and named after its original location moves to the home village of the winner and still continues today.

In 1676 the Finsbury Archers distributed tickets inviting competition for prizes at the Eleven-Score Target for a fee of 20 shillings. (T. Roberts in *The English Bowman* credits the Finsbury Archers with establishing target sizes of 4 inches at 100 yards, 3 inches at 80 yards, and 2 inches at 60 yards.) The distance of 220 yards could be

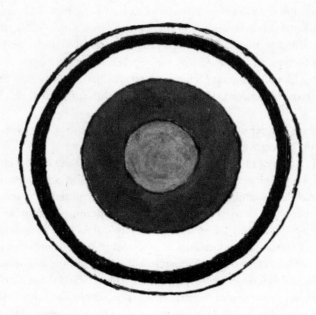

A target used by the Finsbury Archers and the Lancashire Bowmen, the earliest example of the modern type target. This heralded the end of the old archery.

reduced at the discretion of the Captain (winner of the previous competition) by ten yards every few rounds or so. The first man to hit the gold won the Captain's Prize. The target was like the one used by the Lancashire Bowmen, and each ring had a prize assigned to it. There were spoons of varying values, a hit in the outer white earning a horn spoon. The Captain had the privilege of shooting first and went around the target by the left. The Lieutenant, who had shot the second best arrow in the previous competition, shot next. All other entrants drew lots for shooting order. This was important as only the first hit in a ring was counted. When all the prizes were won, the game was said to have been 'shotten down'.

Archery was on its way to becoming a gentlemen's sport or social event. In 1844 the York Round would be instituted with its 72 arrows at 100 yards, 48 at 80 yards and 24 at 60 yards, designed to fill a sunny Sunday afternoon and provide a bit of suspense for the participants. After the adoption of such multi-arrow rounds with points assigned to each coloured ring, at measured distances, it was natural that shooting style would be changed to suit the altered situation, one not ideal for instinctive aiming. The man who made these changes was Gerald Ford. The bow was no longer used for hunting or warfare, and men seldom tried to hit a mark at more than 100 yards. Except for isolated or traditionally minded groups, the old archery had passed from England.

In Cheshire and Lancashire, long renowned for their archers, the old ways continued for a time. The 'Paper Game' of Cheshire and Lancashire continued until fairly recently as a well-recorded survival of a mediaeval-style shooting game. There were seldom more than three pairs of arrows allowed on each side and the marks were pasteboard squares pinned to the butts. The archers drew lots to determine shooting order, which was maintained throughout the contest regardless of hits. Only arrows 'in the inches', the paper square, were counted. The game was shot at distances of 30, 60, 90 and 120 yards with different sized pasteboard squares and different specified weights of arrows at different lengths: Compare the sixteen-inch paper at 120 yards with today's standard target of four feet at 100 yards.

Length		Paper size (inches)	Arrow weight (old silver weight)
roods	yards		
4	30	4	5 s 6d
18	60	6	4s 6d
12	90	12	3s 6d
16	120	16	3s 6d

'Markers', men who signalled the results of the shots, were used at the twelve and sixteen rood lengths at which distances it is difficult to see where the arrows have hit. A marker appears at a crossbow butt in an illustration of 1450, and such markers were also used in crossbow shooting in the Alps.

The marker carried a white wand held briefly near each arrow. The best arrow was indicated by the wand being shaken thrice over the head, the second best by its being shaken toward the ground. When the paper was pricked he uncovered and bowed once for the outer circle, twice for the white and thrice for the pin. The wand was moved upwards for over arrows, horizontally for wide arrows and downwards for short arrows. Butts were arranged at 30-yard intervals.

In Flanders, where archery was a popular pastime, 'goose-shooting' was practised. Originally, the living goose, except for its head, was enclosed in a turf butt. The archer who first hit the goose's head, received the goose as a prize. The game was later played without using the goose as a mark.

24

HUNTING

The hinds were held in the valley with hey! and ware!
The does driven with din to the depth of the dale,
Then the shimmering arrows slipped from the bowstring and slanted,
Winging their way from every tree in the wood,
Their broad heads piercing the bonny flanks of brown;
The deer brayed and bled, as on the banks they died.

Sir Gawain and the Green Knight[49]

In the early Middle Ages, man was engaged in a battle with nature that has since resulted in some kind of victory: to carve out a living space, to protect his crops and livestock from birds and animals as well as to provide meat for his table. However, for the nobility, hunting was a popular diversion. It was considered a means of keeping in readiness for warfare, the true function of the noble, and could be a dangerous pastime; Charlemagne was once badly gored in the thigh while trying to kill an aurochs with a sword from the back of a horse. There was also the danger of the arrows of other hunters as noted by Count Gaston de Foix in his fourteenth-century book *Le Livre de Chasse*.

The two basic kinds of hunting were falconry and venery, venery being further divided into the chase and the hunt. In the chase, the game was pursued, usually with dogs; it was in the hunt that bows and arrows were used. Naturally these were not the only hunting weapons; much hunting was done with spears and swords, as well as bait, nets, fences and traps. The usual form of hunting for the nobility was 'bow and stable' in which archers took up fixed positions while deer were driven past them. However, some bowmen ranged forests stalking their prey and 'shot at view', much like some of today's bow hunters.

De Arte Bersandi, written by Guicemas, a German knight, describes the huntsmen of the early Middle Ages. They were well paid and were even sometimes of knightly rank. A huntsman's duty was to bring venison to his lord's board, but he also had to be adept in the use of both bow and crossbow as well as able to cut arrow shafts and make bowstrings if necessary. He had to train his scent hound, a *brachet*, to seek out red or fallow deer, while ignoring roe deer, and to follow a blood trail. He had to know how to sound the various horn signals, a series of short and long blasts similar to Morse code. He supervised his archers, men camouflaged in green tunics, hats and hoods, who each had to have a quiver with five arrows for the deer, and three darts (bodkins) for self defence, or two flat headed arrows (blunts) for shooting birds. *Le Livre de Chasse* advised not only green clothing for camouflage but green bows and crossbows as well.

Ideally, three archers and three horsemen accompanied the huntsman in the forest while the brachet ranged freely until deer were sighted. Then, the brachet leashed and carried on the crupper of one of the horses, the horsemen would begin to circle the deer on the downwind side. The archers, concealed by the horses, were assigned their places behind trees. The deer had learned to flee at the sight of a man but did not recognise a horse or a horseman as a danger. The horsemen would continue to circle until they came upwind of the deer, when they began to gradually move the deer towards the waiting archers, careful not to make it flee in panic. Wounded deer that fled were tracked by the brachet.

In the great royal 'bow and stable' hunts, the Yeoman of the King's Bows had the duty of preparing the royal blind and occupying it until the monarch's arrival. For the King and his friends, the morning might begin with a picnic in the forest while the hunt itself began with 'the quest'. Several huntsmen, each with a scent hound such as a 'lymer', set out to locate the deer, leaving a trail of small broken branches for the archers to follow. They estimated the size of the deer from its tracks and droppings, some of which were gathered in the hunting horn to show the lord, who would decide if it was worth hunting that day. If the hunt went ahead, the green-clad archers would wait motionless at their chosen trees with arrows half drawn until the game was driven past them by the huntsmen advancing on foot with pairs of lymers. Deer wounded but fleeing would be tracked by the archer with his bloodhound, and finished off with a hunting knife. The deer's belly was slit open and the organs removed; these were the portion of the huntsman. The meat was then divided and the dogs were permitted to feast on bread thrown in the bloody abdominal cavity.

Rather than taking part in these active hunts, mediaeval ladies were sometimes provided a comfortable and convenient place from which to shoot at deer driven into nets or other enclosures, where they could be killed at the noblewomen's leisure.

Hunts became much more elaborate after the crusades began. Like the Saracens, many Europeans came to rely on packs of hounds to pursue and even kill their quarry, and Saracen falconry was introduced into Europe as well. In England, where nearly all men and many women were skilled with the bow, archery retained more popularity than on the continent.

For many kings, hunting was an overriding passion and they established royal forests and game parks to make it more enjoyable. The Ardennes was originally established as Charlemagne's hunting preserve, with foresters posted to guard the entrance trail. He was particularly fond of hunting in his youth and chased deer, boar and wild oxen with javelin and 'small bow and short or long arrows'.

The Anglo-Saxon kings of England were also keen hunters. Alfred the Great was a most expert and active hunter before he was even twelve, and excelled in all branches of the art. Even Edward the Confessor, whose temperament seemed more that of a churchman than a king, loved to follow a pack of swift hounds in pursuit of game and to cheer them with his voice. His successor, Harold Godwinson, rarely travelled without his hawks and hounds.

The Anglo-Saxon Chronicle informs us that the Norman usurper William the Conqueror made large forests for deer and enacted laws that whoever killed a hart or hind would be blinded. He also forbade the killing of boars and hares.

> He made great protection for the game
> And imposed laws for the same,
> That who so slew hart or hind
> Should be made blind.

William established the New Forest, comprising some tens of thousands of acres from which area many Saxons were forcibly evicted. Some habitations were permitted in the royal forests, but those who lived in them, though allowed to carry bows and blunts, were forbidden to carry arrows with sharp steel arrowheads. Furthermore, though they could gather dead branches for firewood, they were forbidden to take living branches or wood. Their pigs or cattle were not to graze when the deer were fawning, and their dogs had to have the three claws in their forepaws clipped so that they could not run after game.

William's son William Rufus, was killed in the new Forest under mysterious circumstances by an arrow supposedly shot by one Wat Tyrell, a nobleman visiting from France. Some interpreted his death as divine retribution for the means by which his father had established the New Forest. Rufus' cousin Richard was also killed by an arrow shot by one of his knights while hunting. This did not stop Henry I, Rufus' successor, from constructing a park at Woodstock, 'walled about with stone, seven miles in compass, and placed therein, besides great store of deer, divers strange beasts, such as lions, linces, porpentines and such other.' The presence of exotic animals in mediaeval hunting stories is therefore not necessarily fantasy; the royal court was situated at Woodstock in the early fourteenth century.

Both Henry II and his one-time friend and nemesis Thomas Becket were enthusiastic hunters. Becket visited Paris in 1157, with grooms and hawkers with hounds and gerfalcons in his extensive baggage train. He clearly ignored those who felt that hunting was not for the clergy. Hunting, hawking or dicing had been forbidden to priests during the reign of King Edward, but Henry II relaxed the game laws, permitting an archbishop, bishop, earl or baron to kill one or two deer in the sight of a forester if one was present. If not, a horn had to be sounded to be free of suspicion of poaching. John Kirkby, the fighting Bishop of Carlisle, poached a royal doe from Sherwood Forest but was pardoned, perhaps because of prior military service against the Scots. Edward III, even on his military campaigns in France, brought his hunting staff with him and went hunting every day he could.

The epic poem the *Nibelungenlied* (*The Song of the Nibelungs*), written in the early thirteenth century, describes Siegfried's last hunt in the Wasken Woods and illustrates the sumptuous pleasure of the hunt for the nobility.

It was a royal hunt for boar, bear and bison with spears. They arose early and loaded their hunting gear on pack horses for they meant to cross the Rhine. The horses also carried bread, mead and spiced wine, meats and fish and other provisions. They made camp on a broad island at the edge of the green forest near the place where the game could be started. On this occasion rather than choose a leader, they divided men and hounds and hunted separately. Siegfried took one huntsman with a tracking dog to lead him to the game. Siegfried, on horseback, killed such game as the hound flushed with sword or with sharp arrows. After he felled them they put the hound on its leash. He killed bison, elk, aurochs, shelk, and boar and bear. One loud blast of the horn signalled for the return to camp. This blast was answered by the huntsmen.

How splendidly he rode to camp! His spear was large, sturdy, and broad. A fine sword hung down to his spurs, and he carried a. handsome horn of red gold. I never heard tell of better hunting gear. He wore a cloak of black pfellel silk and a hat of rich sable. Oh, what costly borders he had upon his quiver! A panther's skin formed its covering for the sake of the sweet fragrance. And he carried a bow which no one could bend but himself except with a windlass. His hunting garb was all of otter (ludern) skin, with inserts of other-coloured furs from head to toe, and from the shining fur there gleamed on either side many a golden clasp. He carried Balmung, a broad and handsome sword. So sharp were its cutting edges that it never failed when wielded against a helmet. The splendid hunter was proud and gay. Since I must tell you everything, to the smallest detail: his precious quiver was full of good arrows, the heads mounted in gold and at least a hand's breadth wide. Whatever he pierced with them was soon doomed to die. So the knight rode along in hunter's fashion.

Not everyone found hunting so laudable. John of Salisbury, a twelfth-century critic of hunting, wrote:

In our time, hunting and hawking are esteemed the most honourable employments, and most excellent virtues, by our nobility; and they think it the height of worldly felicity to spend the whole of their time in these diversions; accordingly they prepare for them with more solicitude, expense, and parade, than they do for war; and pursue the wild beasts with greater fury than they do the enemies of their country. By constantly following this way of life, they lose much of their humanity and become as savage, nearly, as the very brutes they hunt. Husbandmen, with their harmless herds and flocks, are driven from their well cultivated fields, their meadows, and their pastures, that wild beasts may range in them without interruption. If one of these great and merciless hunters shall pass by your habitation, bring forth hastily all the refreshment you have in your house, or that you can readily buy, or borrow from your neighbour; that you may not be involved in ruin, or even accused of treason.

By the thirteenth century, there were dozens of royal forests in England. Verderers were assigned to take care of the vegetation, ensuring that no one cut the timber, branches or undergrowth that gave the animals shelter, while foresters were to protect the game, apprehending poachers.

Henry I employed four huntsmen as well as four horn blowers, 20 sergeants (beaters), several assistant huntsmen, a variety of dog handlers, a troop of mounted wolf hunters, and several archers, one of whom was also the King's bow bearer. Similarly Henry II's hunting staff was like a small army. It included hornblowers, fewterers (who slipped the hounds) leading the greyhounds and the lime-hounds and the brachets; the berners, who fed the hounds; the wolf hunters with their 24 running hounds and eight greyhounds; the archers; the chief huntsman and his knights and the 20 sergeants of the hunt and a host of underlings.

These men wore clothing of Lincoln or Kendal green (so named from their places of manufacture) or of russet brown to match the woods according to the season. Caped hoods were a traditional part of hunting atire. In addition to the camouflage offered by green or brown clothing, hunters used branches and leaves to conceal themselves, sometimes holding branches in their mouths to break up the telltale glare of the face, sometimes with faces blackened.

Also traditional was the hunting horn for signalling the dogs or other hunters. Various calls were used such as 'recheat', three short blasts for the assembly of the hounds. In the ballads, Robin Hood uses this signal to summon his outlaws when he needs their help. The horns were usually made of cowhorn, but sometimes of elephant tusk, often beautifully carved; these were called 'Oliphants'. The horns were fitted with metal bands, sometimes of gold, and hung low from a baldric crossing the body.

Hunting dogs were provided with collars to which a ring was attached. The fewterer had a length of line, one end of which was tied to his upper arm. The other end of the line was passed through the rings in the collars of one or several dogs and held in the hand. The dogs were let slip simply by releasing the end of the line. Two dogs on the line ere called a brace, three were a leash.

Various breeds of dogs were used, both sight or 'gaze' hounds, and scent hounds. The most important were the greyhound or levrier, the lymer and the brachet. The greyhound runs mute and follows game by sight rather than scent. They were larger than modern greyhounds, and were trained either to simply to pursue the game, or to kill. The lymer was a bloodhound kept on a leash and used to locate game, to follow a wounded animal, or to finish a wounded stag at bay. The brachet was a long eared scent hound, supposedly the ancestor of the modern pointer and was similar to the braque, which is still bred in Portugal. The alaunt was a large, fierce dog, similar to a German shepherd, usually employed in boar hunts.

A lone archer could use a lymer to track a deer and keep it at bay until he could shoot it. Archers in groups usually waited for the deer to be driven past by huntsmen and dogs. Even the spaniel imported from Spain was used in deer hunting in England in Elizabethan times. A wounded deer will frequently attempt to make its escape in the water, and trained spaniels were employed to get them back on land.

The favoured game animal was the deer, both for sport and meat. Three species of deer were hunted: the red deer, the fallow deer and the roe deer. The red deer were the largest and most preferred, rather larger than they are today with their range and food supply in the forests reduced. Their summer coat is reddish brown, becoming brownish grey in the winter. The male is named according to the development of its tined antlers: a calf a few months old is called a 'knobbe,' the second year a 'brocket' (spike buck), the third year a 'spayad,' the fourth year a 'staggard' and the fifth year a 'hart'. In the sixth year it becomes a 'stag'. The 'Hart of Ten' with antlers of ten tines was considered the most worthy quarry.

Fallow deer are not native to northern Europe, but were introduced to England from the Mediterranean, perhaps as early as Roman times. This deer is a smaller species than the red deer. Its summer coat is a reddish fawn with white spots and a white line along the flanks. The winter coat is darker and the spots disappear. The male is named according to the development of its palmate antlers in a mediaeval poem of Sir Tristram:

The first yeere, a Fawne
The second yeere, a Pricket
The third yeere, a Sorell
The fourth yeere, a Sore
The fifth yeere, a Bucke of the first head.
The sixth yeere, a Bucke or a great Bucke.

For only two species of deer we have here more than a dozen distinct names familiar to any mediaeval man considered a gentleman. These should help clarify various references in old writings on hunting.

The smallest species was the roe deer. In eighteenth- and nineteenth-century Britain these were almost extinct except in the Scottish Highlands. Its summer coat is short and bright fox-red, the winter coat a dark speckled greyish fawn with a conspicuous white tail patch. The female is called a roe, the male a roebuck and the young are called kids. The meat of all species of deer was called venison.

Another animal favoured for meat and more dangerous sport was the boar. These animals have a coat of greyish hair and large, sharp, curved tusks, capable of disembowelling an unwary hunter.

Smallbows, longbows and crossbows were all used in hunting, and the many illustrations in *Le Livre de Chasse* mostly show crossbows. As firearms came into general use, skill with the handbow diminished and the more user-friendly technology of the crossbow became more popular. It was in England that the longbow remained longest in use, except for isolated areas like Scotland or Lapland. In the sixteenth century, Thomas Elyot wrote of longbowmen:

… for being industrious they killed their game further from them (if they shot a great strength) than they can with a crossbow, except it be of such a weight that the arm will repent the bearing thereof twenty years after.

Crossbows were also noisier than handbows, which was why when steel ones became general in military circles, sportsmen continued to use ones of composite construction so as not to startle their prey.

Large game was hunted with broadheads and with 'angell-hedes', the angle of barbs of which was 90 degrees. Heads of these types, up to four fingers wide, are both described and pictured in *Le Livre de Chasse*. There were also chisel-shaped heads on crossbow shafts for hamstringing game. The forked heads had still another purpose. 'For geese or other large birds they should be double forked, sharp, and strong, to cut a wing or neck clean off.' A hit with a broadhead could not be depended on to bring down a strong flyer like a large goose immediately, for 'notwithstanding she be hurt or shot through, she will fly off and die in another place.'

Small game such as hares, squirrels and birds was hunted using less powerful bows called 'birding bows' used with blunt arrows or bolts.

> Many must go together to hunt them and must carry dogs with them. The squirrels take refuge in trees, and … since it is too troublesome to climb every tree, that labour must be supplied with Bows and Bolts, that when the squirrel resteth, presently he may be thumpt with the blow of an arrow; the Archer need not fear to do her much harm, except he hit her on the head; for by reason of a strong back-bone and fleshy parts, she will abide as great a stroak as a dog.

Hares might be flushed by greyhounds and shot with blunt arrows. 'Burders' and 'fowlers' aided farmers by catching birds of prey with falcon nets or disposing of smaller seed-eating birds with crossbows.

Le Ménagier De Paris, written around 1393, advises ladies wishing to stock the larder with birds to use falconry in conjunction with archery. 'For this purpose you may carry a bow and bolt in order that, when the blackbird takes shelter in a bush and does not quit it for the hawk which hovers over and watches it, the lady or damsel who knows how to shoot may kill it with the bolt.'

Birds were also commonly hunted with stonebows or stone casting crossbows called rodds. These weapons could shoot stones with great accuracy and were equipped with sights. The hunter's mark was the eye of the woodcock or other bird; in Shakespeare's *Twelfth Night* Sir Toby cries, 'Oh, for a stone bow, to hit him in the eye.'

Hunters could get close to waterfowl using a stalking horse, as recommended by Gervase Markham in his 1684 book *The Art of Archery*. Birds or animals that would take flight at the sight of a man, see no danger in a slowly moving horse, 'an old Jade trayned up for that use which will gently walke up and downe in the water; and then you shall shelter yourself and your Peice behind his fore shoulder.' Lacking a horse, the hunter could take 'pieces of oulde canvasse, and having made it in the shape or proportion of a Horse, let it be painted as neare the colour of a Horse as you can devise.' Similar pictures or dummies were used in hunting deer, and are pictured in Gaston de Foix's *Le Livre de Chasse*.

Gaston de Foix remained the standard authority on the hunt during the late Middle Ages and the Renaissance. However, since his book is largely derived from the earlier

Roi Modus, the bowhunting section of the latter is reproduced here to instruct us in the finer points of bowhunting in thirteenth-century France. In it, King Modus's scholars demand to know how archers take stand to shoot deer in a forest. Modus replies:

This mode of hunting may be practiced two ways, either with hounds or without. When an archer designs to hunt in a thicket where he perceives game is harboured, let him carefully notice from what point the wind cometh, that he may place himself with advantage, and so the animals may not get vent of him. And if several archers follow this chase together in an open country, they must station themselves much farther apart than where the trees and underwood are more abundant. The chief forester who manages the dogs should be on horseback, and his hounds must be taught to couch and cower down, until he has appointed for each bowman his respective station. This done, if the cover be large and thick, they must let loose from three to five dogs, according to its extent. Those who are appointed to drive the deer should now talk loudly and call to each other, that they may not attempt to pass between them. When an archer espies a deer approaching his stand, he must order himself after this fashion: Let him endeavour to keep out of sight as much as possible, while he raises his bow perpendicularly, holding the drawing hand with the arrow ready nocked, directly before his face; and if the animal continue to approach without stopping, he should very silently and cautiously extend his arms, and draw his bow softly, that the arrow may be pulled up to its head, before the game come near; and his bow should be very weak and gentle so that he may hold it drawn a reasonable space; and he must pull the bowstring ever to his right ear; and whilst the deer is passing by a few paces, the archer should follow him with his bow, drawing and redrawing the shaft. Then, having made sure of his aim, he is to let fly with a sharp and steady loose. If the beast come very leisurely, and in a direct line, the hunter must aim his arrow straight at the breast: but if it cross him unexpectedly on the right or left hand, let him shoot in a slanting direction behind the shoulder, about the centre of the ribs, allowing the game to pass him a few paces, as before mentioned. And now I will set forth why the crafty and cunning archer should ever do thus: for to shoot in any other manner is wholly unsportsmanlike, and a violation of the laws of archery, for these four reasons following: firstly; should the arrow pass straight through her body, it may fail to wound a vital part, and the deer will not die near so quickly as when shot obliquely just behind the shoulder, and in the direction of the heart. Secondly; because, having seen the archer, she will make a bound, and most probably cause him to miss his aim. Thirdly; from the flurry produced by her sudden appearance, he cannot point his arrow so deliberately as when shooting after her. Fourthly; if the game cross the hunter very swiftly, and at any considerable distance from his stand, the arrow shot in a direct line may fail to reach it before it passes by. Thus have I explained the reasons why the hunter should manage his bow according to the peculiar circumstances of the case. And if the deer at which he aimed be struck by the arrow and mortally wounded, the huntsman should whoop loudly for his bloodhound, which is abiding with the other dogs. Let him also blow a note upon his horn, to warn his comrades to cast down the blinks. Should the wound, on the contrary, be only a slight one, not the bloodhound only, but the other dogs must be slipped, the forester on horseback spurring after them with all the speed he may. And now I will explain how the cunning archer may discover, by the colour of the blood which falls from the stricken deer, whether the wound be fatal or not. When dark red, and slightly covered with froth, it is a sure token that the arrow has met her in a good place, and she shall die quickly. Item, if the blood be clear and thin, with a few bubbles on its surface, be satisfied that your arrow, having struck upon a bone, has done little hurt. If the game be hit in the belly, then small portions of grass or other food, on which she has been feeding, shall flow with the blood. When this is the case, you may allow her to repose a considerable time before laying on the bloodhound, for two reasons: firstly, because she cannot live long thus; secondly, because where she lyeth down, she will remain, and permit the hunter to take her. But if, when you follow with the bloodhound, she should happen to spring up from her lair, loose four or five steady dogs, and you shall see her taken with much pleasure. If the arrow enter at the loins, she will die in an hour. If at the chine, between two joints, she will void herself and fall, but not die. If among the great ribs, in a slanting direction towards the shoulder, she shall die briefly; but if the arrow points towards the haunches, she shall run a long time. If struck high up behind the shoulders, she shall not die; but if lower down towards the ribs, instant death follows. If in the middle of the neck, death will not ensue; nearer the setting on of the head, your weapon shall be fatal. If the arrow enter right through the neck, three fingers from the shoulders, that is among the vitals, she shall fall instantly. An outside wound in the thick part of the haunch is not mortal; but on the inner part of the same, just the reverse. Lastly, an arrow passing directly through the throat severs the windpipe, and causes instant death.

He then reveals how to hunt in woods at stand, without a pack of dogs.

When the archers have taken their stand, as before indicated, the chief forester should station those who are to drive the deer right across the thicket, at a stone's throw from each other; then should they gradually walk towards the archers, whistling and shouting as they proceed, to alarm the herd. And when a deer is struck, he who is inclined to the love of archery should have with him one good dog trained to hunt upon the blood. And farther, I will describe other things peculiar to this mystery. First, then, the bow with which an archer shoots at stand, should be more elastic and easier to draw, than that used by him who shoots at view, or when a beast is in chase, for three reasons: because he who shoots with too strong a bow, will be compelled to incline his body forwards from the tree, and thus expose himself to the view of the approaching game; because he cannot hold the arrow when drawn up to the head, for any length of time; because his bow hand will be unsteady, and his loose uncertain and irregular. These are the reasons why every archer who shoots at stand, should be master of his bow. There are yet other requisites for a chief of the game; viz: a file wherewith to make his arrow heads sharp and pointed, some spare strings carried in his pouch, and a coat of green; or, in summer and autumn, of russet colour, resembling that of the woods.

The second chapter 'shall treat of killing deer with the bow, by riding in upon them unawares'.

When archers go to the forest to take deer after this manner, two horses will be amply sufficient; for where there are more, the game, becoming restless, straightway decamps. Two mounted foresters, skilful in discovering the haunts of deer, each followed by a small party of archers, are to proceed into those glades and open woodlands which afford an easy passage to the horses; and if they discover the herd feeding at a distance, let them ride cautiously one a little in advance of the other. On arriving as near as prudence will admit, both archers and horsemen should stop. The former then station themselves in a semicircle, about a stone's throw apart, and so as to gain the vent of the beasts; their bows, ready braced, are to be held perpendicularly before the body, with an arrow on the string, the right hand should hold the nock of the arrow before the archer's face, very near to it; and they are to remain in this position, keeping their eyes fixed on the deer. In the mean time, the two mounted foresters, having made a large circuit; on arriving opposite the archers, should walk their horses forwards in a direct line. The deer, startled at their appearance, will rush towards the ambuscade, when each bowman, singling out the one which likes him best, discharges his arrow with a cool and deliberate aim. Such as do not fall directly, are tracked by the bloodhound, kept waiting at some convenient spot.

The third chapter treats of shooting deer at view, both on foot and on horseback.

The foot archer who designs to shoot at view, must order himself in the following manner:- let him seek the game among the forests, with bow in hand, and shafts buckled under his belt. And here the bow may be much stronger than that used by the archer on horseback, for three reasons: because he will have to take aim from a greater distance; because his mark being a flight shot, he may extend his arms more fully, and lay his body in the bow; because he will have no occasion to hold the arrow drawn up, even for an instant, as he is directed to do when at stand. On discovering a stag, let him forthwith brace his bow, and place an arrow upon the string, approaching him as near as he can; and if the stag raise up his head to gaze around, at that instant must he pull the string to his ear, and having drawn and redrawn the arrow for an instant, to secure his aim, he is then to let fly. If the shot take effect, the archer should speedily fetch his bloodhound from the place where he left it. The sportsman who shoots at view on horseback, must provide himself with some sober jade, that will, when necessary, remain quiet without moving. As soon as the game is in sight, let him brace his bow, which should be a weak one; then placing his arrow on the string, he is to hold both in his left hand, by throwing the fore-finger over the arrow to secure it, and guide the horse with his right. Then, putting him to the gallop, the archer should make a wide circuit around the whole herd, in order to select the best opening through which to direct his shot. If the deer grow restless and alarmed, which he will be presently aware of, by their raising up their heads, let him halt until they recommence feeding. When he perceives they are quiet, he may approach very cautiously, until in a favourable position for shooting; in other words, until he can discern the side of the fattest of the herd fully exposed to his arrow let him then halt, and handle his weapons. Now, the skilful archer will so order himself, that he may conveniently draw his bow behind him, and not on one side, or directly in front, supporting himself in the left stirrup, which should be a little shorter than the other. Let him shoot with all his force, drawing the arrow fully up to its head, and levelling his bow-hand at the spot where he wishes to pierce the game. If the shot be fatal, he may go and seek his bloodhound, as before said, or slip his deer dogs, which latter will be better able to pull down the stag, in case he be but slightly hurt.

The fourth chapter considers shooting in covert during windy weather.

The best season is from the middle of August to the middle of September, for two causes; because in these months deer are yet in full season; and because they go forth very early in the morning, and bray so loudly at one another, as to be heard afar off. A strong wind, accompanied by rain, is, for two causes, the most favourable weather for this kind of shooting: the deer being then more a-foot, and less able to discern the archer, by reason of the force of the wind. Let the hunter proceed alone, early in the morning, creeping from stand to stand, through the overgrown bushes of that part of the forest where he suspects the game is harboured. Having got sight of a stag, he cannot be too wary; if seen, it is all over with him, his shot is spoiled. But should he succeed in creeping unperceived within range, let him kneel behind a bush, and there brace his bow; then placing an arrow on the string, he is to hold both of them in the left hand, while with each blast of wind he changes his position, taking notice if the animal continues to feed. When two stags are braying and fighting together, the hunter may approach exceedingly near; indeed, it often happens that they are so blinded by fury as to be easily killed with a sword. And when the archer has got so near that he cannot possibly miss, let him move cautiously from his hiding-place and discharge his arrow. This is best done whilst kneeling on one knee, the bow being short and weak. He should hold a small green branch in his mouth to conceal his features, and the habit he wears must be the colour of the woods. In a country well covered with lofty trees, stalking will afford the archer much diversion. Procure a piece of linen sufficiently large to admit the figure of a hind being painted on it, and fasten its extremities to a couple of poles, like those of a stalking horse. The hunter keeps this device extended, while he advances very cautiously down wind upon the deer, which he discovers by looking through the eyelet-holes made in its centre. Let him creep from tree to tree under cover of his disguise, until within bow-shot; then fixing the poles in the ground, so that the painted deer may be fairly displayed, let him rise cautiously and shoot over the upper edge of the cloth. This is a very agreeable mode of hunting, and the archer cannot fail of sport in a country tolerably well furnished with stags.

What is the pastime of shooting wild boars at soil? Modus replies, that to shoot at soil is the fifth chapter of archery, 'and the finest sport a single archer can enjoy.'

> The proper season extends from mid-October to the end of November. And now it is proper the archer be informed that 'a soil', in hunter's language, means a standing pool of mud and water. Thither the boars assemble while roaming in search of food, to drink, wallow, and rest therein. Having discovered such a place, look out some moderately sized tree, growing on the edge of the water, and as nearly as possible opposite to the path by which wild boars make their approach. Then select a bough of four forks, a couple of feet at least from the ground, which may serve for a seat. And now I will inform you why it is necessary to be placed thus high. Rest assured, if the wild boars are near, either with the wind or against it, they will neither see nor smell the hunter, who is lifted above the ground. Mount then, to your seat, with your bow ready bent, and a good tough-shafted arrow, well headed and sharpened. Keep good watch, looking narrowly around, and there is a certainty of sport, for not only wild boars, but every other description of game, will pass by your hiding place, and you may kill them quite at hand; more especially the former, for they will dash into the pool, and wallow therein before your eyes.

'To kill a hare on her form is a pleasant diversion in a favourable country.'

> The season for this sort of hunting is the month of April, when hares resort at daybreak to the green corn, to feed thereon. Let the archer mount on horseback, and ride forth, bow in hand, with a varlet at his side, leading a brace or a leash of greyhounds. Then let him ride up and down the corn, until he espy a hare, when the hounds are to be placed in front, that the sight of them may occupy her attention. And as soon as she sees the dogs, straitway will she tap with her foot among the corn, a sure sign that she is squatting close: then make a wide circuit, with the bent bow in your left hand, and an arrow nocked upon the string; draw up and shoot, without stopping the horse and know, that as soon as the hare espies the dogs, she will allow the hunter to approach as near as he listeth. This is a marvellously pleasant amusement in a country abounding with hares. And now my friends and pupils, ye will be duly qualified and skilled to practice and enjoy all the pastime which I and Queen Racio have taught; provided ye give heed unto our words.

Hares and coneys (rabbits) were the most popular small game hunted with blunt arrows or bolts or with hounds. Hunting seasons covered nearly the entire year except for 'Fencer Month', from two weeks before Midsummer Day to two weeks after, during which time no game might be killed. The seasons, like many events in mediaeval times, were marked by the religious calendar.

Hart and Buck	Nativity of St John the Baptist (24 June) to Holyrood Day (14 September) or end of Fencer month (8 July) to Holyrood Day

Hind and Doe	Holyrood Day to Candlemas (2 February)
Roebuck	Easter to Michaelmas (29 September)
Roe	Michaelmas to Candlemas
Boar	Nativity of Our Lady (8 September) to Candlemas
Hare	Michaelmas to Candlemas
Coney	all seasons

Besides those listed above, still other animals were worthy prey. Before their extinction in the Middle Ages, aurochs were the largest and most dangerous game animal native to continental Europe. This wild ox had great horns which made the largest drinking vessels. Wolves and foxes were hunted for sport, hides and for population control or extermination; the latter was sadly successful in most parts of Europe. Although William the Conqueror set a penalty of blinding for anyone who killed a deer or boar in his vast deer preserve, rights of 'warren' were often granted to kill foxes, hares, badgers, of whose skins bolt quivers were made, squirrels, wild cats, martens and otters, that he considered pests.

Most kinds of birds were hunted: swans, herons and storks, as well as geese and ducks. Archers would use blunt arrowheads or stonebows to avoid unduly tearing up the game, or forked heads to cut off a wing of a flying goose or swan. Among the smaller birds were partridge, quail, woodcock, doves, crows, blackbirds and larks. All these kinds of birds were not only hunted, but also eaten, even by nobles. In Italy the custom of eating songbirds continues, much to the anguish of many bird lovers in northern Europe who find bird songs diminishing as more and more birds that fly south for the winter do not return each year.

Apart from the nobility who hunted for sport, and the poor who hunted for food, some men were professional hunters. Ordinarily they were interested in obtaining fur, especially in the northern regions of Scandinavia and Russia, which was then traded to all parts of Europe. Not as much fur was used in the Middle Ages as is popularly supposed, and its use was regulated by law. For common people, only lamb, hare and fox were permitted. Barons were permitted vair, grey, sable and ermine. Vair, used in the linings of mantles and surcotes and on caps, was made from the skins of northern arboreal squirrels, the upper bluish grey fur, called grey or gris, and the white underbelly also called vair, cut separately and sewn together to form the patterns of vair and countervair, familiar to students of heraldry. Finns or Lapps were the major suppliers of the skins of these squirrels, which they hunted with blunt arrows for meat as well as fur. The fur of martens was used in royal sable mantles.

In addition to the pleasures of the hunt, the nobleman (and the outlaw) also took much pleasure in dining on the game he bagged. Venison was the favourite repast. In 1429 the coronation feast of Henry VII included 'venyson rosted and frument with venyson'. In 1458 Froissart attended a great feast in seven courses for the King of France and his court. The feast was given by our old friend Gaston, Count de Foix, and Prince de Viane, and as we might expect, enormous quantities of game and poultry featured. Some recipes of the period (some prepared in the kitchens of Richard II) that we would not be surprised to find on the table were as follows.

Venison or Beef Steak

Take venison or beef and slice and grill it up brown. Then take vinegar and a little verjuice and a little wine, and put powdered pepper thereon enough and powdered ginger. And at the dresser strew on powdered cinnamon enough, that the steaks may be all covered therewith and but a little sauce. And then serve it forth.'

Mediaeval recipes give the ingredients but do not tell how much of each to use. 'Verjuice' was the juice of such sour fruits as crab apples, green grapes or gooseberries, sometimes fermented, used in preparing meat, fish and eggs. The 'dresser' referred to was the serving table on which the food was placed by the kitchen staff to be picked up by the service personnel.

Frumenty

Take wheat picked clean, hulled, winnowed and washed. Then boiled until it bursts, beaten up with milk, mixed with yolks of eggs, heated but not burned, coloured with saffron, seasoned with sugar and salt and served.

Venison was commonly served with frument or frumenty, the dish resembling cream of wheat or American grits. Frumenty may be prepared today from cracked wheat (bulgur wheat).

Venison in a Pasty

Take haunches of venison, parboil it in fair water and salt. Then take fair paste and lay thereon the venison cut in pieces as thou wilt have it and cast under it and above it powder of ginger, or pepper and salt mixed together. And set them in an oven and let them bake til they be enough. Parboiling should be at barely a simmer, to prevent too much loss of juices which should be kept for later use.

These were the venison pasties so loved by Friar Tuck in the Robin Hood ballads similar to Scottish Forfar Bridies. The 'fair paste' is pastry dough rolled into a disc. After laying on the contents it is folded double, the edges dampened and pressed together to seal. This should be pierced with a knife to allow steam to escape. Half an hour in a hot oven should be enough baking. Both fresh and salt venison, highly seasoned with pepper and ginger, was put into pasties, which were made to be eaten hot or were filled up on cooling with clarified butter for a cold bakement. A fifteenth-century recipe from Harleian Collection manuscript No.279 is for a venison pie much like the venison pasty above.

Venyson Y-bake

Take hoghes of Venyson, & parboyle hem in fayre Water an Salt; & whan the Fleyssche is fayre y-boylid, make fayre past, & caste thin Venison ther-on; & caste a-boue an be-nethe, pouder Pepir, Gyngere, & Salt, & than sette it on the ouyn, & lat bake, & serue forth.

This time venison shanks, parboiled in salted water, are cut up, placed on a disc of dough and spiced with a mixture of pepper, salt and ginger. It is not clear if the venison is to be covered with more dough or perhaps formed into a pasty. It is then baked in the oven until the crust is lightly browned.

Sometimes deer carcasses, after being hung for several days, were roasted whole on a spit. Basting was done with butter, oil, fine suet rendered up with cinnamon or simple salt and water. Roast venison was eaten with a strong pepper and vinegar sauce (*poivrade* or *peverade*) or salt and cinnamon, or powdered ginger. An Elizabethan sauce was composed of vinegar, sugar, cinnamon and butter boiled together. Charlemagne's huntsman brought him his roasts on a spit, which he preferred to the boiled meat advised by his physician. Freshly killed deer were sometimes immediately salted for preservation.

Roe Broth

Take flesh of boar or roe-buck; parboil it in small pieces, seethe it well in half water and half wine. Take bread and grind it with the same broth and add blood. Let it seethe together with Powder-fort [strong powder] of ginger or of cinnamon and mace with a great proportion of vinegar and currants.

Venison could also be boiled, with parsley, sage, ground pepper, cloves, mace, vinegar and a little red wine.

Noumbles

Take noumbles of Deer or of other beest; parboyle hem; kerf hem to dyce. Take the self broth or better; take brede and grynde with the broth and temper it up with a good quantity of vinegar and wyne. Take the onyons and parboyle hem, and mynce hem smale and do ther-to. Color it with blode and do ther-to powdor fort and salt, boyle it wele, and serve it forth.

The noumbles, or humbles, were the organs such as the heart and kidneys, traditionally allotted to the huntsman. Robin Hood ballads state that he served noumbles to his 'guests'. One form of 'powdor fort' would be ginger, mace and pepper ground together.

Humble Pie

Take your humbles being parboiled, and choppe them verye small with a good quantity of mutton suet and halfe a handful of herbes following; time, marjoram, borage, parseley and a little rosemary, and season the same being chopped, with pepper, cloves and mace, and so close your pie and bake him.

Pork Loin in Boar's Tail Sauce

First put the loin in boiling water, then take it out and stick it all over with cloves. Set it to roast, basting it with a sauce made from spices: that is, ginger, cinnamon, cloves, grains, long pepper, and nutmeg, moistened with verjuice, wine, and vinegar: and baste with this without first boiling it. And when the roast is done, boil it together. This sauce might also be thickened with breadcrumbs.

Wild boar, though not as much loved as venison, was a favourite meat especially when in season in late autumn.

The culinary and other delights of the hunt were difficult to resist for many Englishmen, all of whom had longbows and knew how to use them, and for the forest outlaws, in trouble with the law in any case, they were a necessary means of survival. Of course arrows with steel broadheads were not permitted to commoners within the royal forests although blunt arrows were allowed. 'Arkes et setes hors de foreste, et en foreste ark et piles.'

The poacher, like the nobleman, preferred venison. Since his risk was considerable in any case, he might as well go for the best. Such deer as wandered beyond the pale, outside the confines of the doubtful sanctuary of game parks, were fair game, but many men did not care to wait for them to come out. Poachers were armed with handbows or arbalests for the game, and whatever other weapons they deemed necessary to protect themselves against the foresters. Some used hounds. Scotland's forest laws, the 'Leges Forestarium', required that 'a man following his dog into the king's forest must divest himself of bows and arrows or bind them with his bowstring.' Swineherds were permitted entry to get acorns but their dogs had to be 'lawed', their claws cut off to the skin.

Some bands of outlaws, as in the ballads of Robin Hood or Adam Bell, who faced death in any case if caught, simply lived in the royal forests and took such deer as they wanted. Outlawry meant being deprived of any legal protection so that anything done to an outlaw had no legal penalty.

When a poacher was caught, penalties could be severe. Cnut, England's Danish king, permitted every freeman to hunt on his own lands but poaching in the royal forests was severely punished. For a first offence a freeman lost his liberty, and a villein his right hand. Being caught a second time was likely to mean death. Some poachers were killed out of hand when caught in the act. An under-keeper to Thomas, second Lord of Berkeley 'slew one Clift stealing deer, with a forker out of his crossbow'. Another of Thomas' servants found a man netting hares in his master's wood and killed him with an arrow. It was perhaps because of poachers that in his 1590 book, *Certaine Discourses Military*, John Smythe's gamekeeper promised to always have in readiness 'one able bow of yew and a sheaf of arrows, with a bracer and shooting glove, a sword and a dagger'.

In his Forest Charter, Henry II relaxed the severity of these punishments, rescinding those depriving the poacher of life and limb. However, if caught in the act he would be subject to a heavy fine, and in default of payment be imprisoned for a year and a day, after which he should find surety for his future behaviour or be banished from the land. As is usual in instances in which punishments are terribly severe but convictions are few, poaching continued. During the reign of Henry VII, 'Robin Hood bands' with masked or blackened faces 'were killing the king's deer with impunity, with none to say them nay.'

Apprehending poachers in the royal forests was the duty of the green-clad foresters, some mounted, who patrolled the royal forests armed with quarter staves, swords, bows and arrows. Foresters served under wardens and the chief forester would be resident at the nearest castle. Few ballads are sympathetic to foresters. At best they are portrayed as just doing their job, at worst as arrogant, bloodthirsty bullies, known for extortion and other infringements of the law, including poaching themselves. Local villagers tended to favour the poachers. They saw nothing, heard nothing, and failed to raise the hue and cry required by law.

Forests granted to barons were not under royal forest law and less severe punishments were specified. However, the baron's foresters could arrest poachers when caught in the act.

Dog draw
Stable stand
Back berond
Bloody hand

This old rhyme lists conditions under which a man in a hunting preserve would be considered a poacher: pursuing a deer with a dog; being settled to shoot; carrying a deer on his back; and being caught 'red-handed'. The malefactor would be held in prison until a fine was paid to the baron. In the Scottish ballad of Johny Cock, the gentlemanly poacher is told:

> There are seven forsters at Pickeram Side,
> At Pickeram where they dwell,
> And for a drop of thy hearts bluid,
> They wad ride the fords of hell.

Johny is later attacked by the foresters as he lies sleeping with his dogs beside his kill. In *Robin Hood's Progress to Nottingham* there is another conflict:

> Robin Hood he would to fair Nottingham
> With the general for to dine,
> There he was ware of fifteen forresters,
> And a drinking beer, ale and wine.

Their insolent baiting of young Robin results in them being terminally silenced by the latter's arrows.

The foresters' job could be dangerous. In May 1246, in Brockingham Forest near Beanfield, the foresters William, Roger and Matthew were on the alert for potential poachers who might take advantage of the cover provided by the newly green foliage. Word had come to their ears of poachers in the vicinity with greyhounds come to slay the King's deer and at last their vigil was rewarded as five hunting greyhounds came into view. The foresters caught four of them but the fifth, a tawny one, escaped. After taking the dogs the foresters returned to the forest and again lay in ambush. This time they saw the tawny greyhound again and they saw 'five poachers in the lord king's demene of Wydehawe, one with a crossbow and four with bows and arrows, standing at their trees. And when the foresters perceived them, they hailed and pursued them.' The records of the court continue:

> And the aforesaid rnalefactors, standing at their trees, turned in defence and shot arrows at the foresters so that they wounded Matthew, the forester of the park of Brigstock, with two Welsh arrows, to wit with one arrow under the left breast, to the depth of one hand slantwise, and with the second arrow in the left arm to the depth of two fingers, so that it was despaired of the life of the said Matthew.

The foresters continued their pursuit of the poachers who turned and fled into the depths of the forest and, as night fell, made good their escape. Matthew died of his wounds but the poachers were never taken.

In times of peace poachers could expect little mercy; however, during times of war a poacher or an outlaw might get a pardon, even for murder, in return for military service.

25

WARFARE

Certes the Frenchmen and Rutters deriding our new archerie in respect of their corslets, will not let in open skirmish, if any leisure serue, to turn up their tailes and crie: Shoote English, and all because our strong shooting is decaied and laid in bed. But if some of our Englishmen now lived that serued King Edward the third in his warres with France, the breech of such a varlet should have been nailed to his bum with one arrow, and an other fethered in his bowels, before he should have turned about to see who shot the first.

William Harrison, *Description of Britain*[50]

It was the English who recognised the full and terrible potential of the use of archery in warfare, and the English archer of the Hundred Years War had no equal in all of Christendom. Archers formed by far the bulk of English armies for centuries. Although nobles and even kings were practised in the use of the bow, military archers were usually men of lower birth. Early statutes required a man to arm himself according to his income, and those with higher incomes, usually derived from land holdings, appeared for military service with costly armour, horses, swords and lances, while the common folk used the bows and arrows they were required to have for local defence. Uniforms were not yet general though some archers wore 'liveries', suits of clothes provided by their lords or home districts.

In the earlier Middle Ages armies were mustered by conscription, the old feudal levy system, and the soldiers had to be released at harvest time. Levies were abolished by Edward III and his archers were volunteers – and decently paid ones at that – recruited for service under contract to a nobleman or to the King himself. One archer was enlisted to stay with Edward's army 'until he had shot away his arrowes'. Officially, there were to be three archers to each lance, or man-at-arms, but there were sometimes fewer, usually many more. Some knights, like the one described in Chaucer's *The Canterbury Tales*, had a single archer in their service.

The best amongst them were called yeomen, men pledged to the service of a lord. The word had the connotation of solid dependability and was also respectfully applied to peasants who worked their own piece of land, a rise in status for many serfs who survived the Black Death.

> These were they that in times past made all France afraid and albeit they be not called 'Master', as gentlemen are, or 'Sir' as to knights appertaineth, but only 'John' and 'Thomas' etc., yet have they been found to have done very good service. The kings of England in foughten battles were wont to remain among them who were their footmen, as the French kings did amongst their horsemen, the prince thereby shewing where his chief strength did consist.

The preferred archers were tall, strong, and between 18 and 46 years of age. They were known for their belief that they were the finest men in the world as well as for their steadiness under attack and grim determination in their advance. Welsh archers were included in early English armies but after 1401, all had to be native Englishmen.

As discussed in previous chapters, the English archer was practised to shoot hard and fast and far, and to make his mark up to the full range of his flight arrows. In an emergency he could shoot two or three arrows at once. His back and shoulders were strong from his years of practice and he was used to walking and running from retrieving his arrows at the very long distances he shot.

The yeoman did a lot of walking. Although there eventually were mounted archers, most were on foot, and they trudged from one campaign to the next. Burgundian armies, mostly mounted, were ordained to march at least five leagues daily for two days, being permitted to rest on the third day if necessary.

The archer's spiritual needs were seen to by a chaplain. When the Englishmen first learned the size of the French forces at Agincourt in 1415, they lined up for last rites, and before the battle, heard more than one mass.

When it came to more earthly needs, English soldiers often had to fend for themselves. While expeditions were initially well supplied with food and wine, the yeoman's food and drink was foraged when possible, and this was the job of the archers and other foot soldiers. At the beginning of the Hundred Years War, France was ideal for foraging, but in a land overrun with armed men, forage was sometimes scarce and each '*chevauchée*,' the mounted raids conducted for plunder and devastation, reduced it further. Big-bellied cogs of the Hanseatic League sailed southward, their holds full of stockfish, unsalted dried haddock and cod from Norway. This was the emergency ration of the English army; but preparing the hard stockfish required time and labour. After the French instituted a scorched earth policy, roots and bark became part of the archer's diet. Only as a last resort would a mediaeval soldier drink water. Archers in the Dover Castle garrison had a daily ration of five pints of wine.

When an archer entered military service little additional training or conditioning was necessary, apart from learning to take his place in a formation rather like a modern infantry company. A 'centenier' was responsible for the 100-man training unit, a 'vintinier' for 20 men, and a 'decentenier' for a ten-man squad. In *Certaine Discourses Military*, John Smythe noted that archers could stand eight or ten deep in their 'herse' formations, in rank and file, and shoot over each other's heads. 'Archers of the first sort' presumably were in the first rank where they could shoot point blank when the enemy was close enough. Archers were expected to shoot at least ten aimed arrows a minute (a minute was first recognised in the fifteenth century). The Duke of York struck off four of his 300 archers who failed the test following the 1415 siege of Harfleur that began Henry V's French campaign.

Crossbows were the favoured missile weapon until Edward III made the change to longbows. In 1192 Richard the Lionheart, learning of an impending attack by Saladin's forces at Jaffa, had placed his outnumbered infantry for defence. Tent pegs were thrust into the ground to impede a cavalry charge. A line of spearmen knelt behind their long shields planted in the ground, their spear butts against the earth, the spearheads at the height of a horse's breast. Behind them stood two lines of 400 crossbowmen, the first line to shoot and the second line to cock and reload. They repelled seven charges of Saracen horsemen who finally abandoned the attack.

The Black Prince had as many archers as men-at arms but in the later army of Edward IV, archers outnumbered men-at-arms by ten to one. When attack was imminent and circumstances permitted, the archers took up positions on an elevation with the wind and sun at their backs so that the range of their arrows would be increased and they would not have to shoot into the sun, the enemy being of course in reversed circumstances. In early pitched battles archers were devastating to enemy infantry but were vulnerable to cavalry attack. In response, before Agincourt, Henry V ordered that each archer provide himself with a six-foot square or round staff pointed on both ends. The archers set these pointing forward, the points waist high, targeting the French horses. After Agincourt each archer carried a pair of six- or seven-foot wooden stakes tipped at both ends with pointed iron ferrules. These were attached together and hung over the shoulder, one before and one behind. To drive in the stakes without blunting the points, the archer carried at his back a lead maul with a five-foot handle. The leaden head was bound with iron bands and the maul, that could weigh as much as 25lbs, was also used as a weapon at close quarters; it could crush in a knight's helmet like an eggshell.

Ditches might be dug before the stakes to form a further obstacle, the earth removed being piled on the archer's side of the ditch. At the Battle of Crecy in 1346, archers dug potholes a foot wide and a foot deep to impede a mounted attack and 'caltrops' were strewn about to cripple the horses. These were made with four pointed iron spikes, one to always stand upright.

Archers were generally positioned in relation to the 'battles', the rectangular bodies of dismounted knights and men-at-arms. Separate formations of archers were placed either in the vanguard, in the rear, in 'wings' or 'sleeves' at the sides of the battle, or in forlorn hopes, small groups advanced and detached from the main body. When the enemy also had a large number of archers, archers were usually placed in the vanguard, the result usually being a bloody slaughter on both sides. A nearly contemporary illustration for Jehan de Wavrin's *Chroniques D'Angleterre* shows a vanguard three or four ranks deep, in front of and separated from the main battle. Polearms are shown within the formation indicating that the archers were mixed with other infantry. Archers in the forward slanting wings could shower an enemy attack against

Mediæval commanders ordered their squadrons of archers to support the main battles of men-at-arms in—
the rear
sleeves
the van
wings
or
'forlorn hopes

the main battle with a hail of arrows on the flanks until the last moment. Formations were as much as eight or ten men deep.

A 'herse' formation is mentioned by the chronicler Froissart, writing in the fourteenth century, but it has not been determined exactly what he meant by the term. Herse may mean 'hedgehog' or 'harrow' and most harrows of the period are shown as a squared lattice construction with pegs at the junctures. This would mean a formation of rank and file, not staggered ranks.

A detailed description of such a formation in William Neade's 1625 book *The Double Armed Man* may describe an earlier practice. The archers take up a square formation, files straight, line by line. The men in the first rank shoot breast high, the men in the second rank raise their bowhands to the height of the leaders' heads. Roving was practised in order to learn to judge distance accurately. The range of their arrows was 18–20 score while fire arrows, each carrying an ounce of 'fire work,' could be shot 12 score. The last arrow was loosed when the enemy had closed to 5 score yards.

Before the charge of the enemy knights, English archers sometimes had to shoot it out with opposing archers or crossbowmen. They usually prevailed in a contest of this kind unless they faced other Englishmen, but at Verneuil in 1424 they found themselves facing Scottish archers in the service of the French. The English archers, in wing formation, planted their stakes 'in the English fashion' and advanced with shouts. Jehan de Wavrin, a seasoned Burgundian veteran who had survived Agincourt on the French side and Patay on the English side, wrote that they 'began to shoot against each other so murderously that it was horrible to watch.'

When enemy forces had approached to about 400 yards, the archers prepared to shoot, spilling their arrows on the ground, or sticking them upright before them. At this range they chose flight arrows with light barbed heads that were not meant to

During the Wars of the Roses, English archers faced other English archers. Note the sword and buckler combination. (British Library Board)

pierce armour, but 'to gall or astoyne the enemy'. These arrows were meant primarily for the horses.

On command, the archers each took one pace forward and shot 'wholly together' in volley and the first shower or drift of arrows shot in high arc hit the attacking formation. A shower was not a random barrage at any range; each arrow had its chosen mark. A single arrow, shot 200 yards or so, seems to fly almost lazily, looking deceptively harmless. A man has time to dodge it or deflect it with his shield. It is even possible to catch it in the hand. A volley of arrows is a bit different. A man dodging one arrow merely places himself in the path of another.

> Our archery was such, that the arrows, flying in the air as thick as snow, with a terrible noise, much like a tempestuous wind preceding a tempest, they did leave no disarmed place of horse or man unstricken.

Sir John Smythe noted in the waning days of English military archery that an arrow would still kill or wound in any part of its flight:

> If in their descents they light not upon the enemy's faces, yet in their lower descents they light either upon their breasts, bellies, codpieces, thighs, knees, or legs, and in their lowest descent fall even to the very nailing of their feet to the ground.

Horses struck by the arrows became completely unmanageable. With the barbed arrows jouncing in their flesh, they galloped aimlessly in terror or bucked and kicked until their riders were thrown. A French chronicler wrote that 'the Englishmen's bearded arrows drove the horses mad.' It was said that the outcome of a battle could be told at the sixth arrow.

When the enemy had advanced to twenty score, 240 yards, the heavier sheaf arrows were clapped across the great longbows and seconds later they struck home. This was the range at which the skill of an archer was measured, the effective range for the armour-piercing arrows. Armour light enough to be practical in combat could not be made thick enough to offer sure protection against the can-opener effect of a heavy bodkin. Now the real carnage began. At maximum range the archers all shot upward at an angle of about 45 degrees for longest distance. As the distance reduced, the men in the front ranks lowered their elevation and those in the rear ranks raised theirs so that the charging knights were subjected both to arrows falling from above as well as being shot directly at them. Froissart wrote of Poitiers, where the Earl of Oxford ordered the archers to shoot for the horses, that the archers 'shot so thick that the Frenchmen wist not on what side to take heed'.

An impression of the devastation of massed shooting can be conveyed by simple numbers. Consider an English force of 150 archers and 50 knights, a typical proportion, in a good defensive position, each archer being equipped with the standard sheaf of 24 arrows and being able to shoot an aimed arrow every six seconds. Opposed to them a formation of 600 enemy knights, odds of four to one. But if these knights could not cover 400 yards in less than two and a half minutes, they and their horses stood to absorb 24 'drifts' totalling 3600 aimed arrows before they had even gotten close enough to use their weapons.

From archers ordered on the wings of a battle, arrows would be coming at a knight from both sides when he was close enough to couch his lance. If he was still able, he thundered on, dodging, jumping or stumbling over fallen kicking, screaming horses and comrades, doubtless alternating curses with prayers to his God for the chance to skewer at least one or two of the archers on his lance. Then he would reach the ditched hedge of stakes where he had to make the quick decision either to continue his charge, uselessly impaling his horse in the process, or to stop, discard his useless lance, and fight hand-to-hand with the fresh knights and billmen now joined by nimble archers who had cast aside their bows and taken up their swords, axes, mauls and daggers, or even their stakes to be used as weapons.

The reader may get the impression that archers could hardly be beaten, and indeed at the Battle of Crecy, the English defeated the attacking force at odds of seventeen to one, primarily through use of archery. There were even reported instances of individual archers positioned on hummocks in marshy areas. There, more or less invulnerable to mounted attack, they could strip to the waist for unencumbered shooting. But archers were not invulnerable, and the Burgundian Jehan de Wavrin wrote; 'I am of the opinion that the most important thing in battle is the archers, but they must be in the thousands, for in small numbers they do not prevail.'

At the Battle of Nogent in 1359 the English had, as usual, chosen favourable ground for defence, but French reinforcements advanced behind shields large enough for a man to be completely protected from arrows. John Smythe relates that French commanders in Edward III's time

... caused their footmen (although they were as well armed for the defense of their
bodies and heads as footmen nowadays are) to carry pavises of seven feet long, and a
foot and a half or two broad, with little holes toward the upper end armed with steel
for them to look through, which pavises did cover their faces and all other disarmed
parts even down to their toes.

The French broke through the archers and routed the entire English formation. But
five years later at Auray, frustrated English archers faced with a similar advance cast
aside their bows, rushed the French and killed them with their own axes.

As discussed above, if their defences were inadequate, archers were vulnerable to
cavalry attack. Unsupported by men-at-arms or caught by surprise at close quarters,
they could be overrun and wiped out very quickly, and after Agincourt the French
began to seriously work at catching them by surprise, as at the Battle of Patay, or at
night. Improved ordinance and armour also reduced their effectiveness. Nonetheless,
the archers' only rivals as the supreme infantry force in Europe at this time were the
Swiss pikemen and halberdiers, with whom they did have one encounter (see below).

It was vital for men-at-arms to have the support of archers. Infantry could not
keep up with a rapid mounted advance so as the Hundred Years War dragged on,
horse-archers became more usual and by the end of the war they outnumbered the
unmounted archers. Those recruited in England in 1424 were inspected by commis-
sioners who had to provide lists of names under oath, and check bows and arrows
at each muster. 'All the archers, one after the other, were made to shoot at the butts'
and they had to show that they had sufficient arrows, as well as swords, bucklers, caps,
cloaks and proper liveries. Each was also required to bring his own horse to muster
on pain of a possible fine of half his pay. They wore a helmet or steel skull cap fitting
close to the head, and had a coat of mail and some body armour. Each man carried
his bow and a quiver of 24 arrows on his back or at his right side, but arrows used
in action were held under the sword belt. Eight of his arrows were long-range flight
arrows. Although these men usually fought on foot after reaching the battlefield, they
also shot from horseback. As we have discussed earlier, while a longbow is manageable
on horseback, smallbows may also have been used by mounted men.

Mounted Scottish archers served with Charles the Bold, Duke of Burgundy. His
ordinance of 1473 specified field training; archers were to be drilled in dismounting,
drawing their bows, advancing briskly to shoot while retaining formation. Pikemen
who preceded them were to kneel, with pike points at the level of a horse's back
while the archers shot over their heads. The archers' horses were tied by their bridles
in groups of three to the saddle bow of their commanding man-at-arms' page who
followed closely behind. In defence, archers were to form a circle or square, again
behind the pikemen, who were to pursue the enemy should they retreat. Alternatively,
archers were to defend themselves standing back to back.

In the early days of the Hundred Years War, the yeoman might have seen sea duty.
Before the actual fighting, there was much difficult manoeuvering of the square-
sailed craft to gain the advantage of wind and sun. Cannon were not used on ships
before Tudor times and sea battles were fought out with slung stones and boulders,

A sea battle, perhaps Sluys, during the Hundred Years War. The ship belongs to the Earl of Warwick and flies his banner as well as his pennon displaying the bear and ragged staff badges. (Beauchamp Chronicles, 1485. The British Library)

quick-lime, timbers and bars of iron dumped on the enemy ship, as well as the arrows and quarrels of archers and crossbowmen which, with the stones of the slingers, were the only effective missile weapons. In addition to picking off men, archers used fire arrows to ignite unfurled sails. On the 'carracks,' much used in the Hundred Years War, archers were stationed by preference in the raised castles fore and aft, and in the crow's nest. On the *Mary Rose*, wooden screens protected the archers in the castles. Sliding panels enabled the archers to shoot between them.

Men-at-arms were useless except during a boarding. When two opposing ships got close enough, iron grappling hooks attached to chains were thrown out to pull the ships together, and the men-at-arms attempted to board and capture the enemy ship. Sometimes ships changed hands more than once in the course of a battle. Sea fights were always fiercer than fights on land because retreat and flight were impossible. The entire crew of a captured ship was usually killed to prevent them from retaking the ship.

During the Battle of Sluys in 1340, the French had chained their ships together to form a floating fortress as the Vikings had done in times past. On one end, 20,000 Genoese crossbowmen were stationed on captured English ships. The English arranged their fleet in the formations used in land battles: men-at-arms in the middle squadron, archers and crossbowmen in squadrons on each flank, and a fourth squadron in reserve. The English loosed 'an iron shower of bolts from crossbows and arrows from bows' enabling English men-at-arms to board the French vessels and send the French crewmen to a watery grave.

Archers and crossbowmen as well as slingers were also useful in both besieging and defending castles and walled towns. The proud feudal barons of England were not easy to control and were a constant threat to law and order and at times to the king himself. So it was that Henry II placed the building and occupation of castles under his own power. A written licence to 'crenellate' was issued only to such barons as he trusted, crenellations adding greatly to the defensibility of a castle. (Crenellations formed an 'embattled' edge as part of the defensive structure atop walls.)

The part of the wall that was crenellated was the 'parapet', the upper part of the curtain wall that screened the wall walk and provided protection for the defenders in that position. This arrangement had been used since Norman times. The solid portions were called 'merlons', the open parts were called 'embrasures' or 'crenels'. The whole structure constitutes the 'battlements'. In the merlons, in the towers where the spiral staircase gave access and in the curtain walls where one or two passages ran the length of the wall, might be arrow loops. These were vertical openings about a yard long and only a few inches wide on the outside but broad at the inside of the thick wall to offer a wider field of vision and shooting for the archer or crossbowman, an angle of perhaps 90 degrees. Those with a sloping fishtail opening at the bottom allowed for better downward shooting. Some arrow loops in the form of a cross were occupied by three archers at the same time. These might have round openings called 'oilets' at the four ends, as can be seen at Warwick Castle.

While an arrow loop made a pretty narrow target of a man behind it, it must be remembered that an attacking archer who could split a wand could also put an arrow through the narrow opening. Crossbowmen on the wall walk could shoot from an embrasure, then duck behind a merlon for reloading. If the missiles of the attacking archers and slingers became too effective, the archers could use the arrow loops in the merlons. During attacks the embrasures might be provided with 'hoardings', protective wooden shutters hung on hinges from the top that would be raised when the crossbowman or archer was shooting.

In addition to the usual crossbows, 'ballistae' – large heavy crossbows that had to be rested on the parapet – were also used. These were necessarily shot from an embrasure with an assistant cocking a spare bow behind a merlon. The device used for this was a heavy standing wooden apparatus with a long lever, the short end of which hooked onto the bowstring. The similar 'springalds' cast a javelin that could skewer three men at a time.

A well kept fortification would be kept clear of trees and brush within a bowshot from the walls to deprive attacking archers of cover, but archers advancing under cover of mantlets could get close enough to shoot fire arrows to burn the wooden gate. If the castle was of the type with round towers projecting from the corners of the wall, the defending archers had a good clear enfilading shot at anyone right up to the foot of the wall, at which point the attackers would also be bombarded with boulders, timbers and quicklime dropped from the parapet. Inside, murder holes in the floors enabled defenders to shower attackers with arrows, spears and boiling water. If the besiegers made it inside the walls, more difficulties awaited them. Narrow staircases wound upwards in a clockwise spiral giving the advantage to the defending right-handed swordsman or archer while the attacker was hampered by the wall. At the top of the stairs a low doorway made it necessary for an attacker to stoop, placing his head and neck in position for beheading.

Rather than attempting a frontal attack on a well-defending castle or town, some commanders had their miners dig tunnels to undermine and collapse walls or blocked the inflow of supplies to starve the inhabitants into submission, unless time was of the essence. The attacking army often pitched camp a 'little more than a bowshot' from the wall and waited for the defenders' supplies to run out. To command access, wooden towers constructed from locally available materials were built around the castle or city and manned with archers. Other archers shot arrows over the walls with propaganda leaflets tied to the shafts.

In a determined attack, siege engines like 'trebuchets' might be constructed from local materials and brought into play, casting huge boulders to breach the walls. Alternatively, movable siege towers called 'belfreys' were constructed to the height of the castle wall. They were usually covered with fresh hides so they could not easily be burned, and provided with wheels so they could be rolled forward. These towers were partly manned with archers whose job was to keep the defenders occupied, enabling men-at-arms in the upper part of the tower to gain the battlements. Froissart describes such belfries at the siege of Reole in 1345, this time used to provide cover for miners digging tunnels to undermine the wall.

> ... the Englishmen that had made in the mean space two belfries of great timber with three stages. Every belfry in four great wheels, and the sides towards the town were covered with cure-boly (hides) to defend them from fire and from shot, and into every stage there was pointed an hundred archers. By strength of men these two belfries were brought to the walls of the town for they had so filled the dikes that they might be brought just to the walls. The archers in these stages shot so wholly together that none durst appear at their defence unless they were pavised by shields; and between these two belfries there were two hundred men with pick-axes to mine the walls, and so they brake through the walls.

Attacking crossbowmen, especially vulnerable while cocking their crossbows, sometimes used pavises or mantlets for protection. Pavises were provided with a movable prop so they could be stood upright on the ground. After cocking, the crossbowman could shoot over the top of the pavise or through a small peep hole in it. Mantlets were larger wooden shields, sometimes on wheels, which would be used in a siege, sometimes by longbowmen as well as crossbowmen.

In attacks archers were ordered to set up their shouts to stimulate their courage and cow the enemy. The archers' shout described by Froissart was 'hahay, hahay!' perhaps derived from driving game. At the First Battle of St Albans (1455) at the beginning of the Wars of the Roses, the Earl of Warwick's archers sounded their trumpets and raised the shout, 'A Warrewe, a Warrewyck, a Warrewyck!' as they nocked their arrows.

Archers on the ground busied themselves picking off exposed defenders or dropping arrows inside the walls. These might be fire arrows, with small barbed heads to

The Earl of Warwick,
supported by a
vanguard of archers
facing a vanguard of
crossbowmen, one of
whom has already been
repaid for his temerity.
(Courtesy of the
British Library Board)

stick and hang in a hoarding, a thatched roof, timber or clothing while they burned. The barrage of arrows and slung stones would be intensified when the scaling ladders were used to gain the parapet. When a castle or city refused to surrender, and was finally taken at the cost of lives and material, little mercy was shown the defenders by the victorious commander, and the archers frequently indulged in an orgy of rape and pillage.

Surprisingly in this brutal time, the knights, who somewhat corresponded to present-day military officers, often did all in their power to prevent this or at least to curb the worst excesses, especially protecting noblewomen, such as when Edward III occupied the castle of Pois and found it deserted except for two noblewomen 'who would have been raped by the low-born archers had not two noted knights … rescued them.'

During the frequent and sometimes lengthy truces during the Hundred Years War the English archers returned to England. Many of these veterans wandered the roads with beggars and other indigents of no fixed address until such time as hostilities were resumed. This vagabondage had become more common following the years of the Black Death when the labour force was reduced by half and a common man could find employment elsewhere than his birthplace. A law of 1376 forbade ordinary vagabonds to misrepresent themselves as discharged archers, gentlemen or men-at-arms, which some found it profitable to do.

During the periods of truce not all the fighting men freed of military obligations went home. Some preferred to continue with their life of pillage and did so privately as *ecorcheurs*, or enlisted as mercenaries under commanders of Free Companies who sold their services to the highest bidder throughout Europe. These had already been in existence at the end of the thirteenth century. Some served in Italy in the White Company, the condottiere of Sir John Hawkwood under contract to one city state or another. Hawkwood got a good price because, unlike many of the companies, he provided dependable service. The Florentines erected a statue to this condottier who maintained their independence. Being English and a war veteran, Hawkwood employed 2500 cavalry and 2000 longbowmen while the notorious Fra Moriale, who had been expelled from the Order of St John, had 7000 mounted men-at-arms and 2000 crossbowmen in his Grand Company. No other condottier but Hawkwood used longbowmen.

Archers were also sent to the assistance of kings in other lands. English archers served in Norway, Brittany, Italy, Spain and even Africa, and in Burgundy 3000 English archers formed the flower of the infantry of Charles the Bold in his final conflict with the Swiss Eidgenossen at Morat. These archers, caught by surprise, died by Swiss pike and halberd. As a result, archery fell out of favour with continental princes but in the Britain, the use of archery and the Wars of the Roses, continued.

Military Archers' Equipment

The soldiers were clothed in a kind of thick felt, and coats of mail as ample as they were strong, which protected them against arrows. I have seen soldiers with up to twenty-one arrows stuck on their bodies marching no less easily for that. They on the contrary pierced us with their spears, killing horse and rider at the same time.

Baha ed Din[51]

'Make glad chere,'sayd Lytell Johan,
'And drese our bowes of ewe,
And loke your hertes be seker and sad,
Your strynges trusty and trewe.

A Lytel Geste of Robyn Hode

Some mediaeval illustrations show archers in full armour. Noblemen like William the Conqueror and Strongbow, who took pride in their archery skills, of course wore the armour befitting their station. Archers of the lower classes had less protection, the nature of which was specified by the villages, towns or lords who supplied it.

Each English archer carried his archery equipment and his other weapons. A 'livery' bow, his yew war bow, was provided by the crown for foreign service, as were his arrows. The bow was longer than he was used to, which lessened risk of breakage at crucial times. He was issued one or two sheaves of 24 arrows of which six or eight were flight shafts. It was boasted that 'every Englysshe archer beareth under hys girdle XXIIII Scottes,' a life for each arrow. The arrows were sometimes bundled into a sheaf or garb bound together with a thong and tied at or carried under his belt at his right side. A pull on a slipknot would spill them at his feet in time of need. Extra sheaves of arrows were transported in the supply wagons.

Two dozen arrows may not seem like many, but they were enough in most situations; cumulative muscle fatigue makes it difficult to shoot many more than this from a powerful bow within a few crucial minutes. This said, at the Battle of Morlaix in 1342, the archers were said to have 36 arrows each, and during the Battle of Poitiers in 1356 archers had to go onto the battlefield to retrieve arrows, even resorting to tearing them from the bodies of the wounded and dying. In 1355 the Black Prince requested 1000 bows and 2000 sheaves of arrows from the king's ordnance, but fewer were delivered.

Inside his helmet or under his armpit, the archer carried several spare strings, adjusted as to length, whipped and ready to clap on the bow at a moment's notice. Some archers, taking no chances, kept two strings on the bow at once, using one for shooting while the second hung slack, although,

> In warre, if a string breake, the man is lost; and is no man for his weapon is gone: and although he have two stringes put on at once, yet he shall have small leisure and lesse roome to bend his bowe; therefore God send us good stringers both for warre and peace.

The spare strings had yet another use; that of binding the hands of knights who had been taken prisoner. Ransom payments for captured noblemen were amongst the more lucrative fringe benefits of mediaeval warfare and this was not considered dishonourable as long as the prisoner was treated decently. One businesslike French nobleman even had the sum of his ransom engraved on his helmet. At Poitiers some archers had as many as five or six prisoners, and the prospect of an early retirement. Of course a captured archer was worth no ransom and would seldom survive. The opportunity for plunder was an added attraction for the archer and during the Hundred Years War nearly every woman in England was said to have received clothes, cutlery, furs or various household articles from France.

The archer's additional weapons were a sword and buckler or an axe, or at least a dagger. A mediaeval man was not really dressed without a dagger; even waiters at royal banquets carried long double-edged *baselards*. In 1512 archers sent to Guyenne also carried halberds that were placed on the ground when they used their bows.

In early mediaeval battles, archers, not usually involved in hand-to-hand combat, had little defensive arms apart from perhaps the aforementioned dagger or sword.. Protection later increased and archers came to have helmets in the style of the time as well as jackets or vests to protect the torso. Twelfth-century archers and crossbowmen of the crusaders were equipped with mail 'hauberks' (mail shirts), padded and quilted linen or leather, and iron caps.

These garments provided the protection of padding and/or metal. 'Haketons' or 'gambesons' were padded and quilted garments originally worn under armour to absorb the shock of a blow and, more heavily padded, were also used as outer garments by the infantry. 'Jacks' were made of from 10 to 30 layers of linen cloth, sometimes padded, sometimes with small steel plates. 'Brigandines' had small plates riveted inside canvas with a cloth or leather covering. 'Coats of plates' were similar, but with larger plates. These garments had short, half, or full sleeves, or none. Some were quilted vertically, or criss-cross, or not at all. Some were fastened with an off-centre row of buttons. French crossbowmen were additionally armed with an '*ensis*' or '*spata*' (sword), '*couteau*' (dagger), and sometimes a '*bloquerium*' (small shield or buckler).

In 1316 each 'layman in the realm having £10 in goods shall have for his body in defence of the realm a sufficient haketon, a basinet [a light helmet with a rounded or pointed top], gloves of plate, a spear and a sword.' However in 1415 the English archers that formed Henry V's 'yew hedge' that came ashore at St Vaast-La-Hague were not impressive. They were described as with 'bare feet and no shoes, scruffy doublets made of old bedding [actually layered used linen makes better armour] a poor iron skullcap, a bow and quiver of arrows in hand and a sword hanging at their side'. At Agincourt as described by Jehan de Wavrin who saw them from within the French ranks, they were 'for the most part in their doublets, without armour, their hose rolled down to their knees and having hatchets or great swords hanging at their girdles; some were barefooted and bareheaded, others had caps of boiled leather and others of osier, covered with harpoy [skins] or leather.' This shabby state is partly explained by the severe dysentery with which many of the English were afflicted at the time. The tops of the hose were sometimes unfastened for freedom of movement; in this case it was done for a more unpleasant reason.

After the slaughter at Agincourt, Charles VII reorganised his army and instituted the corps of 'francs archiers' who were armed with sword, dagger, bow and side quiver or crossbow garnie. They wore the brigandine or a heavy linen lined jack and the simple steel cap was replaced by the newly fashionable 'salade' (a helmet with a flared tail). Later versions of the salade, which also formed part of the knightly armour, had a visor with eye slits. Mounted archers had brigandines or good jacks with mail haubergeons (a shorter and sleeveless version of the hauberk), and leg armour, as well as the salades (*sallets*). Henry V required his mounted archers to have 'good jacks of defense, salads, swords, and sheeves of 40 arrows at least.'

At this time Charles the Bold reorganised and modernised the Burgundian forces, issuing a series of ordinances. A 'lance,' a 9-man unit, was to be formed of a man-at-arms, three mounted archers, a mounted 'coustillier', a mounted page or valet, a handgunner, a crossbowman, and a pikeman on foot. Later, some archers on foot were added. A 'coustillee' was a weapon between a sword and a dagger in length. The mounted archers had a bow and 30 arrows, a long, sharp, two-handed sword and a long double edged dagger. A blue and white jack with a red St Andrew's cross protected and identified them. Men-at-arms were issued a vermilion velvet St Andrew's cross.

Later requirements specified a brigandine over an aketon, splints (armour of metal strips attached to a leather base) for the arms, a 'gorgerine' or neck defence, a sallet, dagger and a lead hammer and a bow and quiver hanging behind. English archers also carried the lead mallets mentioned earlier to hammer in protective pointed stakes.

A year later there were more adjustments. This time a brigandine or sleeveless mail shirt under a 10-layer jack was specified. In the 1473 ordinance of Maximin de Treyes, Charles specified that his mounted archers should have a horse worth at least six francs, should wear a visorless sallet, a 'gorget', (the gorget was a late mediaeval plate collar protecting the neck and adjoining chest and shoulders; a similar mail defence was called a 'standard'), sword and dagger, forearms armoured so as not to impede shooting and knee-length boots with short spurs. The then fashionable piked toes were prohibited, as were puffed out doublet sleeves. Mounted crossbowmen were also to wear a brigandine or corselet, light armour on the arms, a gorget, a sallet and the same short spurs as the mounted archers. Further changes were not made, due to the death of Duke Charles, killed by a Swiss halberd at the Battle of Nancy in 1477.

Dominic Mancini described Richard III's English archers he observed in the 1480s.

> Only the wealthy had iron armour, the ordinary soldiers preferring tunics stuffed with tow, which reached down to their thighs. Indeed the common soldiery have more comfortable tunics that reach down below the loins and are stuffed with tow or some other soft material. They say that the softer the tunic the better do they withstand the blows of arrows and swords. The more tow there was, the better they were able to withstand blows.

These were jacks or haketons, presumably with the White Boar badge.

In 1481 John Howard, the later Duke of Norfolk, lent to one Harry Mainwaryng 'a peir of brigandines keuvred with purpil velvet, a salate, a standart, a chief [sheaf] of arrows, a peir of splentys [splints] and his jackette and a gusset [a section of mail]'.

The best archers of the mercenary Hawkwood's White Company (see p.203) had polished steel breastplates (hence the name), iron caps or helmets and mail gloves. Two men were assigned to each lance to withstand the first shock of an attack. Mounted archers had two horses each.

An ordinance of Louis XI of France (1461–1483) gives specifications for sleeved jacks, in the style of that time, of 25 or 30 layers of cloth with stag skin covering the torso. Used cloth, being more supple, was preferred, and mediaeval linen from London was finer than the usual found in today's stores. Such a jack, though made without metal plates, was considered proof against stabs or arrow wounds and reproductions have proven hard to penetrate.

The jack was to be made in four quarters, seams at sides, front and back. It would be laced in front, with an extra piece behind the opening of the same thickness as the jack and the sleeves. A standing collar, made like the rest of the jack, was not to be so high in back as to interfere with the tail of the sallet. The armhole of the roomy sleeves was to be large and placed near the collar, not on the shoulder bone. It was to be broad under the armpit and full under the arm.

An engraving by Albrecht Dürer of Irish (or perhaps Scottish) fighters *c.*1531. One carries a smallbow. Of the five arrows in his girdle, one is a swallowtail broadhead, one is a forker amd one is a silver spoon head for butt shooting. The sword pommel is a distinctly Irish type. (bpk. Berlin/Art Resource NY)

To give ease and comfort, the jack was to be worn over a 'pourpoint,' a doublet designed to attach 'chausses', mail leggings reaching to the knee or ankle. This pourpoint was to be of two folds of cloth without sleeves or collar, only four fingers broad on the shoulder.

In 1512 a German writer described Henry VIII's army parading in France. He saw big strong men with a captain to every hundred. Some had English bows, some crossbows. Almost all wore long white coats edged with green cloth. They also had breastplates and steel caps. The following year Henry's forces faced those of King James IV of Scotland. Lord Dacre's forces included 'the bows of Kendal stout, with milk-white coats and crosses red'.

In 1531, although English infantrymen were beginning to use firearms (harquebuses) they were still equipped in the old style with a bow, sword, buckler, celata (salade) and a two-pronged stake to resist a charge from the enemy's horse. In 1547 the archer in the 'trayned bands' was required to have a bow, a sheaf of arrows and three bow strings in a waterproof case, a good sword and a short dagger, a helmet, vambraces and a leather or mail jerkin, on pain of punishment.

In 1577 archers from Yorkshire were to have bow, arrows, case, coat of plate, sword dagger and girdle, shooting glove, bracelet (bracer) and string, skull (steel cap) and a Scottish cap to cover it.

Before the 'trayned bands' were disbanded in 1598 by Elizabeth I, it was recommended that the archers

> … should have good bows, well nocked, well stringed, every string whipped in the nock, and in the midst rubbed with wax, bracer and shooting glove, some spare strings trimmed as aforesaid; every man one sheaf of arrows, with a case of leather, defensible against the rain whereof eight [arrows] shall be lighter to gall or astonish the enemy before they shall come within danger of harquebus shot. Let every man have a brigandine or a little coat of plate, a skull or hufkin. A maul of lead and a pike with a hook and dagger. Also a good sword.

While helmet styles changed through the centuries, bow and arrow styles and the amount of defensive armour for archers changed little.

26

ARCHERS OF THE GUARD

The yeomen of the guard were archers all.
A hundred at a time I oft have seen,
With bowes and arrowes ride before the queen,
Their bowes in hand, their quivers on their shoulders.

Taylor, *The Water Poet*[52]

Throughout the time of military archery, archers played an important role in protecting their leaders. During the Dark Ages, kings and chieftains maintained small groups of warriors as elite trained units to form the core or cadre of an army as well as to protect their lord. In 1130, the Norman King Roger of Sicily used Saracen archers in his bodyguard. Frederick II, the Holy Roman Emperor, also formed his guard of Saracen archers from Sicily as well as using Saracen contingents militarily.

Throughout the mediaeval period and until the present day, tall strong archers were preferred as royal bodyguards. Henry II, the first English monarch to establish a lifeguard, formed it of 50 tall archers. King John placed the archers of the royal bodyguard as well as all servants involved with the royal hunts under the constable and under him, a marshall. His son Henry III had some 20 Picard bodyguards armed with the newly popular crossbows. In 1334, John Ward, king's archer, and 99 mounted archers from Cheshire formed the royal bodyguard for Edward III, and in 1346 Chester provided an additional 100 special archers for the bodyguard of his son, the Prince of Wales, later known as the Black Prince.

His son Richard II, having taking the throne as a child, had been dominated by his 'protectors' and advisors. As soon as he could, he formed a bodyguard of king's archers. Following his father's example, he chose archers from Cheshire as well as from Wales and Ireland, and outfitted them in green and white livery. A core unit of 300 was organised in seven watches under noble captains who wore the badge of the White Hart on their left shoulder. Their men wore silver or gold crown badges. These Cheshire Archers of the Royal Bodyguard formed a substantial private army to contend with the private armies of unruly barons who chose to consider the King's

archers as low-born ruffians. Richard, however, granted his archers many privi-
leges. This was well advised, as he found himself in need of their protection. At the
Parliament of 1397 Richard had to arrest popular nobles who had plotted against him
and there was 'some bustle':

> The King's archers in number four thousand, compassed the Parliament house
> thinking that there had been some broil, or fighting, with their Bows bent, their
> Arrows notched, and drawing, ready to shoot, to the terror of all that were there; but
> the King coming pacified them.

In the end, Richard's archers were unable to save his life. But during the rebellion
against Henry IV, one of Percy's Cheshire archers put an arrow into the face of the
16-year-old Prince Henry at the Battle of Shrewsbury in 1403, leaving him scarred
for life.

Henry V, following his victory at Agincourt, had so many French prisoners that
they outnumbered his own men. Fearing a renewed attack he ordered all prisoners killed except those of the highest rank. The expected ransoms of these noble
prisoners meant a secure future for any archer holding one, and even Henry's threats
to hang anyone who refused, failed to spur on his men to the killing. Finally, 200 of
Henry's blue and white liveried archer bodyguard, sworn to personal loyalty, did the
job and prisoners were 'sticked with daggers, brained with poleaxes, slain with malles'.

Charles VII, after becoming king of France formed the corps of Francs-Archiers
and, impressed by Scottish bravery at Verneuil, also formed a bodyguard of Scottish
archers, *La. Compagnie des Gardes Ecossoises*. In 1449 he entered Rouen followed by his
Grand Guard of archers and crossbowmen. Matthew de Coussy wrote that they wore
'sleeveless hoquetons coloured vermillion red and green, decorated in gold, with
plumes in matching colours'.

Louis XI continued to keep an archer bodyguard. These men, The Hundred and
Twenty Archers of the King of France's Guard, carried a 'glaive' or perhaps a 'voulge'
or 'guisarme' when not carrying a bow. The glaive, a pole arm with a single edged
blade and a circular steel plate at its base to stop a parried blade, was also used as a
parade weapon. These were used much like a quarterstaff, one hand at the middle,
the other hand between the middle and the end of the staff could be shifted to the
other end for cutting or thrusting. In combat it was placed on the ground when
using the bow.

Charles V, as heir of Burgundy, adopted the archer bodyguard with their 'couteaux'
(glaives). His nephew, Maximillian II, introduced his 'Hartschiere' bodyguard, later
the 'Arcierenleibgarde,' to the Viennese imperial court, replacing the spear-carrying
Hapsburg Guards. The word 'hartschier' is a German corruption of the English word
'archer', and their glaives were known by the German term 'kuse'.

In 1468, Edward IV had a royal bodyguard of 200 archers. The only other standing
army at this time was the Calais garrison. In 1485 Henry VII formed the Yeomen of
the Guard of 50 tall, picked Lancashire archers. Like Cheshire, Lancashire was noted
for its archers. By 1501 the now 300-man Yeomen of the Guard wore the Tudor livery

of white and green in vertical stripes, embroidered on chest and back with the red rose of Lancaster within a vine wreath. The archer guard of Henry VIII still wore white and green for the latter's 1514 French campaign. At the siege of Terouenne, Henry had 600 archers of his guard 'all in white gaberdines and caps'. These yeomen were clad in red for ceremonial occasions. A contemporary painting of Henry's procession to the Field of the Cloth of Gold shows red tunics with black bands at the hem and sleeves, with the gold crowned Tudor Rose on front and back.

Henry was accompanied by 60 mounted archer guardsmen at the Field of the Cloth of Gold. At one point during the festivities, the carriage of the King and Queen halted. Blocking the path were 200 tall yeomen with green hoods and bows and arrows. Their leader stepped forward and announced himself to be Robin Hood. He whistled and all 200 loosed their arrows at once, and he whistled again and they shot again. 'Their arrows whistled by craft of the head so that the noise was strange and great.' Then Robin Hood took the King and Queen with her ladies to the greenwood, the yeomen blowing horns as they went.

> They came to an arbour made of boughs with a hall and a great chamber, and an inner chamber very well made and covered with flowers and sweet herbs, which the king much praised. Then said Robin Hood; 'Sir, outlaws' breakfasts is venison, and therefore you must be content with such fare as we used.'

Henry had a great interest in the stories of Robin Hood, and must have appreciated this entertainment laid on by the Yeomen of the King's Bows.

The ballad *Flodden Field* relates the story of one yeoman of Henry's guard, Long Jamie Garsedd. Stung by taunts of cowardice by his fellow yeomen against himself and the Earl of Derby who had brought Jamie up, he 'sticked two and wounded three', and had with drawn sword in hand, fled to the Earl of Derby. A messenger came from the king to demand that Jamie be delivered up for hanging. The Earl and other noblemen came with him to plead for his life. Jamie told how the Earl had raised him and taught him to shoot and reminded the King how he had come into his guard.

> Then after, under Grenwich upon a day,
> A Scottish minstrel came to thee,
> And brought a bow of yew to drawe,
> And all the guard might not stir that tree.
> Then the bow was given to the Earle of Derbye,
> And the Earl delivered it to mee.
> Seven shoots before your face I shott,
> And at the eighth in sunder it did flee.
> Then I bad the Scot bow down his face,
> And gather up the bow, and bring it to his king,
> Then it liked your noble Grace
> Into your guard for me to bring.

The King, eventually convinced that Jamie has acted justifiably, pardons him.

Scotland also had a royal bodyguard of Scottish nobles sworn to remain at the monarch's side in time of danger. The Ettrick Forest archers, called 'the Flowers of the Forest,' were officially known as the Archers' Guard. After the Battle of Flodden in 1513, the English had to clear away the corpses of these men to reach the body of the slain James IV. The archers had kept their oath to protect him until death. They are remembered in the tune often played by tartan-clad pipers to this day, 'Flowers of the Forest'.

Back in England, Edward VI, Henry VIII's ill fated son, kept a journal. In an entry of 14 May 1550 he states:

> There mustered before me a hundred archers, two arrows apiece, all of the guard; afterwards shot together, and they shot at an inch board, which some pierced quite, and stuck on the outer board; divers pierced it quite through with the heads of their arrows, the boards being very well seasoned timber.

Queen Elizabeth I continued the tradition, forming her bodyguard of tall archers. She doubled their number and liked to be surrounded by her archers in all public processions. Despite this, Elizabeth, who had once declared bows and arrows to be 'God's special gift to our nation', and who had once much encouraged the practice of archery, abolished the use of archery in the 'trained bands'.

In today's England, the guardsmen at the Tower are descendants of Henry's yeomen, and the Royal Company of Archers guards the Queen in Scotland. They still shoot with longbows somewhat after the old fashion, but they set their clouts at 220 yards, and try for no farther mark. A bodyguard of Scottish archers for the Queen of England! Ascham would turn in his grave.

27

COGNIZANCES: LIVERIES, BADGES AND STANDARDS

The white Lion is leyde to slepe
through envy of the Ape clogge,
And he is bownden that our dore should kepe
that is Talbott good dogge.[53]

English political poem

They had bows of ewe and strings of silke,
Arrows of silver chest,
Black hats, white feathers all alike,
Full deftly they were drest.

Robin Hood and Queen Katherine[54]

Cognizances were means of visual identification. While nobles were individually recognised by their arms on shields, banners and surcotes, the lower classes were identified by group. Crusaders were marked by crosses. The monastic military orders, Templars, Hospitallers and Teutonic Knights bore respectively, a red cross on a white surcote, a white cross on a black surcote and a black cross on a white surcote. In preparation for the Third Crusade, an English and French council established that Frenchmen were to wear red crosses sewn to their garments, the English were to wear white ones and Flemings to wear green, serving to differentiate by kingdom and language.

Edward I provided arm pieces of cloth with the red cross of St George to both English and Welsh in his army. During his 1282–83 campaign against the Welsh, white clothing was issued for winter warfare in Snowdonia.

In later wars, the Swiss were marked by couped white crosses, as on today's Swiss flag, Burgundians by red or black saltires. Englishmen during Henry V's invasion of France were required to wear a large red cross in front and back, the cross of their patron St George, while Frenchmen were identified by white crosses, reversing the previous system. Infantry of the City of London in the time of Henry VIII wore white tunics with the red cross plus the addition of an upright red sword on the right breast, the arms of the City of London to the present day.

The *flechas,* the sheaf of arrows, was the badge of Queen Isabella of Castille, coloured red. A badge of Prince Arthur, Henry VIII's brother, was a sheaf of arrows that included a sword.

During the Hundred Years War, feudal levies were abandoned in favour of a paid volunteer army, each noble to provide a certain number of archers and others. The nobles began to provide their men with livery clothing in the noble's identifying colours, usually one or two, sometimes three, not related to the tinctures of his arms. For the Plantagenets from Henry II to Edward II the colours were white and red. For Edward III they were blue or red. The Black Prince, Edward Prince of Wales, outfitted his contingent of Cheshire archers in parti-colour liveries: woollen hose, 'cortepy' (short coats) and 'chaperons' (hoods) in the Welsh colours of green and white, green on the right, white on the left. Cheshire was a border area and some of these men, like the honoured 'Black Bowmen of Llantrisant', were Welsh. All units from Cheshire and Flint during the reign of Edward III were so liveried, the clothing being delivered at points of array, or sometimes in London. Richard II continued his father's tradition, taking the livery colours of green and white, and outfitting his Cheshire archer bodyguard in green and white livery, as mentioned in the previous chapter.

In 1345 Parliament decreed that troops for the French wars were to be dressed in a uniform manner but in 1390, nobles were prohibited from giving liveries to 'any varlet called a yeoman archer nor to any one below the estate of squire', family servants excepted. This was because the formation of private armies was becoming a threat to other citizens. Men might wear liveries of their towns or districts or of their craft companies. In 1445 Coventry called out 100 archers under their own captain. The archers were provided with red and green sashes, while the captain received one of green, violet and red. Bowyers and fletchers were given the right to wear liveries

A broad arrow ermines, the heraldic badge of the chief herald who accompanied King Edward III on his expedition to France.

of their respective colours in 1319 and were exempted from the 1411 statute meant to regulate landowners' liveried private armies. Their liveries, worn on all great city occasions, were a chaperon for free craftsmen and a gown for leading members.

Livery colours included the usual heraldic tinctures of white, yellow, black, blue, red, green and *purpure* and the less common 'murrey' or 'tenné', a burgundy and tawny orange, or sometimes even pink. Bowyers wore black and white, and fletchers wore blue and yellow chaperons. When two colours were used, the tunic or jack was often divided down the middle, half one colour, half the other. Sometimes the colours were in stripes.

Badges were heraldic charges that marked a lord's possessions and were used to identify adherents, servants and yeomen in his service. He might have several badges, inherited or newly devised, one of which was used on the livery of his fighting men. The badge, usually embroidered or appliquéd, was borne on the front and back of a tunic or jack, or a smaller one on the front of the left shoulder, or even on a baldric of the livery colours. Some were made of lead or pewter to sew onto the garment. Below are some examples:

Richard II	a white hart, green and white livery
Earl Rivers	a white scallop shell with rays, green livery
Earl Douglas	a red heart, blue livery
Edward IV	a gold sun in splendour, murrey and blue livery
Richard III	a white boar, murrey and blue livery. (Richard was said to have ordered 13,000 of these badges for his coronation.)

The Calais levy of 1470 was given red jacks with White Rose (Yorkist) badges. Of the noble houses, both Warwick and Stanley used liveries of red. Warwick's 'servitures were apparailed in red cotes embroudered with white ragged staves', while the gold griffin's claw erased identified Stanley's men. Likewise, Talbot and Stafford both clad their men in red and black, Talbot's men were marked by a white talbot courant, Stafford's men by the gold Stafford knot.

In 1533 the Earl of Derby called for archers in white jackets with his 'bage of the leggis of Man' of red cloth on breast and back. This is the emblem of three conjoined armoured legs that now appears on the Manx flag.

Barnard's Roll, compiled to list members of the army accompanying Edward IV to France, lists each knight, the archers and others in his retinue, and includes a sketch of the knight's badge that identified his men, such as the heart of Douglas and the black bull of Hastings. At times during the Wars of the Roses the use of liveries was prohibited to curb hostile private armies, and Henry VII put an end to liveries and private armies except in the service of the crown.

A battle standard, carried by a warrior of known courage, was a long tapering flag, usually swallow-tailed, that marked the position of the commander and formed a rallying point for his men. Next to the staff would be the cross of the kingdom's patron saint. The remainder of the flag would be divided lengthwise into the livery colours, and edged 'compony' with a fringe of the same colours and charged with the lord's badges, including the one that marked his men. The standard might also display a motto in diagonal stripes. The badge could also appear on a pennon of the livery colours, on a guidon or on a badge banner, so that a glance at a soldier was enough to determine where he belonged. Preparation for a battle with displayed standards, guidons, banners, 'pavons' and pennons presented a gorgeous riot of colour. Heralds that accompanied Edward IV's 1475 expedition to France bore the badge of the chief herald, 'a broad arrow ermines'.

28

ARCHERY AND THE NOBILITY

King Sigurd said 'There does not seem to be a more lordly and useful sport than to shoot well with a bow; I think that thou canst not stretch my bow, even if thou didst try it with thy feet.' Eystein answered; 'I am not as strong with a bow as thou, but there is less difference in our ability to shoot at a mark.'

Heimskringla (The Saga of Sigurd the Crusader)[55]

So the English were wont to say, and still say to the French, that the arrow was well shot which was sent up against the king; and that the archer who thus put out Harold's eye won them great glory.

Roman De Rou, Maistre Wace[56]

Even when nobles recognised the importance of archers in their armies, they nonetheless bore some resentment toward those base-born men who could kill their betters from a safe distance and go unpunished; many a noble and king died transfixed by arrows. Noblemen, as English law required, were trained in the use of bows and arrows – the young sons of great lords were to learn 'to feed a bird, to hawk, to know hunting dogs, to shoot bow and arrow, to play chess and backgammon' – as well as the use of sword and lance, axe and dagger. A number of mediaeval manuscript illustrations show knights or men-at-arms using bows and arrows, and the bow bearer of a twelfth-century king or noble was well paid. Pre-Viking Scandinavian graves of Norse princes also show that it was not just poorer men who used the bow; many burials include arrows, often as many as 40, both for war and hunting.

Those nobles who in our romantic imagination lived by the sword, often died by the arrow. Arrows, or more particularly the noble deaths they caused, shaped the course of European Dark Age and mediaeval history, making possible the wholesale conquest of a country, as in 1066, or changing lines of succession, as in the accidental death of William II. What follows are a few examples of those kings and noblemen who were felled by archery, often brought low by those of much lower rank, and whose deaths had political ramifications that defined both their world and ours.

The nobility of Dark Age Europe, in a time when kings were warriors rather than administrators, often fell at the hands of archers. In 633 Offrid, son of Edwin, King of Northumbria, was killed by an arrow during a battle between Northumbria and a Welsh and Mercian alliance. Edmund, King of the Angles, was defeated by a Viking army and executed by being tied to a tree and being shot full of arrows like St Sebastian.

Hakon, a son of King Harald Fairhair of Norway, was fostered with King Athelstane of England. On the death of his father, the young man returned to Norway to claim the kingdom. Although as a Christian he tolerated the heathen practices of his subjects with reluctance, he was accepted willingly and earned the name Hakon the Good, but his reign was contested by the widow and sons of Erik Bloodaxe, another son of Harald. In the unavoidable battle, Hakon fought fiercely in the vanguard, wielding his sword 'Kvernbit' with both hands.

> Then flew an arrow, one of the kind called a 'flein', into Hakon's arm, into the muscles below the shoulder; and it is said by many people that Gunnhild's shoe-boy whose name was Kisping, ran out and forwards amidst the confusion of arms, called out 'Make way for the king-killer' and shot King Hakon with the flein. Others again say that nobody could tell who shot the King, which is indeed the most likely; for spears, arrows, and all kinds of missiles flew as thick as a snow drift.

Hakon's wound was bandaged but the bleeding could not be stopped and he said at last that Erik's sons should be kings over the country but should hold his friends in respect and honour.

> And if fate,' added he, 'should prolong my life, I will, at any rate, leave the country, and go to a Christian land, and do penance for what I have done against God; but should I die in heathen land, give me any burial you think fit.

He shortly died and as fit for a great hero, his men laid him in a great mound in full armour and consigned him to Valhalla.

The Jomsviking Saga tells us that Harald Bluetooth, King of the Danes, made an enemy of one of his followers called Palnatoki who afterward became a chieftain of the Jomsvikings, a society of warriors who lived in an island stronghold and became a power strong enough to challenge kings. Palnatoki took an interest in Swein, an illegitimate son of the King, constantly reminding the boy of his royal blood and when he became a young man, Palnatoki gave him ships. Swein, rejected by his father and resentful, began raiding in his father's kingdom. At nightfall following a sea battle, Swein's ships were pursued into a creek and with the creek mouth blocked by Harald's ships, awaited the dawn while Harald went ashore. But Palnatoki had anchored his ships on the opposite side of the headland and he took up bow and quiver and also went ashore. Harald's men had made a fire to warm themselves and Palnatoki, seeing the fire, moved silently toward it. The king undressed and, kneeling in front of the fire, bent forward to warm his chest and hands, while behind him in the darkness Palnatoki had recognised him, and quietly nocked an arrow. Harald's men suddenly realised that their king lay dead, an arrow head protruding from his mouth, the arrow having passed from his buttocks through his entire torso. His embarassed companions agreed to say that the King had died in battle while Palnatoki returned to his ships to assist Swein, called Forkbeard, who soon became king in place of Harald.

Harald Hardrade (Hard Counsel) was the last of the great Viking kings. Harald's final expedition was an invasion of England with Earl Tostig of Northumbria, who believed himself cheated by his brother King Harold Godwinson. At Stamford Bridge near York, the Vikings were surprised by Godwinson's Saxons. With the Saxons was an excellent archer called Heming, who had left Norway because of difficulties with Harald Hardrade. The Saxons were unable to break through the Viking defence and King Harald asked Heming to shoot the Viking king. But Heming, because his life had been saved by the spirit of St Olaf, had sworn not to kill Hardrade, his descendant. King Harold then pressed Heming to shoot Hardrade enough to mark him.

> Heming then shot at the king with a slotted arrow, and the arrow-head locked itself in his flesh. The king cut the arrow out at once, but because of this it was easy to see the king clearly. Harold Godwinson then shot King Harald through the throat.

Earl Tostig, now commanding the Vikings, refused to surrender. Harold did not ask Heming to shoot Tostig because he did not wish to be the cause of his brother's death, but Heming said:

> It's strange that you are willing to let your men be slaughtered; and I will give him a gift, if you do not forbid it.' The king said; 'I shall not now seek to avenge this man, even if some serious injury is done him'. Then Heming shot Tostig in the eye.

So ended the bloodiest battle that had ever been fought in England.

Meanwhile William Duke of Normandy had readied an invasion fleet and recruited an army; William had a claim to the English throne which he had expected to inherit from Edward the Confessor. William heard of Edward's death while in his hunting park at Rouen.

> He held in his hand a bow, which he had strung and bent, making it ready for the arrow, and he had given it into the hands of a page, for he was going forth to the chase and had with him many knights and pages and esquires.

Of his bow, it was said that nobody but he could draw it, and he could even bend it up and shoot powerfully and accurately while riding at full gallop.

The recently victorious King Harold got word that William's Norman fleet had landed on the English coast and the Saxons made a forced march south to encounter the Normans near Hastings at a position on Senlac Hill. During the battle the

Normans combined cavalry charges with a hail of arrows shot in high arc. The plummeting arrows rained down on the Saxon line. In *Roman De Rou,* a history of the Dukes of Normandy commissioned by Henry II in 1160, Maistre Wace wrote:

> Then it was that an arrow, which was shot upwards towards the sky, struck Harold above the right eye, and that one of his eyes it put out. In his agony he drew out the arrow and threw it away, breaking it with his hands; and the pain was so great that he leaned upon his shield.

Some accounts said that Harold died on the battlefield but others said that Heming helped him from the field and cared for him until his death, then entered a monastery.

William the Conqueror may have been helped to victory by the actions of an archer, but his son and heir, William II (Rufus), was not so lucky. One morning after breakfast, Rufus prepared for a hunt in the New Forest with a guest from France, one Wat Tyrell. The party mounted and rode into the forest where the nobles separated as was customary. Rufus and Tyrell took up their positions on either side of a game trail to wait. As the sun was setting, a stag passed between them and Rufus prepared to loose an arrow. There are differing versions of what happened next. Either the King's bowstring snapped and he called to Tyrell to shoot, or he did loose an arrow that wounded the stag, which fled in terror while Tyrell took aim at a second passing stag. In either case Tyrell's arrow only grazed the deer and lodged in the King's chest. Without a sound, Rufus snapped off the shaft, fell forward and lay motionless. Tyrell, springing to the King's side and finding him unconscious, mounted his horse and galloped for the coast to take the first ship home to France. The King's brother Henry, first in line to the crown, galloped off to secure the royal treasury and left the corpse for later consideration.

Simeon of Durham lists various atrocities perpetrated on the Welsh, including a priest, by the Norman Earl of Shrewsbury on the island of Menavia, commonly called Anglesey:

> At that time Magnus King of the Norsemen, son of King Olaf, son of King Harald, [Harald Hardrade, who was killed at the Battle of Stamford Bridge] having added to his empire the Orkney and Menavian islands, came thither in a few vessels. And when he brought his vessels to land, Hugh Earl of Shrewsbury with many armed soldiers met him on the very shore, shot by the king himself, on the seventh day after he had practised this cruelty on the aforesaid priest.

Divine retribution is implied.

Gilbert Fitz Gilbert de Clare (Strongbow) was made Earl of Pembroke in 1138. His son, Richard Fitz Gilbert, who inherited the earldom as well as the name 'Strongbow', conquered most of Ireland in 1170, and is in fact more often associated with the name in modern times. At the age of eighteen Richard, a strong young man noted for having unusually long arms, was said to be master of a bow that no other man could fully draw. When he led the first Norman invasion of Ireland with 200 men-at-arms and 1000 archers, he often dismounted and used his bow among the archers and crossbowmen in his army.

Richard the Lionheart spent his last years in Normandy protecting his continental kingdom from the French. Learning that a gold sculpture had been dug up near the castle of Chalus, which was under his jurisdiction, and finding that the lord of the castle refused to surrender the sculpture, Richard laid siege. On 26 March 1199 he rode out to reconnoitre with his crossbow and protected only by an iron headpiece and rectangular shield, he rode close to the walls. A crossbowman, shielding himself with a frying pan, loosed a bolt that penetrated Richard's shoulder just below his neck. He broke off the shaft but delayed treatment until the siege ended with surrender ten days later. The defenders were all hanged except for the defiant crossbowman Bertram de Gourdon. He was brought before Richard who pardoned him and granted him 100 shillings. Finally, Richard had the arrowhead cut out and bandaged, but blood poisoning had set in and he died in his mother's arms. The crossbowman was flayed alive. Some thought that Richard's death was divine retribution for his liberal use of crossbowmen and his personal use of that weapon, contrary to the papal edict of 1139.

In 1295 King Edward I led an attack on Scotland. The following year, from the Red Hall, the guild hall of Flemish settlers in Berwick, a Flemish crossbowman shot Edward's cousin Richard of Cornwall through his helmet visor and into his brain. Following a siege, Edward killed hundreds, possibly thousands, of innocent townspeople, partly it is argued in revenge for his cousin's death.

At the same time the shadowy figure of William Wallace was making his presence known in Scotland. Very little is known about him, as much of what was later written was based on a fifteenth-century poem by 'Blind Harry', who took a great deal of artistic license. However, Wallace was said to be an archer who obtained his living by means of his bow, the youngest son of a minor laird, who killed an Englishman and became an outlaw. He took part in the fight against the invading English forces, one story stating that he once took an English arrow under the chin, through a collar of steel, which wounded his neck but he killed the English archer with his sword. He was eventually executed but lives on in the popular imagination as 'Braveheart', a heroic if somewhat romanticised figure about whom we really know very little.

.   In 1307 Robert the Bruce, allied with the Black Douglas, took up the fight and harried the English in a guerilla campaign. One morning, while outside his temporary camp for his morning ablutions and accompanied only by a page, he saw three armed men approaching and recognised a kinsman and his two sons. Bruce had been warned that they intended betrayal. He always carried his great sword hanging at his neck, but borrowed a bow and arrow from his page and warned him to stand well back. He told the three men to halt but they kept coming, saying that they had news of the English. Bruce then shot the father, who had a sword in his hand, through the eye and he fell backward. The elder son, armed with sword and axe, sprang forward with axe upraised but Bruce cut him down with a blow of his own sword. The second son attacked with his spear, but Bruce cut off the point of the spear and killed him before he could draw his sword.

Not long afterwards, Bruce, with 300 men, moved south into Galloway. The English learned of his whereabouts and dispatched 1500 hand-picked knights who, because of rocky terrain, decided to attack on foot. Bruce was warned barely in time for his men to prepare themselves. As the English charged, Bruce seized a bow and arrow from one of his archers and shot the arrow through the throat of the enemy leader. Then Bruce seized his banner and led the charge against the English knights, who fled.

Present-day archery experiments have had little success in piercing plate armour but well armoured mediaeval nobles are often recorded as having suffered wounds or death from arrows that managed the feat. At the Battle of Crecy English longbowmen shot arrows into the throat and thigh of King Philippe VI of France and killed his horse under him with their arrows. Simiarly Joan of Arc wore full plate armour; she took an arrow in the shoulder at close range, not a serious wound but enough to put her out of action briefly. At the siege of Paris she took a crossbow bolt through her thigh while her banner bearer had his foot nailed to the ground by one bolt and took a second in the forehead when he raised his visor to pull out the first.

In 1333 at Halidon Hill the Earl Douglas, galled by the rain of English arrows that 'flew as thick as motes in a sunbeam', drew his sword and led some 80 armoured horsemen in an attack on the archers but, despite his excellent new armour, he received five arrow wounds, one of which took out an eye, and was taken prisoner with his followers. In 1346 at Durham, King David II of Scotland was also wounded by an arrow in the eye.

In an early battle of the Wars of the Roses, the First Battle of St Albans, the royal army came under surprise attack by a force of the Earl of Warwick allied with the Duke of York. In a hail of arrows, four of King Henry VI's bodyguards died instantly while the King himself, standing beside the fallen royal banner, took an arrow through the flesh between neck and shoulder. The Duke of Buckingham took an arrow 'in the vysage' and Stafford had one through his hand.

Henry VII took part in shooting matches and shot at the butts with a crossbow. He participated in shooting matches that were part of the festivities celebrating Henry's marriage to Elizabeth of York, which united the Yorkist and Lancastrian factions. Both his sons, Arthur and Henry, practised and enjoyed archery. Henry was the stronger of the two and was a superb archer. He practiced archery shooting at rounds in the gardens behind Hampton Court and took great pride in his skill and once king he was said to outshoot the yeomen of his guard. Paulus Jovius wrote; 'No man in his dominions drew the great English bow more vigorously than Henry himself, no man shot farther or with more unerring aim.'

In 1513, while Henry VIII was invading France, King James IV of Scotland led a military expedition into England. An English force of billmen, archers and men-at-arms met him at Flodden. Both sides had cannon. The English archers were hampered by rain and a contrary wind but although the arrows had little effect against the then excellent armour of the Scottish nobles, they decimated the pikemen in the shiltrons. James's body was found beneath the bodies of his loyal archer bodyguard. Despite his superb armour, he had taken several arrow wounds, one in his head which may have been the cause of his death, and a gash in the neck and left hand from bills or swords. Flodden was the last major battle in which archery played a significant but perhaps not a decisive part.

One mediaeval archer was rumoured to have changed history without using his bow. King Louis XI of France had to pay an annuity to King Edward IV of England, but chuckled as he privately referred to Edward as 'Blayburgh'. This was in reference to Blackburn, a common archer rumoured to have been admitted to the bedchamber of the King's mother, the Duchess of York, during the absence of the Duke, pretender to the crown of England. Her son Edward fought his way to the kingship and was a successful ruler, siring two sons. On Edward's death, his brother Richard, Duke of Gloucester, official protector of the two princes, announced that Edward had not been the true son of the Duke of York and therefore his kingship as well as its inheritance by his sons was invalid. Richard imprisoned the boys in the Tower of London and took the crown as Richard III, setting the stage for the last act in the Wars of the Roses and the coming of the Tudor dynasty.

29

ROBIN HOOD AND WILHELM TELL

All they schot a bowthe agen,
The screffes men and he;
Off the marke he welde not fayle,
He cleffed the preke on thre.

Robin Hood and the Potter

Robin Hood

According to a recent poll, Robin Hood is the most popular folk hero in the world. A newspaper review of the film 1976 *Robin and Marian* sought to explain the enduring fascination with the character:

> lthough there is not much hard evidence to prove he ever existed, the hauntingly beautiful legend of Robin Hood endures. And it's not difficult to know why. The wonderful ingredients of the myth; stealing from the rich to give to the poor, an arcadian setting in the gentle woods, the love of a fair lady, the quintessence of male comradeship, are too rich to ignore.

Since *Piers Plowman* was written over 600 years ago, and presumably for many years beforehand in the oral tradition, Robin Hood ballads, stories and films have been produced unceasingly. From this outpouring of sometimes very fanciful material, it is difficult to find if there is any historical basis for the figure. Sadly, Maid Marion does not appear in the oldest ballads, and the fictional Robin, who because of his veneration of the Virgin Mary would not permit a woman to be molested, seemed to have had no love interest apart from a dalliance with the Sheriff's wife in *Robin Hood and the Potter*.

Having left the King's service, Robin Hood returns to the forest of Barnsdale, kills a deer and sounds his horn to summon his old outlaw band. He is again acknowledged as their lord.

It is likely that the character we now know as Robin Hood evolved through the adaption and combination of many stories concerning outlaws and historical figures across England, and that by the time such stories were put down on paper, the deeds of many had been assigned to one character, the details of his life being adjusted and added to by successive generations. The fact that he appears in the historical record centuries after those who inspired the original tales must have lived, and that the writers clearly considered him to have been a real person, is a testament to how ingrained the stories had become in the public mind. One of the abiding attractions to these accounts is that they reflect the reality of the times, often allowing Robin Hood to be neatly slotted into real historical events, and the leaders of real bands of outlaws to take or be assigned the title by chroniclers.

In Andrew Wyntoun's *Chronicle of Scotland* written in about 1420 is the following passage, under the year 1283.

Lytil John and Robyne Hude
Waythmen ware commended gude;
In Yngliwode and Barnysdale
Thai oysyd all this time thare trawale.

The date 1283, 137 years before the chronicle was written, falls during the reign of Edward I, at which time there was particular danger from outlaws in the vicinity of Sherwood Forest, Barnsdale being a forest area just north of Sherwood. During the reign of Edward I, three ecclesiastics journeyed from Scotland to Winchester. They had with them a guard sometimes of eight archers, sometimes of twelve, or farther south, none at all, but when they passed from Pontefract to Tickhill, the number was increased to 20. Tickhill is on the edge of the wooded Barnsdale area; clearly the clerics had reason to believe that the area was especially dangerous and so reinforced their bodyguard accordingly.

Another account of Robin is in John Major's *Scotichronicon*, a chronicle of Scotland written in 1521. The book is no longer in existence but is quoted in a later book, Richard Grafton's *A Chronicle at Large, mere History of the affayres of England* of 1568.

About this time [1189] as sayth John Major in his Chronicle of Scotland, there were many robbers and outlaws in England, among which number, he especially noteth Robert Hood, whom we now call Robyn Hood, and little John, who were famous thieves. They continued in woodes mountaynes and forestes, spoyling robbing, namely such as were riche. Murders common lv did they none, except it were by the provocation of such as resisted them in their rifelynges and spoyles.

And the sayde Major sayth that the aforesaid Robin Hood had at his rule and commandment an hundred tall yomen, which were mightie men and exceeding good archers, and they were maintained by such spoyles as came to their hands: and he sayth moreover, that those hundreth were such picked men, and of such force, that four hundreth men, whosoever they were, durst never set upon them. And one thing was commended in him, that he would suffer no woman to be oppressed, violated or other-wise abused. The poorer sort of people he favoured and would in no-wise suffer their goodes to be touched or spoyled, but relieved and ayded them with such goodes as he gotte from the riche, which he spared not; namely the rich priestes, fat abbotes, and the houses of riche caries. And although his theft and rapyn was to be contemned, yet the aforesaid aucthour prayeseth him and sayeth, that among the number of theeves, he was worthy the name of the most gentle theefe ...

In this account, the bare facts are at least inkeeping with conditions of the time.. There were many bands of forest outlaws in England, as long as there were sizable forests. The claim that Robin's men could handle odds of four to one should raise no eyebrows in view of the fact that military longbowinen triumphed over odds of twenty to one and that the Swiss infantry more than once unhesitatingly and successfully took on odds of ten to one.

That outlaws robbed the rich is not surprising either; they were the obvious target. If Robin (or his inspiration) gave money to the poor and permitted no woman to be molested, one can put it down to the fact that an outlaw or guerilla band without popular support had poor prospects for a long life. This has been recognised in our times by Sicilian bandits as well as Yugoslav and Vietnamese guerillas. However, Major's 1521 account differs on the dating of the 'real' Robin Hood, which is an issue which crops up repeatedly in the historical record.

In his 1568 book Richard Grafton provided an explanation of how Robin came to be an outlaw.

> In an olde and auncient pamphlet I find this written of the sayd Robert Hood This man, sayeth he, descended of a noble parentage; or rather, beying of a base stock and linage, was for his manhood and chivalry advanced to the noble dignitie of an erle … But afterwards he so prodigially exceeded in charges and expenses that he fell into great debt, by reason whereof so many actions and sutes were commenced against him, whereunto he aunswered not, that by order of lawe he was outlawed for a lewde shift, and as his last refuge, gathered together a companye of roysters and cutters, and practised robberyes and spoyling of the kinges subjects, and occupied and frequented the forestes or wild countries.

Here were reasons for becoming an outlaw that a spendthrift nobleman could understand. The forests and wild countries mentioned are the adjoining forests of Sherwood and Barnesdale. Another chronicler adds Ingliwood, or Inglewood, as Robin's base.

In 1323 following a Lancastrian rebellion, Edward II made a royal progress through York, Lancaster and Nottingham. He was in Nottingham in November and December of that year, leaving shortly before Christmas. In the documents of the Exchequer covering that period is a startling entry. Listed are the names of about 28 *vadlets, porteurs de la chambre* of the King who received 3*d* a day for their services. One of these names is 'Robyn Hode'. The entries run from 24 March to 22 November in 1324, being payments to valets for the year preceding. Robyn Hode's pay is docked for 5 days absence in May, again for 8 days in August, for 15 days in October, and another 7 days in November. On 22 November, '*Robyn Hode, jadys un de porteurs, poar cas ii ne poait plus travailler, le donn par comandement, Vs.*'

The entry is in the sort of French still used at that time by the heirs of the Norman conquerors, and we find Robyn Hode unromantically discharged with five shillings severance pay because he could no longer do the work. There is of course no proof that this was *the* Robin Hood, as the name was a common one, and sometimes used as a shorthand term for an archer, the character already having become widespread in English folklaw. However, it is pleasing to note that the accounts perfectly coincide with Robin begging a leave of absence after a year in Edward's service and returning to his outlaw band, as related in the ballad *A Lytel Geste of Robyn Hode*. The position of valet is not so inappropriate as might at first appear for we find that the term applied to chamber servants who also served noble travellers as mounted archers in the capacity of bodyguards, as the Knight's yeoman of *The Canterbury Tales* seems to have served.

Richard Grafton quotes further from his 'olde and auncient pamphlet'.

Fore the sayd Robert Hood, being afterwards troubled with sicknesse, came to a certain 'nonry in Yorkshire, called Birklies, where desiring to let blood, he was betrayed and bled to death. After whose death, the prioresse of the same place caused him to be buried by the highway side, where he had used to rob and spoyle those that passed that way.

Many sites have been claimed as the graves of both Robin Hood and Little John, but obviously none are verifiable. Tradition has it that Robin, while being bled by the abbess of Kirklees nunnery for health reasons, was treacherously overcome by one Red Roger and died after making his last request to Little John:

Give me my bent bow in my hand, and a broad arrow I'll let flee,
And where that arrow lighteth, There shall my grave digged be.

Robin Hood plays were a traditional and important part of the May Day and Wakes Day entertainments not only in England, but also in Scotland, to the vexation of the authorities. The ballads were extremely popular, especially amongst the lower classes over all of Britain in Major's time. Bishop Hugh Latimer once finding himself unable to enter a village church to preach, was told: 'Sir, this is a busy day with us, we cannot hear you, it is Robin Hood's Day.' Later Robin even became popular with nobles. Henry VIII arranged a Robin Hood dance shortly after his coronation and, costumed as Robin Hood, entered the bedchamber of his wife, Catherine of Aragon.

Some Robin Hood ballads were written with the intention of flattering certain audiences, such as tradesmen, who would presumably reward the minstrel. The later ballads are sometimes outright foolish. In none of the older ballads are there any political overtones of Robin fighting guerrilla warfare against Norman oppression, such as have crept into movie versions of the story. These belong to tales of other men of the period such as Hereward the Saxon or Fulk Fitz Warine.

Many people have the impression that Robin Hood was represented as performing impossible feats. The ballads do credit him with being the best archer in his area, though Gilbert of the White Hand is sometimes depicted as shooting just as well. However, the ballads do provide us with useful source material on period archery, as Robin's 'impossible' feats have been shown to be possible by modern archers, and give us an idea of the standards and contests of the time.

Many ballads, especially the later ones, portray Robin as more antihero than superman, describing him as being roundly beaten on several occasions. One ballad goes so far as to have not only Robin but also two of his men severely beaten by a lone ragged beggar he attempts to rob at arrowpoint! Robin's face-saving device in such situations is to invite his adversary to join his band.

Many consider Robin Hood's existence improbable, but such a legend is unlikely to have arisen without a kernel of truth at its base. Whether that kernel was one man named Robin Hood, or whether the deeds of many men were distilled and embroidered over the centuries, we will probably never know.

Wilhelm Tell

The tale will be told of the marksman Tell
As long as the mountains stand on their ground.

Schiller, Wilhelm Tell[57]

Ihr muend net lange warten, wehrend euch bei Morengarten. [You must not wait long, defend yourselves at Morgarten.]

Note on the arrow (see p.230)

The name Wilhelm Tell, or its anglicised form William Tell, is almost as well known as that of Robin Hood, largely because of Friedrich Schiller's 1804 play of the same name. (A Swiss play was produced at the same time, but eclipsed by the great success of Schiller's work.) Schiller, a German poet, grudgingly began the play at the urging of Goethe and others. Wherever there is brutal oppression of a people, especially by a foreign power, the play experiences a revival, for example in Korea whilst a Japanese protectorate. As a result the play has been banned many times by oppressive regimes. It was followed by two Italian operas, the best known by Rossini.

Tell's story appears in several mediaeval Swiss sources such as the *Tellenlied*, a song dating from the 1470s, the *White Book of Sarnen*, written in 1475 by a scribe named Hans Schreiber and Tschudi's *Eidgenossische Chronik*, written in the sixteenth century. Tell is characterised as a strong, independent, professional hunter who spent much time alone in the mountains, or living quietly with his wife and children, staying clear of politics. Schiller, though he apparently never visited Switzerland, drew heavily on the old chronicles, and the section concerning the shooting of the apple is taken almost verbatim from Tschudi's chronicle.

The story is set in the period of the original foundation of the Old Swiss Confederacy in the early fourteenth century, when the Swiss overthrew their Austrian rulers. The events as told by Tschudi in the 1570s are that in Uri, where Tell lived, Gessler, the tyrannical viceroy of the Habsburg Empire, thought of a new way to gratify his thirst for power. Since he could not take the time to be always in the town square to receive the bows of the people he set his hat, adorned with the peacock feathers that proclaimed allegiance to Habsburg, on a pole and gave instructions that the people were to behave toward the hat as they would toward his person, setting guards to enforce compliance.

Tell, visiting the town with his crossbow and his son Walter, did not know of the new regulation and upon ignoring the hat were apprehended by the guardsmen. Gessler was summoned and Tell, with no show of defiance, begged to be excused on grounds of ignorance of the regulation, but Gessler would not miss the opportunity to make an example of Tell. Knowing that Tell had claimed to be able to hit an apple on a stick at a considerable distance, Gessler required that Tell demonstrate his skill, but with the apple on his son's head. Tell begged to be excused from attempting this and even offered his own life, but Gessler threatened to kill both Tell and his son if he refused, saying 'I don't want your blood, Tell, I want the shot.'

Tell placed an arrow in his crossbow and a second arrow behind his collar and levelled his crossbow at the apple at 80 yards. His shot hit the mark but Gessler was not yet satisfied, and having given his word as a knight, before witnesses, to spare Tell's life, wanted to know why Tell had put the second arrow in his collar. Tell replied that it was simply an archers' custom, but Gessler was not satisfied and Tell finally told him that had he missed the first shot, Gessler would have been the second target, and that he wouldn't have missed that one. Gessler immediately had Tell taken prisoner and ordered that he be taken to a dungeon, as he had only promised to spare Tell's life.

Tell was accordingly taken to a boat to be conveyed on the Lake of the Four Forest Places to the tower in which he would be imprisoned, but a sudden alpine storm placed the boat in such danger that Tell's captors released him so he could take the steering oar., as he was known as a strong and capable boatman. He steered the boat to land and lept from the boat with his crossbow. Tell then made his way over the mountains and came to a forest trail where Gessler had to pass, where he waited. When the Viceroy's party came in sight, he levelled his crossbow. Again, he did not miss and Gessler's journey and his life came to an abrupt end.

The Empire assembled a force to punish the mountain herdsmen for the killing of Gessler but the mountaineers had already fortified their mountain fastnesses and a sympathetic knight shot an arrow over their wall. A note on the arrow warned of impending attack and advised a defence at Morgarten. There the proud Imperial force was utterly crushed.

While modern historians generally regard the saga to be fictional, as none of the characters can be proved to have existed, Tell is regarded as a hero in Switzerland, although there is some soul searching over Gessler's manner of death by ambush. The death of Tell's son at the Battle of Sempach has been regarded by some as divine retribution for his father's deed.

30

BALLADS, RELIGION
AND SYMBOLISM

I can not parfitly my Paternoster as the prest it syngeth But I can rymes of Robyn Hood and Randolf Erl of Chestre.

Piers Plowman, The Vision of William[58]

Lythe and listen, gentilmen,
That be of frebore blod.
I shall you tel of a gode yeman,
His name was Robyn Hode.

A Lytel Geste of Robyn Hode

Ballads

Ballads are stories, sometimes quite long ones, written in verse and intended to be sung. The tunes for some of the ballads have survived the passage of time and the reader is recommended to hear them sung to fully appreciate them. Many of the most famous archery ballads, many naturally concerning Robin Hood, were composed during the Middle Ages and Renaissance. Wandering jesters, minstrels or crowders sang them wherever they could find a person or group willing to part with a few coins. Gleemen composed new ballads to please a particular audience, a welcome alternative to the religious morality plays.

Frequently the audiences were common people, who especially favoured the tales about outlaws, which nobles considered a threat. Attempts to suppress such ballads met with little success and men sang of Robin Hood not only in England but also in Scotland, until even the nobility came to appreciate them and commissioned plays based on the stories.

The earliest ballad manuscripts left to us were written down in the fifteenth century when printing presses came into use, but there is little doubt that they originated earlier than that. Three of them are known from one manuscript only, and it is clear that many have been lost. Some of the earlier ones are *A Lytel Geste of Robyn Hode* (composed from at least four even earlier ones), *Robin Hood and Guy of Gisborne*, *Robin Hood and the Potter* and *Robin Hood and the Monk*. Another ballad concerns other forest outlaws, Adam Bell, William of Cloudesle and Clim of the Clough, all outlawed for illegal hunting, who swore brotherhood and took to Inglewood, a forest sixteen miles in length near Carlisle, close to the Scottish border, given by the chronicler Andrew Wyntoun as one of Robin's haunts. They eventually enter the King's service.

Whether or not these ballads are historically accurate, they unquestionably represent the atmosphere of the Middle Ages and the idea of the mediaeval archer as he existed in the consciousness of the common man, who was himself an archer, what author Peter Ackroyd called 'the English Imagination' in his marvellous book *Albion*.

Drayton's *Polyolbion* poem, written a little later than the ballads, portrays Robin Hood as helping the poor and opressed. With excellent archery references, it also includes Maid Marian, who is absent from the earlier ballads.

That lustie Robin Hood, who long time like a King
Within her compasse liv'd, and when he list to range
For some rich booty set, or else his ayre to change,
To Sherwood still retyr'd, his onely standing court,
Whose praise the forrest thus doth pleasantly report.
The merry pranks he playd, would aske an age to tell,
And the adventures strange that Robin Hood befell,
When Mansfield many a time for Robin hath bin layd,
How he hath cosned them, that him would have betrayd;
How often he hath come to Nottingham disguisd,
And cunningly escapt, being set to be surprizd.
In this our spacious isle, I thinke there is not one,
But he hath heard some talke of him and little John;
And to the end of time, the tales shall ne'r be done,
Scarlock, George a Greene, and Much the millers sonne,
Of Tuck the merry frier, which many a sermon made,
In praise of Robin Hood, his out-lawes, and their trade.
An hundred valiant men had this brave Robin Hood,
Still ready at his call, that bow-men were right good,
All clad in Lincolne greene, with caps of red and blew,
His fellowes winded home, not one of them but knew,
When setting to their lips their little beugles shrill,
The warbling eccho's wakt from every dale and hill:
Their bauldricks set with studs, athwart their shoulders cast,
To which under their armes, their sheafes were buckled fast,
A short sword at their belt, a buckler scarse a span,
Who strooke below the knee, not counted then a man:
All made of Spanish yew, their bowes were wondrous strong;

They not an arrow drew, but was a cloth-yard long.
Of archery they had the very perfect craft,
With broad-arrow, or but, or prick, or roving shaft,
At markes full fortie score, they us'd to prick, and rove,
Yet higher then the breast, for compasse never strove;
Yet at the farthest marke a foot could hardly win:
At long-buts, short, and hoyles, each one could cleave the pin:
Their arrowes finely pair'd, for timber, and for feather,
With birch and brazill peec'd, to flie in any weather;
And shot they with the round, the square, or forked pyle,
The loose gave such a twang, as might be heard a myle.
And of these archers brave, there was not any one,
But he could kill a deere his swiftest speed upon,
Which they did boyle and rost, in many a mightie wood,
Sharpe hunger the fine sauce to their more kingly food.
Then taking them to rest, his merry men and hee
Slept many a summers night under the greenewood tree.
No lordly bishop came in lusty Robins way,
To him before he went, but for his passe must pay:
From wealthy abbots chests, and churles abundant store,
What often times he tooke, he shar'd amongst the poore:
The widdow in distresse he graciously reliev'd,
And remedied the wrongs of many a virgin griev'd:
He from the husbands bed no married woman wan,
But to his mistris deare, his loved Marian
Who ever constant knowne, which wheresoere shee came,
Was soveraigne of the woods, chiefe lady of the game:
Her clothes tuck'd to the knee, and daintie braided haire,
With bow and quiver arm'd, shee wandred here and there,
Among the forrests wild; Diana never knew
Such pleasures, nor such harts as Mariana slew.

Archery also appears in poetry, such as *The Song of Roland*, the French epic poem written in the mid-twelfth century. It tells the story of Roland, the nephew of Charlemagne, who leads the latter's rearguard in a campaign against the Saracens. Betrayed by his stepfather, Roland and the rearguard are ambushed in the pass of Roncevaux. Roland is counselled to blow his horn to call back the main body of the army, but refuses. His men are slaughtered and eventually he blows three blasts on his horn to call Charlemagne to avenge him and dies from the effort, facing the enemy.

In the poem, Charlemagne hands Roland his own bow, ready braced, as a token of command. Charlemagne is advised: 'He has been named for the rear guard and no baron of yours can change that now. Give him the bow which you have bent and find him those companions who will be of most help to him.' Charlemagne holds it out and Roland takes it.

Religion

And happed that he saugh bifore hym ryde
A gay yeman, under a forest syde.
A bowe he bar, and arwes brighte and kene;
He hadde upon a courtepy of grene,
An hat upon his heed with frenges blake.

Geoffrey Chaucer, *The Friar's Tale*[59]

Archery is a prominent theme of the Viking religious tradition. Ullr, god of the bow, lived in Ydalir, the yew dales and Vali, a son of Odin, was also skilled with the bow. Skadi, a giantess, loved to go with bow and skis in the mountains and could give skill in bow hunting to ordinary men. By ancient Viking custom, battles were begun by a man throwing a spear or shooting an arrow over the enemy host and calling out; 'I dedicate you all to Odin!' The Huns had a similar custom. The Viking summons to battle was the 'war-arrow', of iron, or of wood painted to look like iron.

> When a man carried war-news he shall raise an iron arrow. That arrow shall go with the lendirmen and be carried on a manned ship both by night and by day along the high road [the sea]. Every man in whose house the arrow comes is summoned within five days on board a ship. If anyone sits quiet he is outlawed, for both thegn and thrall shall go.

In the Middle Ages, every Christian child knew that the rainbow was not the bridge to Valhalla as the Vikings had believed, but God's bow placed in the heavens as a sign to Noah. This was not the only religious connotation of bows and arrows; in fact archery runs through Christian religious symbolism and writings of the time.

The patron saint of archers was St Sebastian. According to legend, he had been a captain of the guard of Emperor Diocletian in third-century Rome. The Emperor, learning that Sebastian was a secret Christian, had him bound to a pillar and shot full of arrows, an image often reproduced in mediaeval art. Found still alive by a peasant, Sebastian recovered, but was later clubbed to death for criticising the Emperor. In religious iconography he is often depicted holding an arrow

Like St Sebastian, St Ursula met her end by the arrow. There are many variations of her story; the eleventh-century chronicle of Sigebert of Gemblours tells us that in the year 453, Ursula, daughter of a prince of the Britons, together with 11,000 white robed ladies-in-waiting, was returning home after a pilgrimage to Rome. Near Cologne, they were captured by a raiding party of Huns. When the virgin Ursula rejected the advances of the Hun chief, she was shot to death with an arrow and all her handmaidens were killed. Ursula is represented in art with a dove and holding an arrow.

In ninth-century England, the Angles were defeated by a Danish Viking army and their king, Edmund, was tied to a tree and shot full of arrows. Edmund was also sanctified. The many mediaeval and Renaissance portrayals of these martyrs often show the types of arrows and bows in use at the time of the artist, as opposed to accurate representations of the weapons that would actually have been used.

Symbolism

> The heddle-rods
> Are blood-wet spears;
> The shafts are iron-bound,
> And arrows are the shuttles,
> With swords we will weave
> this web of battle
>
> 'The Valkyrie's Song', *Heimskringla*[60]

Many mediaeval people sought religious lessons and allusions in nature and familiar activities. Hugh of St Victor found his in hunting, the hind representing the soul, the hunters being the devils, their arrows man's desires, and their nets his senses. Chaucer's *The Canterbury Tales* tell of the meeting of a friar with a demon gotten up as a yeoman hunter, but who was a hunter of human souls.

The weapons of archery could also have symbolic significance. In Wales, a bow of war, a bent bow carried through the land by a runner meant a hostile threat and a call to war, while peace was announced by a runner carrying an unstrung bow, a bow of peace. In Lombard Italy the final act of freeing a slave was escorting him to a crossroad, handing him an arrow as a token of freedom and saying in the presence of witnesses: 'You may take whichever of these four roads you will, you have free power.' Similarly in mediaeval England, a grant of land could be acknowledged by the presentation of a barbed arrow to the king.

31

ARCHERY AND MEDICINE

To Drawe an Arrowhead or other Yron Out of a Wound, take the juice of valerian, in the which, wet a tent and put into the wound laying the said herbe upon it stamped, then make your binder as best fitteth, and by this means you shall draw forth the yron, and after heale the wound.

Sir High Plat, *A Closet for Ladies and Gentlewomen* (1608)

This practice of all other the manliest leaueth no part of the body unexercised, the breast, back, reynes, wast, and armes, withdrawing the thighes and legges with running or going.

Dr Jones, Elizabethan physician

However healthful archery may have been as exercise and sport, in battle it was often deadly. Mediaeval medicine was primitive and men died of wounds that would today be consided minor, often due to infection rather than the damage caused by the fateful blow itself. Kings did not remain behind the lines but had to lead their armies into battle personally, putting themselves in very real danger. The kings Hakon the Good, Harald Bluetooth and Harald Hardrade from Scandinavia as well as Harold Godwinson and Richard the Lionheart were all reported to have died of arrow wounds in battle.

As we have learned, the 'arrow-rain' was the common prelude to Viking battles. At the bloody Battle of Stiklestadir in Norway, King Olaf (later called St Olaf, one of the rare Viking saints) was killed in 1030 in an unsuccessful attempt to win back his kingdom from Canute the Mighty. A man called Tormod Kolbrunarscald fought under the King's banner. He was a *scald* or court poet, which in Viking times was no ivory tower occupation.

He was wounded in the left side by an arrow. He broke off the shaft and went off from the battle and got to the houses and to a lathe; it was a big building. Torrnod had a sword in his hand.

Tormod then went away to a little room, which he entered. Many were already there, sorely wounded men, and there was present a woman who bound up their wounds A fire was burning on the floor and she warmed water wherewith to wash their wounds; Tormod sat down by the door. One came out and the other went in of those who were busying themselves with the wounded men. One of them turned to Tormod, looked at him and said: 'Why art thou so pale? Art thou wounded and why dost thou not ask for a leech?'

After a time a 'leech' was able to attend to his wound.

Then said the leech: 'Let me see thy wounds and I will attend to them.' He sat down and took off his clothes. When the leech saw his wounds, she looked carefully at the wound in his side; she noticed that therein stood a bit of iron but knew not for sure what path the iron had taken. In a stone kettle she had put leeks and other grass, and cooked them together; she gave it to the wounded men to eat and so tried to find out if they had deep wounds, for she could notice the smell of the leek coming out of a deep wound. She brought it to Tormod and bade him eat. He answered: 'Take it away; I have not groats-sickness.' She took a pair of tongs to draw out the iron, but it was fast and would not come out; it stood but a little way out, for the wound was swollen. Then said Tormod: 'Cut the flesh away down to the iron, so that thou canst get at it well with the tongs; then give them to me and let me wrench it.' She did as he said. Then Tormod took the gold ring off his hand and gave it to the leech, bidding her do with it what she would; 'a good possession it is, he said, 'King Olav gave me this ring this morning.' Tormod afterwards took the tongs and wrenched the arrow out; there were barbs on it and on these lay the fibres of the heart, some red, some white. And when he saw it, he said: 'Well hath the king fed us; fat am I still about the roots of the heart!' He then fell back and was dead. Such was the Viking field hospital and the preferred death of a Viking, with a grim jest that men would remember.

In thirteenth-century Paris a deep wound, such as an arrow wound, was kept open with a paraffin tent (a finger of paraffin placed in the wound) with a drain added. Sterile white of egg was applied to prevent infection in piercing and cutting wounds. Other physicians use wine, sometimes heated, to cleanse injuries. Sutures were used to close wounds.

John Bradmore, an English surgeon, devised a tool for extracting embedded socketed arrowheads that were not barbed. His patient was Prince Hal, who had taken an arrow in the face at Shrewsbury. First, dowels of increasing sizes, soaked in honey, which was already known to prevent infection, were used to enlarge the wound. Then the tool, made of a pair of tongs, was inserted and screwed apart to grip the inside of the socket and pull out the arrowhead. A poultice of barley and honey mixed in turpentine completed the treatment, with relief in 20 days.

Centuries later, medical science had advanced little. When Joan of Arc was wounded by an English arrow during a French assault, a French soldier began to chant a charm over the wound, but she stopped him, saying that she wanted no unhallowed cures. Her wound was dressed with olive oil and lard and she recovered to take part in another assault that evening, but so many Frenchmen died of wounds from English arrows that many held the belief that the English arrows were poisoned. This was probably not the case, although arrowheads plated with copper could be toxic. If the arrowhead was not removed before it began to rust, complications could set in even if the wound itself was not serious. Both tanged and socketed arrowheads often came loose from the shaft in the wound. Barbed arrows were especially difficult to remove and were sometimes pushed on through the body, rather than tear up the flesh by pulling them out the way they had gone in.

Ambrose Pare, surgeon for the French Army during the Hundred Years War, wrote of methods of extracting English arrowheads from his countrymen.

If the iron was thus barbed which is often the case with English arrows, and was situated in or near bone, which often happens, in the depth of the muscles of the thigh, arms or legs or other parts which would be far removed, you must not push but rather dilate the wound, avoiding the nerves and vessels, as does the good and expert anatomical surgeon. Also one must apply a dilator to hold the wound open; do it in such a way that you can take the two wings of the barb with pinchers. Keep it firm and pull or draw the three together.

Not to be outdone, the English army also had a surgeon general. Before departure for France he had been authorised to recruit additional medical men who would accompany him but he could find none willing to serve. In France he recruited several assistants who were of little help, as they were required to take their places in the formations of archers. However, Henry V was petitioned to engage twelve surgeons at standard military pay, to accompany his Agincourt campaign. He was also accompanied by an Oxford-educated physician.

In the time of Henry VIII, the value of archery as an exercise not only for getting the body in tone, but also as a definite cure for various diseases, was recognised. In his previously mentioned sermon; Bishop Latimer added:

It is a goodly Arte, a wholesome kind of exercise, and much recommended in Phisike. Narcillius Phiciuus in his booke de triplici uita (it is a great whyle since I redd him now) but I remember he commendeth this kind of exercise and sayeth that it wrestleth against many kinds of diseases. In the reuerence of God let it be continued.

EPILOGUE

The archers came forth, and touched the land first, each with his bow strung and with his quiver full of arrows, slung at his side. All were shaven and shorn; and all clad in short garments, ready to attack, to shoot, to wheel about and skirmish.[61]

Wace, *Roman De Rou*

Now the fire must feed on his body,
Flames grow heavy and black with him
Who endured arrows falling in iron
Showers, feathered shafts, barbed
And sharp, shot through linden shields,
Storms of eager arrowheads dropping.

Wiglaf's funeral oration, *Beowulf*

As we have seen, 'two sticks and a string' had a tremendous influence on the culture, politics, warfare and commerce, as well as the daily lives of both the nobility and the peasantry, of mediaeval and Renaissance Europe. The important role played by those who practised archery (and hunting) and manufactured the equipment can still be seen in many modern surnames, including Archer, Bowman, Bowyer, Fletcher, Arrowsmith, Stringer, Huntsman, Forester, Foster, Hunter and Parker, and the English language has been enriched by associated terms, such as 'making a hit', 'upshot', 'a bolt from the blue', picking a quarrel', 'shot his bolt', 'playing fast and loose', 'caught red-handed', 'made his mark', 'the butt of ridicule', and of course, 'straight as an arrow'.

In England, where nearly all men and many women were skilled at archery for a considerable period, it remained more popular than on the Continent, especially the practice of using the longbow as opposed to the crossbow. Compulsory archery practice did not prevent enjoyment of archery as a sport, and in recent years 'instinctive' or 'traditional' archery has found a new popularity, and many re-enactment groups have a special interest in authentic mediaeval weapons and practice.

For the reader who has been inspired to take up traditional archery, it is now possible to purchase bows, arrows, crossbows and arrowheads made in the true mediaeval fashion, although often a significant financial outlay is required. Unspliced yew self-bow staves, though scarce, may still be had from Italy or Switzerland. Some modern craftsmen offer birch or poplar unfinished arrow shafts, parallel or tapered, self or pieced. Arrows of various styles can be made from birch (a mediaeval favourite) if dowells with perfectly straight grain can be had. Other craftsmen offer reproduction steel broadheads, bodkins and bullet points. Still others provide swan, goose or peacock fletchings as well as the usual turkey. Synthetic bowstring material is now used by many modern archers, but I find it difficult to make bowstrings in the traditional style with it and prefer to use linen or silk thread that may be obtained from old fashioned shoemakers.

The home craftsman wishing to reproduce mediaeval gear outside of commercial sources may find himself on many wild goose chases, both figuratively and literally. Finding suitable raw materials is increasingly more difficult. Domestic geese (whose feathers are suitable for fletching) are normally slaughtered too young to have matured feathers and swan and peacock wing feathers are usually clipped to keep the birds from straying. Similarly cattle horn (for nocks) is hard to get, even from slaughterhouses. Suppliers of seasoned mountain yew suitable for self bows, mostly in Oregon, are few and their stock is expensive. In fact, air dried wood of any kind in mediaeval lists is hard to locate. The surest way to get it is to cut a suitable bolt and wait a few years for it to season, but this demands patience.

Before making or buying any equipment, I would advise buying an inexpensive fibreglass bow and a set of arrows of the proper length to learn to shoot and to find out what strength of bow is suited to your strength. The shooter should be able to perform the act of shooting smoothly and completely but not easily, and able to hold the bow steady at full draw. The bow matched to his strength will give the best results for distance as well as accuracy.

Despite difficulties of materials, it is still possible to learn the pleasure of archery of the old kind. A longbow and sheaf of arrows and the development of skill in their use are, in my opinion, amongst the beautifully perfect things of this world.

And all that with hande-bowe shoteth,
That of heven they may never mysse!

The Ballad of Adam Bell

WAINAMOINEN'S JOURNEY

The *Kalevala* (Land of Heroes) is Finland's great national epic poem. Of ancient origin, it was formerly recited by wandering storytellers. It was said that a mistake in the narrative would cost the storyteller his life. The meter, which Longfellow adapted for his poem 'Hiawatha', helped in memorising this lengthy poem.

Vikings knew the Finns as excellent archers and as sorcerers. Rune VI relates the conflict between a great wizard and a jealous younger one, and the making of a magical crossbow.

Wainamoinen, old and truthful,
Now arranges for a journey
To the village of the Northland,
To the land of cruel winters,
To the land of little sunshine,
To the land of worthy women;
Takes his light-foot royal racer,
Then adjusts the golden bridle,
Lays upon his back the saddle,
Silver-buckled, copper-stirruped,
Seats himself upon his courser,
And begins his journey northward;
Plunges onward, onward, onward,
Galloping along the highway,
In his saddle, gaily fashioned
On his dappled steed of magic,
Plunging through Wainola's meadows,
O'er the plains of Kalevala.
Fast and far he loped onward, A
Galloped far beyond Wainola,
Bounded oer the waste of waters,

Till he reached the blue-sea's margin,
Wetting not the hoofs in running.
But the evil Youkahainen
Nursed a grudge within his bosom,
In his heart the worm of envy,

Envy of this Wainamoinen,
Of this wonderful enchanter.
He prepares a cruel cross-bow,
Made of steel and other metals,
Paints the bow in many colours,
Molds the top-piece out of copper,
Trims his bow with snowy silver,
Gold he uses too in trimming.
Then he hunts for strongest sinews,
Finds them in the stag of Hisi.
Interweaves the flax of Lempo.
Ready is the cruel cross-bow,
String, and shaft, and ends are finished,
Beautiful the bow and mighty,
Surely cost it not a trifle;

On the back a painted courser,
On each end a colt of beauty,
Near the curve a maiden sleeping,
Near the notch a hare is bounding,
Wonderful the bow thus fashioned;
Cuts some arrows for his quiver,
Covers them with finest feathers,
From the oak the shafts lie fashioned,
Makes the tips of keenest metal.
As the rods and points are finished,
Then he feathers well his arrows
From the plumage of the swallow,
From the wing-quills of the sparrow;
Hardens well his feathered arrows,
And imparts to each new virtues,
Steeps them in the blood of serpents
in the virus of the adder.

Ready now are all his arrows,
Ready strung, his cruel cross-bow,
Waiting for wise Wainamoinen,
Youkahainen, Lapland's minstrel,
Waits a long time, is not weary,
Hopes to spy the ancient singer;
Spies at day-dawn, spies at evening,
Spies he ceaselessly at noontide,
Lies in wait for the magician,
Waits, and watches, as in envy;
Sits he. at tile open window,
Stands behind the hedge, and watches
In the foot-path waits, and listens,
Spies along the balks of meadows:
On his back he hangs his quiver,
In his quiver, feathered arrows
Dipped in virus of the viper,
On his arm the mighty cross-bow,
Waits, and watches, and unwearied,
Listens from tile boat-house window,
Lingers at the end of Fog-point,
By the river flowing seaward,
Near the holy stream and whirlpool,
Near the sacred river's fire-fall.
Finally the Lapland minstrel,
Youkahainen of' Pohyola,

At the breaking of the day-dawn,
At the early hour of morning,
Fixed his gaze upon the North-east,
Turned his eyes upon the sunrise,
Saw a black cloud on the ocean,
Something blue upon the waters,
And soliloquised as follows:
'Are those clouds on the horizon,
Or perchance the dawn of morning?
Neither clouds on the horizon,
Nor the dawning of the morning;
It is ancient Wainamoinen,
The renowned and wise enchanter,
Riding on his way to Northland
On his steed, the royal racer,
Magic courser of Wainola'
Quickly now young Youkahainen,
Lapland's vain and evil minstrel,
Filled with envy, grasps his cross-bow,
Makes his bow and arrows ready
For the death of Wainamoinen.
Quick his aged mother asked him,
Spake these words to Youkahiainen For
whose slaughter is thy cross-bow,
For whose heart thy poisoned arrows?
Youkahainen thus made answer:
'l have made this mighty cross-bow,
Fashioned bow and poisoned arrows,
For the death of Wainamoinen,
Thus to slay the friend of waters;
I must shoot the old magician,
The eternal bard and hero,
Through the heart, and through the liver,
Through the head, and through the
shoulders
With this bow and feathered arrows
Thus destroy my rival minstrel.'
Then the aged mother answered,
Thus reproving, thus forbidding;
'Do not slay good Waiiiamoinen,
Ancient hero ot' the Northland,
From a noble tribe descended,
He, my sister's son, my nephew.
if thou slayest Wainamoinen,

Ancient son of Kalevala,
Then alas! all joy will vanish,
Perish all our wondrous singing;
Better on the earth the gladness,
Better here the magic music,
Than within the nether regions,
In the kingdom of Tuoni,
In the realm of the departed,
In the land of the hereafter.'
Then the youthful Youkahaincn
Thought awhile and well considered,
Ere lie made a final answer.
With one hand he raised the cross-bow
But the other seemed to weaken,
As he drew the cruel bow-string.
Finally these words he uttered
As his bosom swelled with envy
'Let all joy forever vanish,
Let earth's pleasures quickly perish,
Disappear earth's sweetest music,
Happiness depart forever;
Shoot I will this rival minstrel,
Little heeding what the end is.'
Quickly now he bends his fire-bow,
On his left knee rests the weapon,
With his right foot firmly planted,
Thus he strings his bow of envy;
Takes three arrows from his quiver,
Choosing well the best among them,
Carefully adjusts the bow-string,
Sets with care the feathered arrow,
To the flaxen string he lays it,
Holds the cross-bow to his shoulder,
Aiming well along the margin,
At the heart of Wainamoinen,
Waiting till he gallops nearer;
In the shadow of a thicket,
Speaks these words while he is waiting
'Be thou, flaxen string, elastic;
Swiftly fly, thou feathered ash. wood,
Swiftly speed, thou deadly missile,
Quick as light, thou poisoned arrow,
To the heart of Wainamoinen,
If my hand too low should hold thee,

May the gods direct thee higher;
If too high mine eye should aim thee,
May the gods direct thee lower.'
Steady now he pulls the trigger;
Like the lightning flies the arrow
O'er the head of Wainamoinen;
To the upper sky it darteth,
And the highest clouds it pierces,
Scatters all the flock of lamb-clouds,
On its rapid journey skyward.
Not discouraged, quick selecting,
Quick adjusting, Youkahainen,
Quickly aiming, shoots a second
Speeds the arrow swift as lightning;
Much too low he aimed the missile,
Into earth the arrow plunges,
Pierces to the lower regions,
Splits in two the old Sand Mountain.
Nothing daunted, Youkahainen,
Quick adjusting shoots a third one.
Swift as light it speeds its journey,
Strikes the steed of Wainamoinen,
Strikes the light-foot ocean swimmer,
Strikes him near his golden girdle,
Through the shoulder of the racer.
Thereupon wise Wainamoinen
Headlong fell upon the waters,
Plunged beneath the rolling billows,
From the saddle of the courser,
From his dappled steed of magic.
Then arose a mighty storm-wind,
Roaring wildly on the waters.
Bore away old Wainamoinen,
Far from land upon the billows,
On the high and rolling billows,
On the broad seas great expanses.
Boasted then young Youkahainen,
Thinking Waino dead and buried,
These the boastful words he uttered
'Nevermore, old Wainanioinen,
Nevermore in all thy lifetime,
While the golden moonlight glistens,
Nevermore wilt fix thy vision
On the meadows of Wainola,

On the plains of Kalevala,
Full six years must swim the ocean,
Tread the waves for seven summers,
Eight years ride the foamy billows,
In the broad expanse of water;
Six long autumns as a fir-tree,
Seven winters as a pebble,
Eight long summers as an aspen.'
Thereupon the Lapland minstrel
Hastened to his room delighting,
When his mother thus addressed him
'Hast thou slain good Wainamoinen,
Slain the son of Kalevala?'
Youkahainen thus made answer
'I have slain old Wainamoinen,
Slain the son of Kalevala,
That he now may plow the ocean,
That he now may sweep the waters,

On tlie billows rock and slumber.
In the salt sea plunged he headlong,
in the deep sank the magician,
Sidewise turned he to the sea-shore,
On his back to rock forever,
Thus the boundless sea to travel,
Thus to ride the rolling billows'
This the answer of the mother:
'Woe to earth for this thine action,
Gone forever, joy and singing,
Vanished is the wit of ages!
Thou hast slain good Wainamoinen,
Slain the ancient wisdom-singer,
Slain the pride of Suwantala,
Slain the hero of Wainola,
Slain the joy of Kalevala.

(Translation by John Martin Crawford, 1888)

NOTES

1 The *Roman De Rou*, a verse history of the Dukes of Normandy commissioned by Henry II, was based on oral traditions passed on through the family of Maistre Wace. Here, Duke William leads his invasion fleet to Hastings.

2 Iolo Goch's description makes it clear that in his time Welshmen had come to use bows of yew and used broadheads in combat.

3 Ascham's advice is helpful to Englishmen who were required by law to purchase bows from licensed bowyers.

4 This verse from the *Rigsthula,* a Norse poem about the origin of different classes of people, illustrates the activities of a young Norse nobleman, including the making and use of archery gear.

5 The arrows given to Robin Hood by the Knight are fletched with brown peacock wing feathers. The silver nocks are something of a mystery. We know that bow nocks were sometimes of silver and brass nocks were used in pre-Viking Scandinavia. One version of the ballad says silk instead of silver.

6 Dominic Mancini, a visitor from Venice and probably a spy, visited England in 1483 during the reign of Richard III. There he observed and reported on Richard's archers.

7 The poem is a somewhat fictionalised mediaeval version of the Battle of Otterborn between 'Hotspur', the son of the Earl of Northumbria, and Scots in the Earl Douglas's lands in 1388. Here, a Northumbrian longbowman, seeing his lord slain, responds with an arrow that pierces a Scottish knight, Sir Hugh Montgomery. Lord Percy was in fact not killed.

8 Drayton refers to bows of the preferred Spanish yew and the celebrated clothyard arrows.

9 Baha ed Din was Saladin's chronicler. This incident occurred during the Christian siege of Acre, which was the beginning of the Third Crusade in which King Richard the Lionheart challenged Saladin.

10 A sheaf of arrows was sometimes carried bound in a leather strip around the foreshaft (*trusyd in a thrumme*) like some found on the *Mary Rose*.

11 In preparation for battle archers are sharpening their 'bearded' (barbed) arrows.

12 This Norse poem is about the great king Atli (Attila the Hun) and the curving bows would probably be composite hornbows, which were known to the Northmen.

13 In this poem, an arrow an 'elle long' (a clothyard) is described as used in hunting.

14 Odericus describes preparations for the hunt in which King William II (Rufus) was killed by Tyrell's arrow.

15 Ludovico Ariosto's huge Renaissance work, all in verse, offers vivid descriptions of shipwrecks, sieges and jousts as well as wild fantasy.

16 A verse from *The Hunting of the Cheviot*, see Note 7.

17 The square arrowheads were a type used in war.

18 This part of T*he Chronicles of the Cid* concerns the Moslem invasion from North Africa and the battle for Valencia at the end of the Cid's life.

19 We see in the papal decree that handbows as well as crossbows were restricted.

20 The Genoese specialised in crossbows, and were employed as mercenaries in northern Europe. However, again according to Froissart, they did not cause much consternation at the Battle of Crecy, 'being very tired and having marched over 15 miles in full armour ... they told the constable they were in no condition to fight. The Count of Alençon said: "This is what happens when you employ such rabble; they fail us in the hour of need."' The crossbowmen, in addition to being asked to fight when exhausted, were forced to do so before they could unload their protective pavisses from the baggage train.

21 In Tudor times, people had not forgotten the Saxon invasions of Britain.

22 *The Battle Of Maldon* is a Saxon poem about an actual battle between Saxon and Viking forces in 991. Saxons had no reputation for military archery at this time so it is unclear who was shooting the arrows.

23 The Battle of Homildon Hill (1402), between the forces of Earl Percy of Northumberland and the raiders of Earl Douglas, was the first major victory for English archery.

24 Gunnar of Hlidarendi, having been sentenced to outlawry, had no legal protection against his enemies, but he was a formidable archer and fighter and chose to remain in Iceland. His story is told in the thirteenth-century *Njal's Saga*.

25 Drayton refers to the era when the best yew came from the mountains of Spain and Italy.

26 Shakespeare knew that archers were to have arrows of their personal draw length to be drawn to the shouldering of the head or the barbs.

27 The *Rigsthula* (see Note 4) notes the making of archery gear at home.

28 Ascham agrees with the findings of centuries of bowyers and archers that yew is the best of all woods for a bow.

29 A Viking skald's comment on the death of Harald Hardrada.

30 Of all the artillers, the stringers were the only ones who needed no tools.

31 This Scottish poem suggests the use of local yew wood and unusual eagle feather fletching.

32 Crossbowmen serving as assault troops.

33 Ariosto's book describes the reality of Renaissance warfare.

34 Henry VIII provided his mistress and later wife Ann Boleyn with the equipment to join him in his beloved sport.

35 Bishop Hugh Latimer, once chaplain to Henry VIII, was burned at the stake in 1555 during the persecution of Protestants by Queen Mary I. He was a passionate proponent of archery, as implied by this sermon.

36 Ascham is here referring to a Byzantine emperor's praise of the long draw to the ear that was probably learned from Hun archers.

37 A sixteenth-century consideration of the archers at the Battle of Agincourt on 25 October 1415.

38 Froissart descibes the beginning of the arrow storm at the Battle of Crecy at which the bolts of the Genoese crossbowmen fell far short while the English arrows did not.

39 While the Sheriff wonders if the disguised Robin Hood can draw the supplied bow fully to his ear, Robin finds it too weak. The best shooting is done with a bow matching the archer's strength.

40 *The Ballad of Adam Bell* is about three forest outlaws. When one is captured while visiting his wife in town, his two friends set out to free him.

41 A lucky day for Robin: silk bowstrings were most prized.

42 Crossbowmen were equipped with protective pavisses. Without them, they were very vulnerable to longbowmen's arrows because of their slow reloading.

43 Marco Polo had ample opportunity to observe Mongol horse-archers during his service with Kublai Khan.

44 The *Rigsthula* describes the young noble both making his archery gear and using it.

45 *The Conquest of Grenada* is translated from a Spanish manuscript of Fray Antonio Agapida. It describes the English contingent under the Earl Rivers who, soon after the victory of Henry VII, helped in the expulsion of the Moors from Spain.

46 In this ballad, Robin and his men form the team of Queen's archers competing with the King's team.

47 Although Markham wrote roughly 100 years after the accepted end of the Renaissance, archery seems not to have undergone much change.

48 A gold and silver arrow was often the appropriate prize for winning a shooting contest.

49 *Sir Gawain and the Green Knight* was written in the latter part of the fourteenth century, author unknown. This hunting scene is the usual bow and stable mediaeval hunt with deer driven past the noble hunters.

50 Many Englishmen regretted the loss of their archers' days of military supremacy.

51 The Saracen chronicler describes the protective garments worn by Richard the Lionheart's men in the Third Crusade.

52 The poem describes the archer guard that accompanied Queen Elizabeth I on her excursions. While at first enthusiastic about archery, she eventually abolished it as a military weapon.

53 This political poem of the Hundred Years War identifies lords by their badges rather than by their names. It refers here to Lord Talbot, England's foremost commander, following his capture by Joan of Arc's army.

54 According to the ballads, Robin outfitted his men in livery, as nobles did.

55 King Sigurd's saga is included in the *Heimskringla*, a thirteenth-century history of the Norse kings.

56 The arrow that put Harold out of action changed English history forever.

57 The play *Wilhelm Tell* by Friedrich Schiller is faithful to the original story in Tschudi's *Chronicle*.

58 As *Piers Plowman* was written in the latter part of the fourteenth century and is the first mention of Robin Hood that we know, it is clear that Robin Hood ballads were well known then. Randolph, Earl of Chester is a character in the poem of *Fulk Fitz Warine*.

59 Chaucer's poem describes a friar's meeting with a demon in the guise of a yeoman hunter hunting for human souls.

60 Vikings believed that Valkyries brought brave slain warriors to Valhalla, there to feast and fight while awaiting the final battle with the giants.

61 A description of the landing of the Norman invasion fleet on the English coast in 1066.

BIBLIOGRAPHY

Ackroyd, Peter, *Albion: The Origins of the English Imagination* (Chatto & Windus 2002)

Anon (trans. Col. H. Walrond, ed. C. Parker), *Lartdarcherie* (1515)

Anon, *Sir Gawain and the Green Knight* (c. late 1300)

Anon, *The Book of Roi Modus and Queen Racio* (c.1370)

Ascham, Roger *Toxophilus* (1545)

Backhouse, Janet, *The Luttrell Psalter* (The British Library Publishing, 1989)

Backhouse, Janet, *Medieval Rural Life in the Luttrell Psalter* (The British Library Publishing, 2001)

Bradbury, Jim, *The Medieval Archer* (St Martin's Press, 1985)

Burke, Edmund, *The History of Archery* (William Murrow and Company, 1957)

Butler, Denis, *1066: The Story of a Year* (Anthony Blond Ltd., 1966)

Cairns, Conrad, *Medieval Castles* (Cambridge University Press, 1987)

Cambrensis, Geraldus (trans. Lewis Thorpe), *The Journey Through Wales and the Description of Wales* (Penguin Books, 2001)

Carew, Richard, *The Survey of Cornwall* (1602)

Chancellor, John, *The Life and Times of Edward I* (Weidenfeld and Nicholson, 1981)

Chaucer, Geoffrey, *The Canterbury Tales* (c.1387–1400)

Child, Francis James (ed.), *The English and Scottish Popular Ballads* Vol. III (Houghton, Mifflin and Company, 1898)

Clark, J.G.D., *Prehistoric Longbows: Proceedings of the Prehistoric Society* (Cambridge University Press, 1963)

Cockerell, Sydney, *Old Testament Miniatures* (Phaidon Press, 1969)

Coggins, Jack, *The Fighting Man* (Doubleday, 1966)

Cummings, John, *The Art of Medieval Hunting: The Hound and the Hawk* (Castle Books, 2003)

de Foix, Count Gaston, *Le Livre de Chasse* (1387–89)

Edge, David & John Miler Paddock, *The Medieval Knight* (Bison Books Ltd, 1988)

Elmer, Robert, *Target Archery* (Derrydale Press, 1992)

Featherstone, Donald, *The Bowmen of England: The Story of the English Longbow* (Jarrolds Publishers, 1967)

Froissart, Jean, (trans. Lord Berners) *Froissart's Chronicles,* four volumes (1369–1400)

Geary, Patrick, J., *Readings in Medieval History* (Broadview Press, 1948)

Geibig, Alfred & Harm Paulsen, *Ausgrabungen in Haithabu* (Wacholz Verlag, 1999)

Gies, Frances & Joseph, *Daily Life in Medieval Times* (Black Dog and Leventhal Publishers)

Gordon, C. D., *The Age of Attila* (University of Michigan Press, 1960)

Grafton, Richard, *A Chronicle at Large, mere History of the affayres of England* (1568)

Hallam, Elizabeth (ed.), *The Plantagenet Encyclopedia* (Penguin Books, 1990)

Hallam, Elizabeth, *The Wars of the Roses* (Bramley Books, 1998)

Hansard, George Agar, *The Book of Archery* (London, 1840)

Hardy, Robert, *Longbow: A Social and Military History* (Arco Publishing, 1970)

Hastings, Thomas, *The British Archer* (1831)

Herrigel, Eugen, *Zen in the Art of Archery: Training the Mind and Body to Become One* (Penguin, 2004)

Hieatt, Constance B. & Sharon Butler, *Pleyn Delit: Medieval Cookery for Modern Cooks* (University of Toronto Press, 1977)

Holt, J.C., *Robin Hood* (Thames and Hudson, 1982)

Kiil, Vilhelm, *Norveg: Hornboge, langboge og finnboge* (H. Aschehoug & Co., 1954)

Koch, H.W., *Medieval Warfare* (Bison Books Ltd., 1982)

Latham, J.D. & W.F. Patterson, *Saracen Archery* (Holland Press 1970)

Longman, W. & Col. H. Walrond, *The Badminton Library of Sports and Pastimes Volume 24: Archery* (Derrydale Press, 1894)

Major, John, *Scotichronicon* (1521)

Markham, Gervase, *Country Contentments* (1615)

Neade, William, *The Double Armed Man* (1625)

Ohlgren, Thomas H., *Robin Hood: The Early Poems* (Rosemont Printing and Publishing, 2007)

Payne-Gallwey, Sir Ralph, *The Crossbow* (Holland Press, 1958)

Phillips E.D., *The Royal Hordes* (Thames & Hudson, 2003)

Phillips, Graham & Martin Keatman, *Robin Hood: The Man Behind the Myth* (Michael O'Mara, 1995)

Pope, Saxton T., *Bows and Arrows* (University of California, 1962)

Riesch, Holger, *Pfeil Und Bogen Zur Merowingerzeit* (Karfunkel Verlag, 2002)

Roberts, T. *The English Bowman* (1801)

Rule, Margaret, *The Mary Rose* (London Ring Publications, 1982) Scott, Ronald & Peter Bedrick, *Robert the Bruce* (New York, 1982)

Seward, Desmond, *The Hundred Years War* (Constable and Robinson, 1978)

Simons, Gerald, *Barbarian Europe* (Trans-life Books, 1968)

Smythe, Sir John (ed. J.R. Hall), *Certaine Discourses Military* (1590)

Soar, Hugh D.H., *The Crooked Stick: A History of the Longbow* (Westholme Publishing, 2004)

Soar, Hugh D.H., *Secrets of the English Warbow* (Westholme Publishing, 2008)

Stow, John, *A Survey of London* (1603)

Stralsi, Nancy G. *Medieval & Early Renaissance Medicine* (University of Chicago Press)

Strutt, Joseph, *Sport and Pastimes of the People of England* (London, 1810)

Sturlason, Snorri (ed. & trans. Erling Monsen & A.H. Smith), *Heimskringla*

Thompson, Maurice, *The Witchery of Archery* (C. Scribners Sons, 1878)

Villani, Giovanni, *Nuova Cronica* (1346)

Wace, Maistre, *Roman de Rou et des ducs de Normandie* (c.1160–1170)

Waring, Thomas *A Treatise on Archery* (1824)

Warner, Philip, *The Medieval Castle* (Penguin Books, 2001)

Wavrin, Jehan de, *Chroniques D'Angleterre* (c.1471)

Wyntoun, Andrew, *Chronicle of Scotland* (1420)

INDEX